SMART *Kids*

A Safe & Civil Schools
Social Skills Curriculum

Susan L. Mulkey

Marilyn Sprick

Published in the United States by
Pacific Northwest Publishing
2451 Willamette St.
Eugene, Oregon 97405
www.pacificnwpublish.com

ISBN 978-1-59909-043-6

Cover design by Hannah Bontrager
Interior design and layout by Natalie Conaway
Illustrations by Benjamin Springer
Additional graphics provided by Clipart.com. © 2010 Jupiterimages Corporation.

Pacific
Northwest
Publishing

Eugene, Oregon | www.pacificnwpublish.com

About the Authors

Susan L. Mulkey, M.Ed.

Susan is an author and trainer in social skills, behavior management, effective instructional practices, reading strategies, classroom coaching, and collaborative teaching. Susan has more than 30 years of experience across several educational settings, including elementary, middle school, and high school. She conducts more than 50 workshops and staff development sessions each year in Utah and across the United States. She spent six years conducting training for the Department of Defense schools in Germany, Japan, and Korea. She is a former project coordinator for a statewide staff development center, university instructor, consulting teacher, and special/general education teacher. She continues to consult independently for schools and school teams participating in Positive Behavior Supports. Susan has co-authored *Teach All, Reach All*; *TGIF: Making It Work on Monday*; *Cool Kids: A Proactive Approach to Social Responsibility*; *One-Minute Skill Builder*; *TRIP: Translating Research Into Practice*; *Working Together: Tools for Collaborative Teaching*; and a video, *Working Together: What Collaborative Teaching Can Look Like*.

Marilyn Sprick, M.S.

With degrees in psychology, education, and special education, Marilyn has worked as a general education teacher, Title 1 learning specialist, and special education teacher. As a consultant, Marilyn has worked with thousands of teachers across the country—adapting curriculum and instruction to better meet the needs of all students. Marilyn is the senior author of the highly effective *Read Well* reading series (K–2), *Read Well Spelling and Writing Conventions* (1–2), and *Read Well Composition* (1). *SMART Kids* has allowed Marilyn the opportunity to apply her knowledge of explicit instruction and programming to helping all children learn skills that develop social grace, encourage friendships, and demonstrate respectful behavior.

From Eugene, Oregon, Marilyn and Randy Sprick co-direct Teaching Strategies, Inc.—a nationally recognized group of consultants who work with schools to improve student responsibility and academic success.

Table of Contents

Table of Contents

Table of Contents

Introduction

What Is *SMART Kids* All About?

SMART is an acronym that stands for **S**ocial Grace, **M**anners, **A**nd **R**espectful **T**alk. We've designed SMART Kids to help you explicitly teach, reinforce, and support the development of social skills with young children. With SMART, your children will learn important social behaviors like how to listen, how to follow instructions, and how to include others. SMART Kids provides you with lessons that result in children who act with social grace, demonstrate good old-fashioned manners, and talk and interact respectfully.

SMART Kids includes fourteen skills that allow people of all ages to communicate effectively and socialize with others. SMART Skills will help your children develop friendships, succeed academically, and secure employment and promotions in the workplace. SMART Skills include verbal and nonverbal communication skills—skills that are best taught while children are still young and learning how to interact with other people and the events that occur around them. SMART Skills are essential learning for all children and youth.

Why Teach SMART Skills?

SMART Kids isn't about manners like how to hold a fork or which fork to use. Instead, SMART is about how we treat others on a day-to-day basis. With cell phones, texting, email, and other technological advances, children can benefit from an education in behaviors that reflect kindness, responsibility, and respect for others—basic social skills that require personal interactions to learn. These social skills will allow you and your children to have fun while teaching and learning academic skills efficiently. SMART Skills open doors for academic learning in your classroom.

Learning how to navigate social interactions is a difficult and complex task. Few of us have been explicitly taught basic manners and how to accept responsibility for our actions. Many of us learned these skills through modeling and the values taught in our homes. By teaching these skills directly at school, we can help reinforce and generalize skills learned at home while concurrently ensuring that all students have the opportunity to learn these skills.

SMART is not a cure-all for fostering appropriate social behavior and responsibility, but can be a powerful beginning. By practicing SMART skills at school and in the home, even your most socially inept students can become adept.

● ········ Why Social Skills Are Important ······· ●

Children and youth who have good social skills:

- Do significantly better in school—academically, behaviorally, and socially

- Develop healthy peer groups and friendships because they are able to show care and concern for others

- Communicate and relate better with sibling and parents

- Stay out of big trouble

- Demonstrate respectful behavior toward teachers and other adults

- Get and keep jobs

Children and youth who have poor social skills:

- May engage in discourteous and disrespectful behaviors—put-downs, insults, threats, trash talk, bullying, pushing, fighting . . .

- May later engage in more serious and violent acts (when discourteous/disrespectful behaviors persist over time and appropriate behaviors are not taught)

- Are often not accepted and avoided by peers

- Are often labeled "bad-mannered," "impolite," or "rude"

- May get poor grades in school

- Are more likely to lose their jobs as adults

What Are Smart Skills?

In most English-speaking countries, social skills include verbal and nonverbal skills. Verbal skills include being able to determine the appropriate thing to say at the appropriate time, being able to communicate and talk in ways that are engaging, having a range in one's vocal tone and quality, and being able to speak in an understandable manner. In a sense, effective social skills are judged by *what* we say, *when* we say it, and *how* we say it.

Social skills vary widely from one culture to another and even have regional differences. For example, in many cultures eye contact is appropriate when listening or engaging in conversations. However, in other cultures, eye contact may be a sign of disrespect.

Verbal Skills: In the United States, people with good verbal social skills are thought to speak with a clear voice, have inflection, speak appropriately to a situation, and have confidence in their voice. People who speak in a monotone, say the wrong thing, speak too softly or too loudly, and speak only on one topic or boring topics are often thought to have poor verbal skills.

Thus, the way we perceive a speaker's voice can lead us to make snap judgments about the person's worth or value, though these are often incorrect.

Nonverbal Skills: Nonverbal behavior is estimated to convey up to 38% of a person's communicative intent. Nonverbal behaviors—things such as eye contact, use of gestures, good posture, leaning toward the person being spoken to, and smiling—constitute good nonverbal social skills when used appropriately. These characteristics when overdone can also contribute to poor nonverbal skills. For example, gestures can be considered too dramatic. Leaning too far forward into someone else's personal space may be considered rude. SMART Skills include steps that give students instruction and practice in verbal and nonverbal behavior. With SMART Kids, your students will learn to use pleasant facial expressions, eye contact, and a calm body posture.

Why Is *SMART Kids* a *Safe & Civil Schools* Curriculum?

Safe & Civil Schools brings educators together at a school and district level to create meaningful improvements in climate, safety, and connectedness. *SMART Kids* fits this picture because it helps you teach the youngest children behaviors that contribute to a positive climate, a safe environment, and a sense of belonging to the school community.

CHAMPS Connections

For schools and teachers using *CHAMPS: A Proactive and Positive Approach to Classroom Management*, 2nd ed. (Sprick, 2009), *SMART Kids* provides model lessons for how to incorporate your school's guidelines for success and implement proactive and positive classroom management principles and strategies included in *CHAMPS*. Sample scripting provides clear examples of the kinds of interactions that promote responsible behavior and prevent misbehavior. (Watch for the CHAMPS Connections in the *SMART Kids* Unit Guides.)

▲
14 SMART Skills at a Glance

Each SMART Unit introduces a new skill while concurrently reviewing old skills. Once a SMART Skill is taught, you will review it in SMART Lessons and in the natural context of your classroom.

Each unit includes:

- A SMART Poster with a Social Story that provides students with steps—the specific behaviors students can practice to demonstrate a social skill.

- A page for each student's *My SMART Book* that includes a positive statement about the new skill. For example, "I can give warm greetings" in Unit 1 and "I can cool down" in Unit 14.

- Recognition Cards awarded to students and collected on a ring throughout the year when skills are used in the classroom

Unit 1 • SMART Greetings

The importance of greetings cannot be over-emphasized. Greet students each day and teach them to greet others.

- A greeting starts each student's day with a positive interaction and a sense of well-being.

- By learning how to greet others, students learn how to initiate positive interactions. A pleasant greeting from young children helps build friendships and a positive outlook.

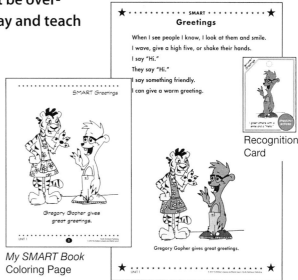

SMART Poster

★ SMART ★
Greetings

When I see people I know, I look at them and smile.
I wave, give a high five, or shake their hands.
I say "Hi."
They say "Hi."
I say something friendly.
I can give a warm greeting.

Recognition Card

My SMART Book
Coloring Page

SMART Greetings

Gregory Gopher gives great greetings.

UNIT 1

Gregory Gopher gives great greetings.

★ UNIT 1 ★

Unit 2 • SMART Looking and Listening

Looking and Listening are basic social skills that allow students to benefit from instruction and develop positive peer relationships.

- By learning to look and listen, students learn how to pay attention.

- Students also learn a skill that is needed to be a good friend. Good friends look at each other and listen to each other.

SMART Poster

My SMART Book Coloring Page

Recognition Card

Unit 3 • SMART Following Directions

SMART Kids learn to follow directions right away—when the directions are given by school staff members and other caring adults they know.

- By learning to follow directions right away, students are learning to cooperate—a critical skill for many jobs.

- By following directions, students help create a positive, productive classroom environment.

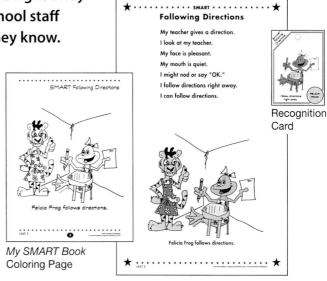

SMART Poster

My SMART Book Coloring Page

Recognition Card

Unit 5 • SMART Polite Requests

SMART Requests are a symbol of social grace and respect for others. SMART Kids make Polite Requests and learn to create positive interactions in multiple contexts.

SMART Poster

Recognition Card

My SMART Book Coloring Page

Unit 6 • SMART Compliments

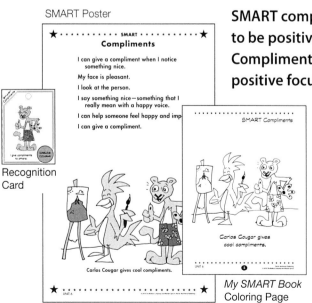

SMART compliments help young children learn to be positive with those around them. SMART Compliments also help children develop a positive focus as they learn to observe and articulate what they like. SMART Kids learn skills that help them develop positive relationships and a positive outlook on life.

SMART Poster

Recognition Card

My SMART Book Coloring Page

Unit 7 • SMART Taking Turns

Taking Turns is a difficult skill for many young children. By teaching SMART Taking Turns, students learn how to behave with maturity and social grace. Taking Turns is a skill that helps children keep friends and cooperate as they work with others.

SMART Poster

My SMART Book Coloring Page

Recognition Card

Unit 9 • SMART Including Others

When students can initiate friendships by starting a conversation and inviting others to play, they help develop peer groups. Research indicates that a sense of group belonging is strongly related to mental health. SMART Kids learn to invite others in and be inclusive.

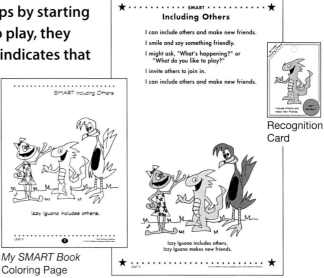

SMART Poster

My SMART Book Coloring Page

Recognition Card

Unit 10 • SMART Friends

SMART Poster

Recognition Card

My SMART Book Coloring Page

"Make new friends but keep the old. One is silver and the other, gold." The lyrics of this classic round speak volumes. Research indicates that students who have positive peer relationships are less likely to experience emotional and behavioral problems. Knowing how to make and keep friends is a precious skill. SMART Kids learn to join in, play nicely, and cheer each other along.

Unit 11 • SMART Accepting "No"

SMART Poster

Recognition Card

My SMART Book Coloring Page

Getting along with family, friends, teachers, and eventually supervisors in the workplace requires the ability to gracefully accept "No." SMART Kids learn that they might want to pout, argue, or whine, but it's best to take a deep breath and say "OK." SMART Kids learn to celebrate No PAWS Days. (P=Pout, A=Argue, W=Whine).

Unit 12 • SMART Cooling Down

SMART Kids learn that everyone gets upset now and again and that's OK. The most important thing is knowing what to do. SMART Kids learn they can take control by counting to three, taking a deep breath, and thinking a happy thought. SMART Kids practice cooling down when they aren't distressed. Then, when they're really upset, they have a strategy for calming down.

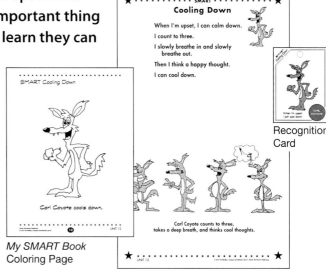

SMART Poster

My SMART Book Coloring Page

Recognition Card

Unit 14 • SMART Apologies

Everyone makes a mistake now and then. Knowing how to make an apology and accept an apology helps students learn to deal positively with things that happen. Making and accepting apologies are demonstrations of social grace—politeness and respect.

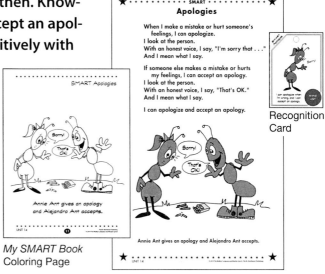

SMART Poster

My SMART Book Coloring Page

Recognition Card

Unit 15 • SMART Interruptions

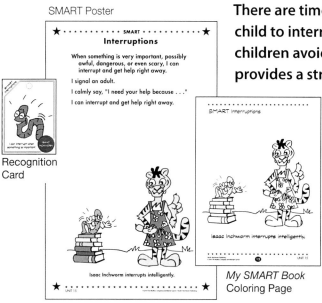

There are times when it is important for a young child to interrupt. Knowing when and how helps children avoid a sense of hopelessness and provides a strategy for getting adult assistance when needed. SMART Kids learn to interrupt *intelligently*—when it's important.

Unit 16 • SMART Disagreeing

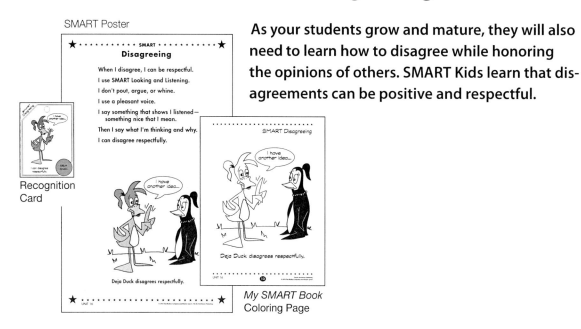

As your students grow and mature, they will also need to learn how to disagree while honoring the opinions of others. SMART Kids learn that disagreements can be positive and respectful.

Unit 17 • SMART Problem Solving

Problem solving is a complex and critical life skill. Getting a start on simple problem solving while children are young helps them learn to deal with problems as they arise. Unit 17 gives kids a start and a positive outlook on problems. "No problem is too big or small for a SMART Kid to solve."

SMART Poster

Recognition Card

My SMART Book Coloring Page

With these 14 SMART Skills, you will overtly teach your students many of the often covert social skills that lead to success in school, at home, and in the workplace. Your kids will be off to a SMART start!

May your SMART Kids go through life with a positive outlook and infinite number of joyful interactions.

What's in a SMART Unit?

Each SMART Unit follows a consistent format for ease of teaching. Each unit begins with a title page and overview, followed by five lessons (each on a two-page spread), and an End-of-Unit Tip.

What's on the Unit Title Page?

Each title page includes Student Objectives—the targeted objective for the unit and those already introduced. Use this page as a handy reference for skills you wish to maintain with prompts, encouragement, and reinforcement.

What's in the Unit Overview?

For your convenience, each overview follows the same easy-to-follow format.

Teaching Objectives: Each overview includes a list of behavioral steps your students will practice. This list also identifies which steps students should be able to use to demonstrate *competency* within the natural setting of your classroom and school.

Teaching Materials: Materials needed to teach the unit are divided into School Materials and SMART Materials. SMART Materials are located on the *SMART Kids* Reproducibles CD.

Teaching Tips: Positive interactions, positive feedback and reinforcement, and ongoing connections to a school's Guidelines for Success are basic instructional principles taught in CHAMPS. Watch this box for examples.

Intervention: For some students, SMART Skills are essentially new. These students may benefit from more prompting and added practice. Watch the Intervention section for simple suggestions.

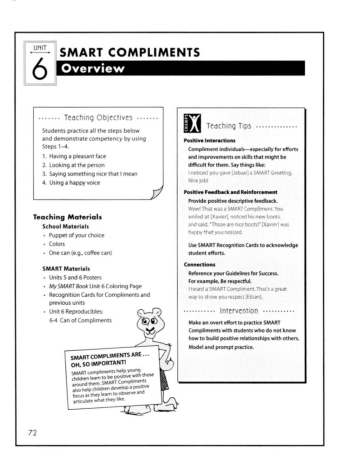

Lesson Planner

The Lesson Planner provides an easy-to-reference view of the lesson activities. This chart also lists materials needed by lesson as well as materials that need to be prepared in advance.

Lesson Planner — UNIT **6**

Lesson	Activities	Materials and Materials Preparation
1	**Model and Explain SMART Compliments** **Introduce Unit 6 Poster** **When to Give SMART Compliments**	**Unit 6 Poster** Reproducible: Print the Unit 6 Poster (2 pages) and affix to 11"x 17" poster board. (Or order premade color posters.)
2	**Practice Unit 6 Poster** **SMART Compliments Description and Modeling** **SMART/Not-So-SMART Teacher Role Playing**	**Unit 6 Poster**
3	**Review Unit 5 Poster** **SMART Polite Requests Role Playing** **Practice SMART Compliments**	**Unit 5 Poster**
4	**Practice Unit 6 Poster** **Reasons for Using SMART Compliments** **SMART Can of Compliments**	• **Unit 6 Poster** • **One can (e.g., coffee can)** • **Unit 6 Can of Compliments** Reproducible 6-4: See Special Preparation Note, p. 80.
5	**Practice SMART Compliments** *My SMART Book* **Unit 6 Coloring Page** **SMART Compliments Checkouts and Recognition**	• *My SMART Book* **Unit 6 Coloring Page** • **Colors** • **SMART Compliments Recognition Cards** Reproducible: On card stock, make several copies of the cards. Then cut and hole punch each card.

73

What's in a Lesson?

Lesson Outline: This box includes an abbreviated lesson plan that can be used during instruction.

Detailed Lesson: Each SMART Lesson also includes a detailed plan that steps out the activity and includes a sample script. The scripting can help you visualize how to directly teach each part of the lesson. The sample dialogues are provided to help you prepare for a lesson. They are not intended to be used during instruction.

For example, in Unit 6, Lesson 1, you will "Model and Explain SMART Compliments" during an activity such as a Read Aloud. Read the script to get a clear idea how to "model" and "explain" this skill.

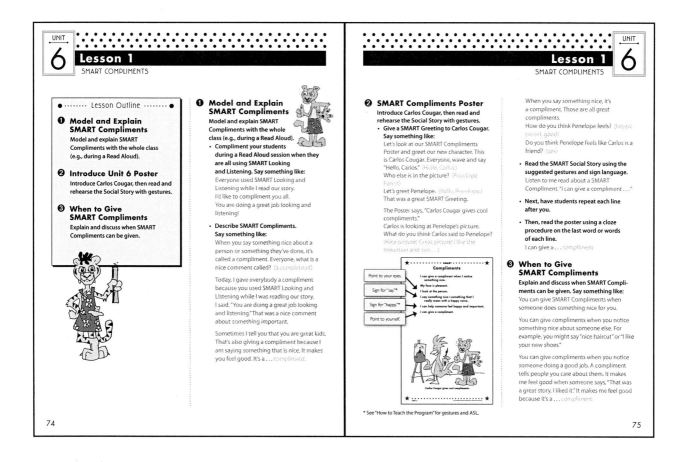

How Are Lessons Sequenced?

Lesson 1: The first lesson introduces the new skill. In Units 1–3, 5–7, 9–12, and 14–17, this includes the introduction of a new poster, suggestions for how to recite the text with gestures, and the introduction of a new SMART Character.

Lesson 2: Students review the poster and practice the new skill with role plays, puppet play, partner practice, and sample scenarios.

Lesson 3: Students review a previously learned skill, and practice the newest social skill.

Lesson 4: Students practice the newest skill, often with a novel activity. (See Can of Compliments below.)

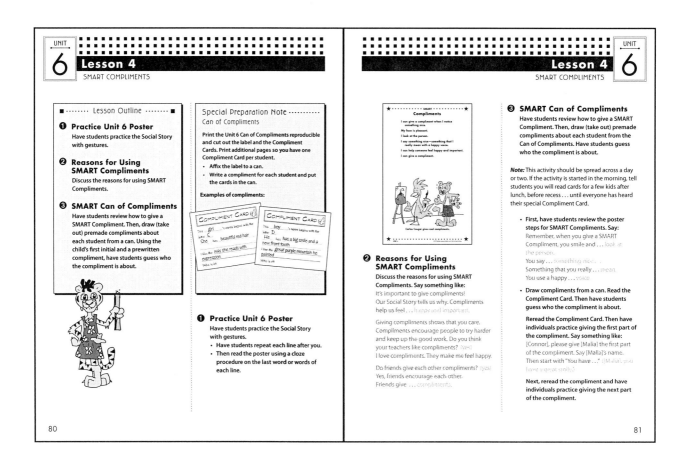

Lesson 5: Students celebrate their accomplishments with a new page in their *My SMART Book*. While students are working in their books, you will check out their new skill and award Recognition Cards.

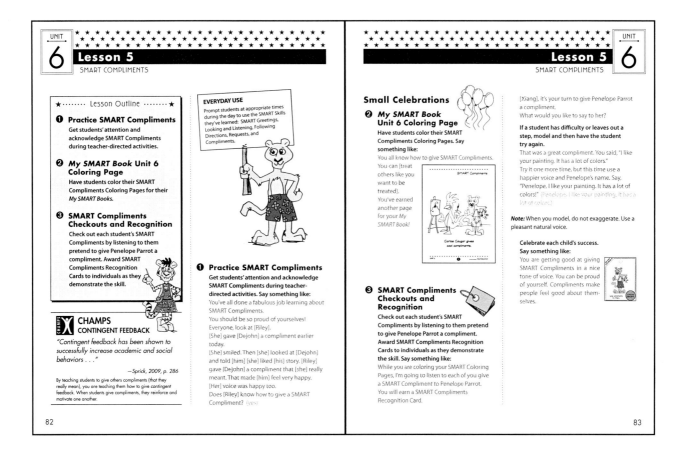

What's Left?

The End-of-Unit Tip provides suggestions for moving forward.

Generalization: Watch this section for how to help students maintain the skill and use it across multiple settings even as you move on to a new social skill.

Intervention: Watch this section for additional tips for helping students who need more practice.

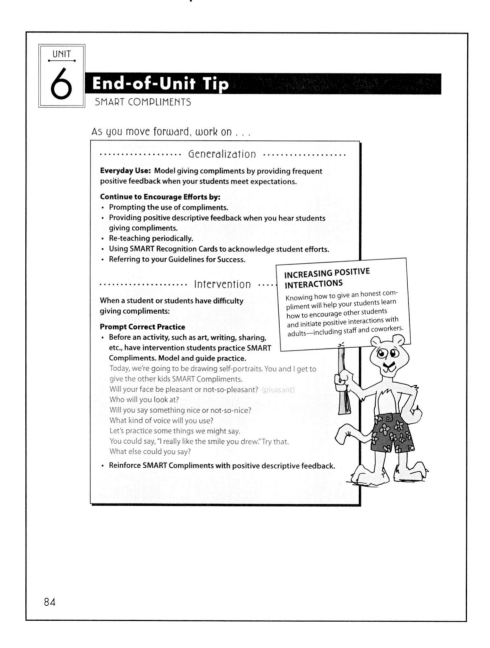

How to Teach the Program

With *SMART Kids,* you can teach proactively. When you teach social skills within a curriculum, your students have the opportunity to learn important social skills during a calm, neutral, and relaxed time.

How Much Time Does it Take to Teach *SMART Kids*?

Eighteen Units: *SMART Kids* is composed of eighteen units, each with five lessons.

- If *SMART Kids* is taught five days per week, the eighteen units can be completed in a semester.

- If *SMART Kids* is taught two to three days per week, the eighteen units can be completed in a school year.

PROACTIVE INSTRUCTION

Social skills are best taught when everyone is happy and open to learning new skills.

Scheduling: Most SMART Lessons require about 15 minutes and are divided into two to four activities. As long as lessons are prepared in advance, you can teach a whole lesson at once or teach the short individual activities as time permits. SMART Activities can make nice sponge activities as long as they are taught in sequence.

How Are SMART Units Constructed and Taught?

Throughout a day, children need multiple social skills to be successful. SMART introduces one new skill at a time so you can focus your instruction and practice on manageable amounts—both for instruction and for learning.

A Focus on Social Stories

Central to each new skill is a social story—a sequence of positive steps that result in successfully engaging in a social skill. Each social story breaks a skill into steps that young children can understand, follow, and learn. Throughout a unit, the social story guides instruction and practice.

For example, the social story for the seemingly simple Unit 2 skill of "Looking and Listening" during a classroom activity is broken into the following steps:

- Sit up.

- Show a pleasant expression.

- Look.

- Listen.

- Keep your mouth quiet.

- Keep your hands and feet still.

Instruction and practice across the unit focuses on guiding students repeatedly through these steps. Once a skill is introduced, you will want to post posters for easy and repeated reference.

★ • • • • • • • • • • SMART • • • • • • • • • • ★
Looking and Listening

Someone is talking to the class.
I sit up.
My face is pleasant.
I look with my eyes.
I listen with my ears.
My mouth is quiet.
My hands and feet are still.
I can look and listen when someone is talking.

Li Lizard looks and listens.

UNIT 2

Instruction and Practice

Each SMART Unit provides explicit instruction in the SMART Skill. During each unit, the SMART Activities lead you through how to:

- Model and describe the skill.

- Discuss with students when, where, and why the skill should be used.

- Engage students in guided practice.

- Provide positive and corrective feedback.

- Learn the difference between using the skill and not using the skill (SMART and Not-So-SMART) behaviors.

- Review with varied activities and celebrate accomplishments.

Modeling of Lessons

In the detailed plans, sample scripting provides you with your own model of how to provide explicit instruction. Because you are busy going about the business of teaching well, the sample dialogues provide you with an idea or vision of how to model and guide practice. In essence, scripts provide advance think alouds for you.

During lessons, you will give directions, model, watch your students, listen, guide practice, and respond appropriately with positive descriptive feedback and gentle corrections. During instruction, follow the Lesson Outlines rather than read the scripts when possible.

Active Engagement

Activities are designed for active engagement.

Group Responses (Verbal and Physical)

Have students practice with group responses. When everyone responds, everyone is engaged. As appropriate:

- Prompt choral responses. Use a quick, simple command such as "Everyone."
- Have students give a thumbs up or thumbs down response.
- Have students follow a direction. For example, say things like: Everyone, touch your nose if you saw a SMART Greeting.
- Have students demonstrate.

Practice With Partners

SMART Lessons include Partner Practice. Students discuss what SMART Skills look and sound like and practice with partners.

Partner Practice gives everyone an individual turn.

Positive Practice and Dramatic Play

SMART Lessons include dramatic play—role plays, role plays with puppets, and role plays with each other.

Games

SMART Lessons also include games to reinforce SMART Skills—Treasure Hunts, Pass the Sack, Five Little Monkeys, and Rock Paper Scissors.

How Do You Teach a Social Story?

For ease of instruction and learning, the social stories present the steps in a logical sequence. A social story often begins with a context, a general body position, and then progresses from head to toe, beginning with general facial expression to eyes, ears, mouths, and then hands and feet.

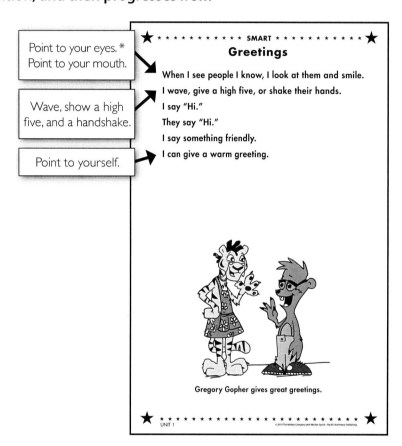

Point to your eyes. *
Point to your mouth.

Wave, show a high five, and a handshake.

Point to yourself.

★ • • • • • • • • • • SMART • • • • • • • • • • • ★
Greetings

When I see people I know, I look at them and smile.
I wave, give a high five, or shake their hands.
I say "Hi."
They say "Hi."
I say something friendly.
I can give a warm greeting.

Gregory Gopher gives great greetings.

★ • ★
UNIT 1   © 2010 The Maskey Company and Marilyn Sprick · Pacific Northwest Publishing

Visual Displays

Ms. Sasha Smart's students demonstrate the skill via illustration.

Gestures and Sign Language

Lesson 1 introduces each social story with simple commonsense gestures. Practice these gestures in advance of instruction.

Beginning with Unit 5, students also learn ten American Sign Language signs. (See p. *f*-27 for gestures and/or go to ASLPro.com for free classroom-based video instruction.)

How to Practice the Social Story

After introducing the skill and poster character:

1. Read each Social Story to your students, using the gestures.

2. Read each line. Have students repeat after you and copy your gestures. For example, with the first line in Unit 3 you would:

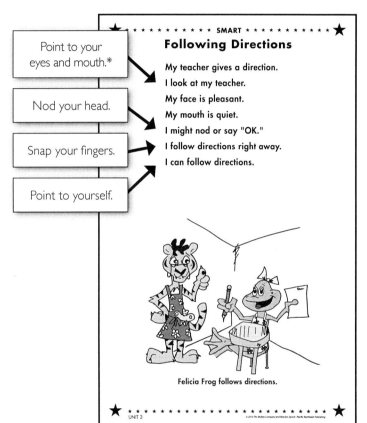

Point to your eyes and mouth.*

Nod your head.

Snap your fingers.

Point to yourself.

★ * * * * * * * * * SMART * * * * * * * * * * ★
Following Directions

My teacher gives a direction.
I look at my teacher.
My face is pleasant.
My mouth is quiet.
I might nod or say "OK."
I follow directions right away.
I can follow directions.

Felicia Frog follows directions.

★ * ★
UNIT 3   © 2010 The Mailbox Company and Marilyn Sprick – Pacific Northwest Publishing

Read: My teacher gives a direction.
Say: Everyone, say that with me.
My teacher gives a direction.

Read and point to your eyes: I look at my teacher.
Say: Everyone, say and do that with me.
Point to your eyes and say: I look at my teacher.

Read: My face is pleasant.
Say: Everyone ... My face is pleasant.

Read and point to your mouth: My mouth is quiet.
Say and point to your mouth:
Everyone ... My mouth is quiet.

A NOTE ON SCRIPTING/SAMPLE DIALOGUE STYLES

Coding for the sample dialogues is fairly intuitive.
- Gray text represents what students say with you.
- Gray text in parentheses represents what students might say without you.
- Open-ended responses are followed by an ellipsis (. . .).
- [Brackets] indicate information you will customize—usually with a student's name in your class.

3. Use a cloze procedure. Begin each line, pause, and then have students finish the last word or words. For example, with the first line in SMART Following Directions you would:

   Say: Everyone, act out the poster with me.

   I'll start a line, and you can help me finish.

   Read and gesture.

   My teacher gives a . . . direction.

   Point to your eyes. I look at my . . . teacher.

   My face is . . . pleasant.

   Point to your mouth. My mouth is . . . quiet.

● · · · · · · · · · · · · ·   American Sign Language (ASL)   · · · · · · · · · · · · ●

1. **Sign for "Please" (starts in Unit 5):** Move your open hand over your heart in a circular motion.

2. **Sign for "Thank you" (starts in Unit 5):** Place the fingertips of your right hand over your mouth. Then move your hand away from your mouth, palm up in front of your chest.

3. **Sign for "OK" (starts in Unit 5):** Fingerspell the letters "O" and "K." (For "K," pointer and middle fingers point up in a "V.")

4. **Sign for "say" (starts in Unit 6):** Put your right index finger in front of your mouth, pointing left, and move your finger in circles outward.

5. **Sign for "happy" (starts in Unit 6):** With an open right hand, touch your heart. Then slide your hand up and off your chest several times.

6. **Sign for "take turns" (starts in Unit 7):** Make an "L" with the thumb and index finger of your right hand with thumb toward chest. Then swing your hand up and out so your thumb faces upward.

7. **Sign for "friend" (starts in Unit 9):** Quickly hook your index fingers together—right over left, then left over right.

8. **Sign for "join" (starts in Unit 9):** Start with your palms out. Quickly bring your hands together, making interlocking circles with each index finger and thumb.

9. **Sign for "sorry" (starts in Unit 14):** Circle your right fist, thumb out, over your heart several times.

10. **Sign for "interrupt" (starts in Unit 15):** Holding your hands flat and thumbs up, bring your right hand on top of your left hand (perpendicular to each other), making a chopping motion.

Note: Several websites have videos that demonstrate how to make ASL gestures. One such website is www.ASLPro.com.

How Do You Teach an Activity?

When preparing to teach, read the description and scripted example. Analyze instruction and practice for:

- Modeling
- Guided practice
- Active engagement

Try to visualize what your lesson will look like.

Example from Unit 1, Lesson 3: What SMART Greetings Look and Sound Like

❷ What SMART Greetings Look and Sound Like

Have students practice SMART Greetings, then share what SMART Greetings look and sound like.

- **Have students practice SMART Greetings. Say something like:**
  Let's all greet [Madison] and make [her] feel welcome.
  [Madison], please go to the door.

p. 8

Everyone, look at [Madison].
Smile and wave. Say "Hi, [Madison]."
(Hi, [Madison].)
Say "How are you doing?"
(How are you doing?)
[Madison], what will you say? (I'm fine.)
I like your smile, [Madison].

p. 9

Have other individuals practice.

- **Have students share with partners what SMART Greetings look and sound like.**
  We're going to tell our partners about SMART Greetings. For example, I might say, "A SMART Greeting includes a wave or a high five."
  Partner 1, tell Partner 2 one thing about how to use a SMART Greeting.
  Repeat with Partner 2.

  [Malia], what did your partner say about how to use a SMART Greeting?
  (Smile when you greet a person you know.)
  That's right! Everyone, show me a smile.

How Do You Encourage Correct Use of a Skill?

When guiding practice and observing students in natural settings, provide positive descriptive feedback, gentle corrective feedback, and correct practice.

Correct Practice

When students practice a skill correctly, acknowledge what they did right with descriptive feedback. Say things like:

[Cailey], I just heard a Polite Request. Your body was quiet. You had a pleasant expression and you said "Please." Let me shake your hand!

Gentle Corrections

When students demonstrate partial competence:

- **Tell students what was right.**

  That was a nice request. I saw quiet bodies. You looked at me, and I heard "Please."

- **Tell students how to make it better.**

  You can make that a great SMART Request by looking at me and showing me a pleasant face.

- **Model the corrected step or help students differentiate between correct and incorrect, if appropriate. You might say something like:**

  Let's try that, but first show me a not-so-pleasant face.
  Now show me a pleasant face.

- **Practice the skill correctly.**

  Try making a Polite Request for free time again.
  Remember—your body is . . . quiet.
  You face is . . . pleasant.
  You look at me.
  And then you start with "May we . . . please have free time."
  That was excellent. I saw pleasant faces.

Repeated Practice

Repeat correct practice in multiple contexts for generalization.

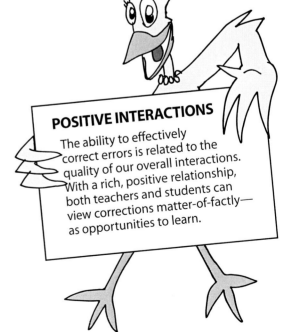

POSITIVE INTERACTIONS
The ability to effectively correct errors is related to the quality of our overall interactions. With a rich, positive relationship, both teachers and students can view corrections matter-of-factly—as opportunities to learn.

How Do You Encourage Students to Generalize Skills?

Once a skill has been taught, it is reviewed in subsequent SMART Units; however, generalization occurs in the natural environment of your classroom.

Once skills are taught, you can easily encourage and reinforce them in the natural course of a day and during special events. Your focus and ongoing attention will help students habituate the skills as well as use them outside of your SMART Lessons.

For example, before reading a story to students, you can prompt with a simple reminder:
This is a great time to use SMART Looking and Listening.

You can also prompt the social skill by reviewing the steps on the related poster.
I'm looking forward to seeing SMART Looking and Listening.
Everyone, should you slouch or sit up? (sit up)
What kind of a face will you show me? Pleasant or not-so-pleasant? (pleasant)
What will you do with your eyes? (look)
What will you do with your ears? (listen)
What will you do with your mouth? (keep it quiet)
What will you do with your hands and feet? (keep them still)

During and after reading a story, you can reinforce with positive descriptive feedback. You can say things like:
I see SMART Looking and Listening. People are sitting up and paying attention! We had fun with this story because you also used SMART Following Directions.

When you see independent use, you can congratulate and reinforce:
Wow! When our principal stopped in to see us, she saw 25 SMART Kids. Everyone gave her a warm greeting and used SMART Looking and Listening. Everyone, thumbs up!

How to Motivate

The single most important element in working with others is developing a rich, positive relationship. Positive descriptive feedback is a tool that will help you build positive relationships while strengthening and reinforcing social manners and respectful talk.

● · · · · · · · · · · · · · SMART Praise · · · · · · · · · · · · · ●

Use positive descriptive feedback:

- Acknowledge and describe how the student used the skill. Catch your kids using SMART Skills and say things like:
  Wow, I just heard a SMART Greeting. You said "Hi" and gave a high five with a smile.
  That was terrific. I just saw . . .

- Show enthusiasm and regard. Make eye contact and smile. Speak honestly with a positive tone.

- Make connections to your Guidelines for Success—remind students that their actions translate into noble concepts like responsibility, respect, kindness, cooperation, and doing one's best.
  I just heard SMART Disagreeing. You had different ideas, but you shared them respectfully.

- Periodically remind students why the skill is important.
  I just heard you give a great compliment to [Abrianna]. That's what friends do. They cheer each other along.

- Encourage self-acknowledgment. Say things like:
  You can be proud of the way you cooled down. Pat yourself on the back.

- Periodically pair tangible rewards with SMART praise.
  I am so proud of the way you apologized when you were wrong. You looked at [Dakota] and [Xavier], said what you did, and then apologized with an honest voice. That was hard to do. I have a SMART Kid Badge for you.

> • ·········· **SMART Reinforcers** ·········· •
>
> **Use tangible, intermittent awards and celebrations. Create a sense of celebration!**
>
> - Periodically reward students (individuals and the class) with a celebration that acknowledges their accomplishments
>
> - Use more frequent intermittent celebrations of success when students are in the early stages of learning a new skill.
>
> - Deliver some rewards unpredictably. This makes them special.
>
> - Use rewards and celebrations sparingly, but as frequently as necessary to motivate students.

SMART Kids Reproducibles

The Teacher Resources folder in the *SMART Kids* Reproducibles CD contains a host of awards and notes ready for you to use.

In Skill Awards and Notes, you will find:

Gregory Gopher's Exceptional Greeter Award
Li Lizard's Looking and Listening Award
Excellence Award for Cooling Down
Problem Solver Award
SMART Home Notes for Following Directions
SMART Kid Notes for Including Others
SMART Kid Notes for Being a SMART Friend

★ ★

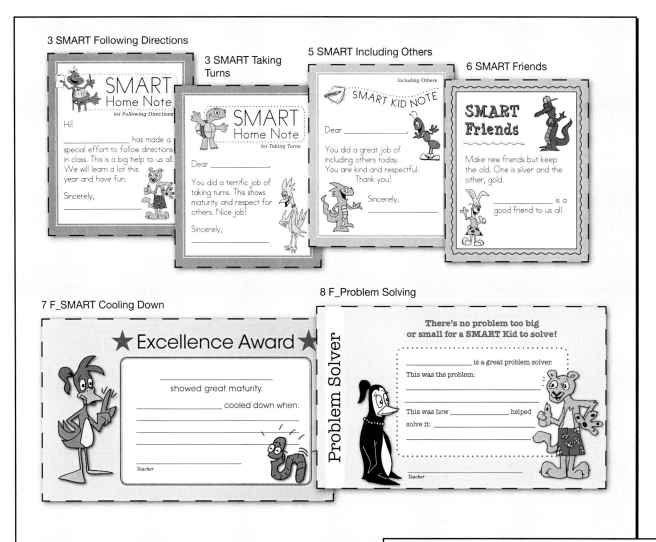

3 SMART Following Directions

3 SMART Taking Turns

5 SMART Including Others

6 SMART Friends

7 F_SMART Cooling Down

8 F_Problem Solving

In General Awards and Notes, you will find:

SMART Home Note
SMART Kid Note
SMART Postcard
SMART Kid Badges
SMART Student of the Week (optional)
Apple Awards (optional)

1 F_SMART Home Note

2 F_SMART Kid Note

Section 5

General Awards and Notes *(continued)*

3 Postcard (front)

3 Postcard (back)

4 Kid Badges

5 SMART Student of the Week

6 Apple Award

In the Unit-Specific Reproducibles Unit 18 folder, you will find:

- Invitations and RSVP cards for the SMART Graduation Ceremony
- Student name tags
- Graduation programs
- Diplomas
- Visitor name tags

Celebrate this SMART Start with a SMART Graduation.

Note: See p. *f*-51 in Section 10: Unit-Specific Reproducibles for thumbnails of the Unit 18 Graduation reproducibles.

Keeping Track of Progress

For your convenience, *SMART Kids* includes two simple record keeping forms—the SMART Checkout Record and the SMART Observation Checklist. These forms are located on the *SMART Kids* Reproducibles CD in Teacher Resources, Record Keeping.

How to Use the SMART Checkout Record

The SMART Checkout Record can be used to keep track of student performance on Lesson 5 Checkouts. For each of the 14 introductory skill units, Lesson 5 provides a scenario in which each student demonstrates his or her ability to perform the new social skill with instructional support as needed.

Checkout Examples:

Unit 1: Have individuals show you a SMART Greeting.

Unit 2: Read a poster to students and have them show you SMART Looking and Listening.

Unit 3: Give a direction such as "Touch your nose" and have students show you SMART Following Directions.

Checkout Rating Scale:

E = Excellent
The student is able to perform the skill independently.

S = Satisfactory
The student is able to perform the skill with minimal prompting. (The skill is likely to continue developing without intervention through basic generalization procedures. See p. f-30.)

N = Needs improvement
The student is able to perform the skill only with heavy prompting and some modeling.

1 F_SMART Checkout Record (page 2)

SMART Checkout Record
For use on Day 5 of each unit

Reproducible 1 (p. 2 of 2)
FILLABLE FORM

Additional Comments

1 F_SMART Checkout Record (page 1)

SMART Checkout Record
For use on Day 5 of each unit

Reproducible 1 (p. 1 of 2)
FILLABLE FORM

Directions: List the date of the checkout. Then record each student's performance. Use the key at the bottom. (You may wish to change ratings as students improve.)

Checkout Date

Students

Greetings
Looking and Listening
Following Directions
Polite Requests
Compliments
Taking Turns
Including Others
Friends
Accepting "No"
Cooling Down
Apologies
Interruptions
Disagreeing
Problem Solving

Teacher _____

Grade _____

Comments

Key: (E) Excellent, (S) Satisfactory, (N) Needs improvement

Because social skills develop over time, you may wish to make additional copies of the form so you can recheck skills and update evaluations.

How to Use the Results

Record-keeping provides you with important feedback. By recording student proficiency levels, you will be aware of:

• Any skill that you need to re-teach to a group of students

• Any student who needs more instruction and practice for improvements to occur

How to Use the SMART Observation Checklist

The SMART Observation Checklist can be used to informally track how well students use SMART Skills in the natural settings of the classroom and school. This checklist is subjective. (You are not formally counting occurrences in a set period of time.) By observing and recording how well students use skills in natural settings, you are keeping a record of how well students are generalizing their skills.

You can use the form once a week or once a month. Set a time for yourself to quickly record your informal observations of student behavior on the SMART Skills you've taught.

Rating Scale

+ = Proficient
The student demonstrates the skill with ease and without prompting. (The student reliably uses the skill on his or her own.)

√ = Developing
The student demonstrates the skill with minimal prompting.
(The student is able to perform the skill but requires reminders.)

– = Beginning
The student needs more instruction and practice.
(If the skill is a high priority, this student would benefit from intervention lessons.)

2 F_SMART Observation Checklist (page 2)

2 F_SMART Observation Checklist (page 1)

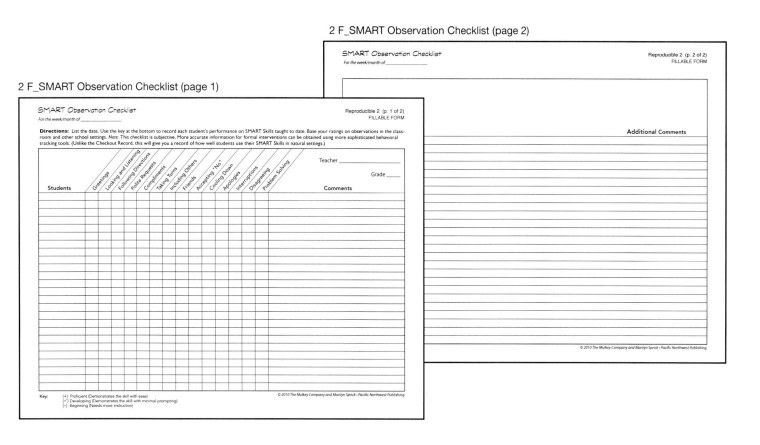

How to Use the Results

The Observation Checklist will help you be aware of student performance on SMART Skills in the natural context of a school day. This will also help you determine:

- Skills you might need to re-teach to a group of students
- Students who can pass a checkout but need more instruction and practice to use the skill in natural settings

Note: This checklist and the SMART Checkout Record are fillable forms. You can type in student names and save a copy to print as needed. See the "Using the CD" file on the CD for more information on working with fillable forms.

Intervention

Some students learn and use social skills easily due to predisposition, family, and or/environmental factors. Other students require extra efforts to become SMART Kids who exhibit social grace, manners, and respectful talk.

● ·······Why Some Kids Need Extra Help ·······●

A student needs intervention when he or she:

- Does not know how to perform the steps in the social skill
- Hasn't had enough practice in different settings to generalize use of the skill
- Is able to perform the skill, but with difficulty
- Is fluent with the skill, but gets more attention and reinforcement for not using the skill

---

When intervention is required, work actively on providing the student with many noncontingent positive interactions. When student-to-teacher and student-student interactions are primarily positive, it is easier for a student to work on difficult skills.

CHAMPS
NONCONTINGENT POSITIVE INTERACTIONS

"Noncontingent attention . . . involves giving students time and attention not because of anything they've done, but just because you notice and value them as people."

—*Sprick, 2009, p. 279*

Noncontingent attention includes greetings, calling on students, and showing an interest in their ideas, feelings, and activities. These rich and positive interactions motivate students to do their best and allow them to tolerate corrections when they are needed. When interventions are needed, rich positive interactions are also needed.

Determine which skill or skills are priorities.

- Consider opportunities for easy success and reinforcement. For example, Greetings may seem to be a low-priority SMART Skill. However, if the student can learn to greet others, he or she can begin the day with many positive interactions. This may therefore be a high-priority skill. Success breeds success.

- Provide more instruction and practice—one-to-one, with a partner, in groups, and in the natural context of the classroom.

- Pre-teach difficult skills in advance of whole class instruction if possible. With this strategy, intervention students can serve as student models.

- Your highest risk students may need scaffolded instruction. If a skill is very difficult for a specific student, you may need to prioritize which steps within a skill you will teach and practice first. Once the student is successful with a few steps, you can gradually add steps.

Acknowledge student efforts with extra Recognition Cards, Skill Awards and Notes, and General Awards and Notes.

Consider setting up a reinforcement system for students who would benefit from added encouragement to use the skill. Reinforcement systems can be set up using materials in the Teacher Resources folder on the _SMART Kids_ Reproducibles CD.

In the Intervention Tools folder, you will find:

> Student Tracker
> SMART Home Ticket
> SMART Home Compliment

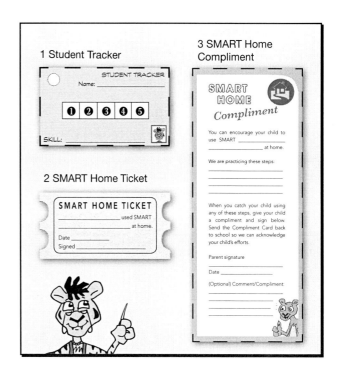

Reinforcement Systems and How to Use Intervention Tools

Reinforcement Systems:

If you decide to use a reinforcement system, be sure to do the following:

- Set up the system so that success is likely.
  The cost of earning rewards should be relatively easy and fast.

- Avoid time limits so that success is always possible.

- Make sure expectations for behavior are clear.

- Continue to provide positive descriptive feedback.

- Once a student is successful, fade the system by increasing the cost of the rewards and the time it takes to earn them. Gradually shift to intermittent rewards.

How to Use Intervention Tools:

- The Student Tracker is worn around a student's wrist or taped to the student's desk. When you catch the student using a specific skill, you punch or mark the Student Tracker. The Student Tracker card can be traded for a prearranged award. (For example, the student might work to be able to eat lunch with the teacher or visit with the principal.)

- Intervention is always the strongest with support and collaboration from a student's family. Enlist their help. Have the family give the student a SMART Ticket when they notice the student using a targeted skill. SMART Tickets can also be exchanged for a prearranged award.

- Students thrive with recognition from the important people in their lives. The SMART Home Compliment encourages families to catch their children using the steps in a targeted skill and give them a much-deserved compliment.

INTERVENTION SPECIFICS
Be sure to watch the End-of-Unit Tips for suggestions on how to help students with specific skills.

Connecting With Families

Mutually reinforcing school-to-home and home-to-school connections can be powerful factors in helping all your students become SMART Kids—children who demonstrate social grace and use respectful talk wherever they are.

To reinforce the school-to-home connection, consider:

- **Implementing a Student-of-the-Week Program.**

  At the end of the week, send home the Student-of-the-Week award with a congratulatory note.

- **Implementing an Apple Tree of Compliments.**

  Send home Apple Awards every couple of weeks. Your children will take great pride in sharing their accomplishments with their families.

- **Sending home a class newsletter.**

  Feature the social skill you are introducing. Include the social story for students to share and practice at home.

- **Sending home Skill Awards and Notes and General Awards and Notes.**

  Young children treasure awards and notes from teachers. By sharing these with families, children are reinforced for their efforts both at school and at home.

- **Making positive phone calls home when you've noticed students making a special effort to use SMART Skills.**

- **Celebrating with the Unit 18 Graduation Ceremony.**

Preparing Materials

1. **Watch the Unit Guides for school materials needed to teach the SMART Lessons.**

    Starting in Unit 1, you will need a puppet.

2. **Locate the Reproducibles CD in the back of this guide.**

    Open the "Using the CD" file for information on how to use the CD. *Note:* Many of the reproducibles are in full color. These can also be printed in black and white.

3. **Set up your SMART Posters.**

     2 SMART Posters

    Each poster is formatted on two 11" x 8.5" (landscape) sheets. These can be printed and mounted on poster board. Full-color 11.5" x 15" posters will be available through Pacific Northwest Publishing in late spring of 2010. Go to www.pacificnwpublish.com for updates.

4. **Make a classroom set of *My SMART Book.***

     3 My SMART Book

    Print and assemble books for each student in your class. *Note:* There are two printing options.

    • My SMART Book
      This version includes a black-and-white cover and coloring pages.

    • My SMART BookAlt
      This version includes a full-color cover (and repeats the same coloring pages).

5. Make Recognition Cards.

 4 Recognition Cards

Each student will collect Recognition Cards on a loose-leaf binder ring (school materials).

Make multiple copies of the cards to pass out when students demonstrate a skill during checkouts and to pass out intermittently when you catch students using the skill during the school day.

6. Set Up Record-Keeping.

 5 Teacher Resources, SMART Checkout Record

Copy and fill in student names by hand or enter student names on the fillable form and print.

7. Set Up Unit-Specific Reproducibles.

 1 Unit-Specific Reproducibles

Print/copy the unit-specific reproducibles and file for future use.

Directions are located on the top of each reproducible and also on the Lesson Planner page for each unit.

8. Make copies of Skill-Specific and General Awards and Notes as appropriate.

 5 Teacher Resources, C Skill Awards and Notes
5 Teacher Resources, D General Awards and Notes

Note: You may wish to make several copies of the SMART Home Notes and SMART Kid Notes—just to have available for a spontaneous note of acknowledgment.

SECTION 10

Index of Unit Reproducibles

We know that every moment you spend with children is a little bit of gold in their lives. With this in mind, we created the *SMART Kids* Reproducibles CD—to make preparation as easy and quick as possible for busy teachers.

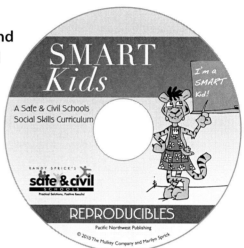

You've already read about and seen:

- SMART Posters
- *My SMART Book*
- Recognition Cards
- Teacher Resources—Record-Keeping, Intervention Tools, Skill-Specific Awards and Notes, General Awards and Notes

What's left? The Unit-Specific Reproducibles!

The Unit-Specific Reproducibles include unique materials designed to keep your lessons easy to teach and interesting for young children. Take a visual walk through this next section to see what's in store for your kids—stick puppets, finger puppets, and teaching props such as Clue Cards, Practice Cards, SMART and Not-So-SMART Cards, Compliment Cards, and more.

1-1 F_Student Greeter Cards

Note: Forms with an **"F"** before the name are electronically fillable forms. You can type directly in these forms and print, or print and then fill them in by hand.

2-2 Faces
(page 1)

2-2 Faces
(page 2)

2-2 Faces
(page 3)

2-2 Faces
(page 4)

2-2 Faces
(page 5)

2-2 Faces
(page 6)

4-1 Greetings Stick Puppets

4-3 Treasure Hunt
(page 1)

4-3 Treasure Hunt
(page 2)

4-5a SMART Not-So-
SMART Cards

4-5b Sharing Book 1

5-4a Practice Cards

★ ★

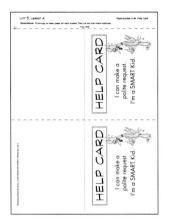

5-4b Help Card

6-4 F_Can of Compliments
(page 1)

6-4 F_Can of Compliments
(page 2)

7-1 Pass the Sack

7-2 Pass the Sack

7-4 SMART Not-So-
SMART Cards

8-2 Treasure Hunt Clue Cards

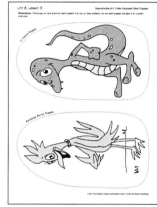

8-3 Polite Requests
Stick Puppets

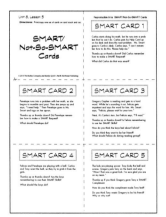

8-5a SMART Not-So-
SMART Cards

8-5b Sharing Book 2

10-3 Practice Cards

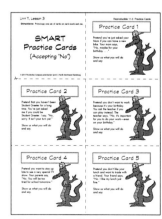

11-3 Practice Cards

Section 10

11-4 No PAWS Symbol (page 1)

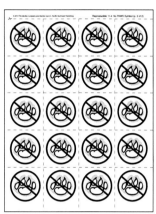

11-4 No PAWS Symbol (page 2)

12-3 Respect and Kindness Scroll

13-2 F_Compliment Cards

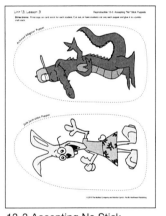

13-3 Accepting No Stick Puppets

13-4 Happy Thoughts

13-5a SMART Not-So-SMART Cards

13-5b Sharing Book 3

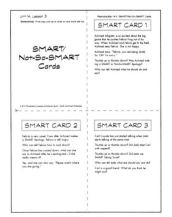

14-3 SMART Not-So-SMART Cards

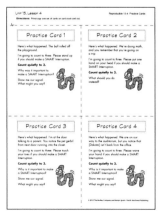

15-4 Practice Cards

16-3 SMART Not-So-SMART Cards

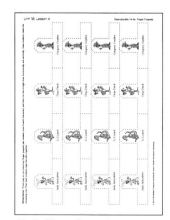

16-4a Finger Puppets

★ ★

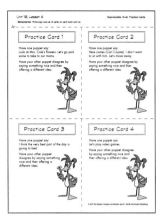

16-4b Practice Cards

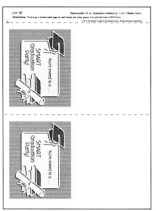

18-1a F_Graduation Invitation
(page 1)

18-1a F_Graduation Invitation
(page 2)

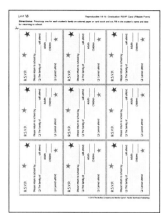

18-1b F_Graduation RSVP Card

18-2 F_Graduation Student
Name Tags

18-3a F_Graduation Program
Option 1 (page 1)

18-3a F_Graduation Program
Option 1 (page 2)

18-3b F_Graduation Program
Option 2 (page 1)

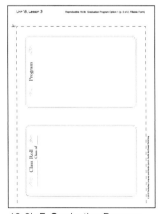

18-3b F_Graduation Program
Option 2 (page 2)

18-5a F_Diploma Option 1

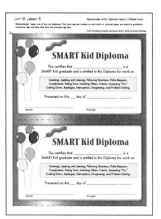

18-5b F_Diploma Option 2

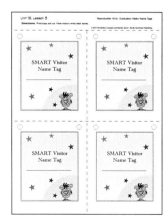

18-5c Graduation Visitor
Name Tags

References

Akin-Little, K., Eckert, T., & Lovett, B. (2004). Extrinsic reinforcement in the classroom: Bribery or best practice. *School Psychology Review, 33,* 344–362.

Anderson, L., Evertson, C., & Emmer, E. (1980). Dimensions in classroom management derived from recent research. *Journal of Curriculum Studies, 12,* 343–356.

Archer, A., & Isaacson, S. (1989). *Design and delivery of academic instruction*. Reston, VA: Council for Exceptional Children.

Babkie, A. (2006). 20 ways to be proactive in managing classroom behavior. *Intervention in School and Clinic, 41,* 184–187.

Baer, G. (1998). School discipline in the United States: Prevention, correction, and long-term social development. *School Psychology Review, 27,* 14–32.

Bandura, A. (1977). *Social learning theory*. Upper Saddle River, NJ: Prentice Hall.

Barbetta, P., Norona, K., & Bicard, D. (2005). Classroom behavior management: A dozen common mistakes and what to do instead. *Preventing School Failure, 49,* 11–19.

Beaman, R., & Wheldall, K. (2000). Teachers' use of approval and disapproval in the classroom. *Educational Psychology, 20,* 431–446.

Beyda, S., Zentall, S., & Ferko, D. (2002). The relationship between teacher practices and the task-appropriate and social behavior of students with behavioral disorders. *Behavioral Disorders, 27,* 236–255.

Binder, C. (1996). Behavioral fluency: Evolution of a new paradigm. *The Behavior Analyst, 19,* 163–197.

Brophy, J. (1981). Teacher praise: A functional analysis. *Review of Educational Research, 51,* 5–32.

Brophy, J. E., & Good, T. L. (1986). Teacher behavior and student achievement. In M.C. Wittrock (Ed.), *Handbook of research on teaching* (3rd ed., pp. 328–375). NY: MacMillan Publishing.

Bullis, M., Walker, H. M., & Sprague, J. R. (2001). A promise unfulfilled: Social skills training with at-risk and antisocial children and youth. *Exceptionality, 9*(1–2), 67–90.

Cameron, J., & Pierce, W. (1994). Reinforcement, reward, and intrinsic motivation: A meta-analysis. *Review of Educational Research, 64,* 363–423.

Caprara, G. V., Barbaranelli, C., Pastorelli, C., Bandura, A., & Zimbardo, P. G. (2000). Prosocial foundations of children's academic achievement. *American Psychological Society, 11*(4), 302–306.

Carr, J., Coriaty, S., Wilder, D., Gaunt, B., Dozier, C., Britton, L., et al. (2000). A review of "noncontingent" reinforcement as treatment for the aberrant behavior of individuals with developmental disabilities. *Research in Developmental Disabilities, 21,* 377–391.

Christenson, S., & Godber, Y. (2001). Enhancing constructive family-school connections. In J. N. Hughes, A. M. LaGreca, & J. C. Conoley (Eds.), *Handbook of psychological services for children and adolescents* (pp. 455–476). New York: Oxford University Press.

Colvin, G., & Sugai, G. (1988). Proactive strategies for managing social behavior problems: An instructional approach. *Education and Treatment of Children, 11,* 341–348.

Colvin, G., Sugai, G., & Patching, B. (1993). Pre-correction: An instructional approach for managing predictable problem behaviors. *Intervention in School and Clinic, 28,* 143–150.

Edwards, D., Hunt, M. H., Meyers, J., Grogg, K. R., & Jarrett, O. (2005). Acceptability and student outcomes of a violence prevention curriculum. *The Journal of Primary Prevention, 26*(5), 401.

Elias, M., & Branden, L. (1998). Primary prevention of behavioral and emotional problems in school-age populations. *School Psychology Review, 17,* 581–592.

Elias, M., & Clabby, J. (1992). *Building social problem solving skills: Guidelines from a school-based program*. San Francisco: Jossey-Bass.

Elksnin, L. K., & Elksnin, N. (1998). Teaching social skills to students with learning and behavior problems. *Intervention in School & Clinic, 333*, 131–141.

Elliott, S. N., & Gresham, F. M. (1991). *Social skills intervention guide: Practical strategies for social skills training.* Circle Pines, MN: American Guidance Service.

Elliott, S. N., & Gresham, F. M. (1993). Social skills interventions for children. *Behavior Modification, 17,* 287–313.

Elliott, S. N., Malecki, C. K., & Demaray, M. K. (2001). New directions in social skills assessment and intervention for elementary and middle school students. *Exceptionality, 9*(1–2), 19–32.

Emmer, E., & Evertson, C. (1981). Synthesis of research on classroom management. *Educational Leadership, January,* 342–347.

Emmer, E., Evertson, C., & Anderson, L. (1980). Effective classroom management at the beginning of the school year. *The Elementary School Journal, 80,* 219–231.

Evertson, C., & Anderson, L. (1979). Beginning school. *Educational Horizons, 57,* 164–168.

Evertson, C., Emmer, E., & Worsham, M. (2003). *Classroom management for elementary teachers* (6th ed.). Boston: Allyn & Bacon.

Gettinger, M., & Ball, C. (2008). Best practices in increasing academic engaged time. In A. Thomas & J. Grimes (Eds.), *Best practices in school psychology V* (pp. 1043–1058). Bethesda, MD: National Association of School Psychologists.

Good, R., & Brophy, J. (2000). *Looking in classrooms* (8th ed.). New York: Longman.

Gresham, F. M. (1996). Best practices in social skills training. *Best practices in school psychology.* Washington, DC: National Association of School Psychologists.

Gresham, F. M. (1998a). Social skills training: Should we raze, remodel, or rebuild? *Behavior Disorders, 24*(1), 19–25.

Gresham, F. M. (1998b). Social skills training with children. In T. S. Watson & F. M. Gresham (Eds.), *Handbook of child behavior therapy* (pp.475–497). New York: Plenum.

Gresham, F. M. (2002). Teaching social skills to high-risk children and youth: Preventive and remedial strategies. In M. R. Shinn, H. M. Walker, & G. Stoner (Eds.), *Interventions for academic and behavior problems II: Preventive and remedial approaches* (pp. 403–432). Bethesda: National Association of School Psychologists.

Gresham, F. M., Sugai, G., & Horner, R. H. (2001). Interpreting outcomes of social skills training for students with high-incidence disabilities. *Exceptional Children, 67,* 331–344.

Gresham, F. M., Watson, S. T., & Skinner, C. H. (2001). Functional behavioral assessment: Principles, procedures, and future directions. *School Psychology Review, 30,* 156–172.

Gunter, P., Coutinho, M., & Cade, T. (2002). Classroom factors linked with academic gains among student with emotional and behavior problems. *Preventing School Failure, 46,* 126–132.

Henderson, A., & Mapp, K. (2002). *A new wave of evidence: The impact of school, family, and community connections on student achievement.* Austin, TX: National Center for Family and Community Connections with Schools, Southwest Educational Development Laboratory.

Johnson, T. C., Stoner, G. & Green, S. K. (1996). Demonstrating the experimenting society model with classwide behavior management interventions. *School Psychology Review, 25,* 199–214.

Jones, Robert N. (1993). Schoolwide social skills training: Providing preventive services to students at-risk. *School Psychology Quarterly, 8*(1), 57–80.

Kerr, J., & Nelson, C. (2002). *Strategies for addressing behavior problems in the classroom* (4th ed.). Englewood Cliffs, NJ: Merrill/Prentice Hall.

Kubina, R. M. (2000). Fluency in education. *Behavior and Social Issues, 10,* 83–99.

Ladd, G., & Mize, J. (1993). A cognitive-social learning model of social skill training. *Psychological Review, 90,* 127–157.

Lampi, A., Fenty, N., & Beaunae, C. (2005). Making the three Ps easier: Praise, proximity, and precorrection. *Beyond Behavior, 15,* 8–12.

Lane, K. L., Givner, C. C., & Pierson, M. R. (2004). Teacher expectations of student behavior: Social skills necessary for success in elementary school classrooms. *Journal of Special Education, 38*(2), 104–110.

Section II

Lope, M., & Edelbaum, J. (1999). *I'm popular! Do I need social skills training?* Unpublished manuscript, Pennsylvania State University.

Madsen, C. H., Jr., Becker, W. C., & Thomas, D. R. (1968). Rules, praise, and ignoring: Elements of elementary classroom control. *Journal of Applied Behavior Analysis, 1,* 139–150.

Mayer, G. (1995). Preventing antisocial behavior in the schools. *Journal of Applied Behavior Analysis, 28,* 467–478.

McGlynn, M. M., & Rutherford, R. B. (2001). Teaching social skills to enrich the lives of children and youth with emotional and behavioral difficulties. *Focal Point, 15*(2).

Miller, D., & Kraft, N. (2008). Best practices in communicating with and involving parents. In A. Thomas & J. Grimes (Eds.), *Best practices in school psychology V* (pp. 937–951). Bethesda, MD: National Association of School Psychologists.

Murray, C., & Greenberg, M. (2006). Examining the importance of social relationships and social contexts in the lives of children with high-incidence disabilities. *The Journal of Special Education, 39,* 220–233.

Rhode, G., Jenson, W. R., & Reavis, H. K (in press). *The tough kid book* (2nd ed). Eugene, OR: Pacific Northwest Publishing.

Rosenshine, B. (1971). *Teaching behaviours and student achievement.* London: National Foundation for Educational Research.

Rosenshine, B. (1978). The third cycle of research on teacher effects: Content covered, academic engaged time, and quality of instruction. In *78th Yearbook of the National Society for the Study of Education.* Chicago: University of Chicago Press.

Rosenshine, B. (1983). Teaching functions in instructional programs. *Elementary School Journal, 83,* 335–351.

Rosenshine, B. (1986). Synthesis of research on explicit teaching. *Educational Leadership, 43,* 60–69.

Rosenshine, B. (1997). Advances in research on instruction. In J. W. Lloyd, E. J. Kame'enui, & D. Chard (Eds.), *Issues in education students with disabilities.* Mahwah, NJ: Lawrence Erlbaum.

Simonsen, B., Fairbanks, S., Briesch, A., Myers, D., & Sugai, G. (2008). Evidence-based practices in classroom management: Considerations for research to practice. *Education and Treatment of Children, 31,* 351–380.

Spence, S. H. (1995). *Social skills training: Enhancing social competence in children and adolescents.* Windsor, UK: NFER-Nelson.

Spence, S. H. (2003). Social skills training with children and young people: Theory, evidence and practice. *Child and Adolescent Mental Health, 8*(2), 84–96.

Sprick, R. (2009). *CHAMPS: A proactive & positive approach to classroom management* (2nd ed.). Eugene, OR: Pacific Northwest Publishing.

Sprick, R., & Garrison, M. (2008). *Interventions: Evidence-based behavioral strategies for individual students* (2nd ed.). Eugene, OR: Pacific Northwest Publishing.

Stormont, M., Smith, S., & Lewis, T. (2007). Teacher implementation of precorrection and praise statements in Head Start classrooms as a component of a program-wide system of positive behavior support. *Journal of Behavioral Education, 16,* 280–290.

Sugai, G., & Lewis, T. (1996). Preferred and promising practices for social skill instruction. *Focus on Exceptional Children, 29,* 1–16.

Sutherland, K. (2000). Promoting positive interactions between teachers and students with emotional/behavioral disorders. *Preventing School Failure, 44,* 110–116.

Trussell, R. (2008). Classroom universals to prevent problem behaviors. *Intervention in school and clinic, 43,* 179–185.

Vincent, C. G., Horner, R. H., & Sugai, G. (2002). Developing social competence for all students. *ERIC/OSEP Digest.*

Walker, H., Colvin, G., & Ramsey, E. (1995). *Antisocial behavior in school: Strategies and best practices.* Pacific Grove, CA: Brooks/Cole Publishing Company.

Weissberg, R., Caplan, M., & Harwood, R. (1991). Promoting competency-enhancing environments: A systems-based perspective on primary prevention. *Journal of Consulting and Clinical Psychology, 59,* 830–841.

SMART Greetings

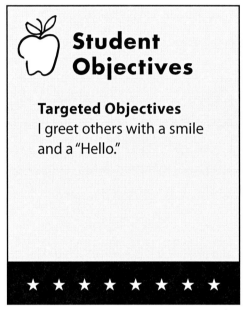

Student Objectives

Targeted Objectives
I greet others with a smile and a "Hello."

Note: Sample scripts or dialogues are provided as a model for how to teach SMART Skills explicitly. Read these in advance of instruction so you can visualize the lesson. Use the Lesson Outlines and your own words when you teach.

UNIT 1

SMART GREETINGS
Overview

······· Teaching Objectives ·······

A warm greeting may include some or all of the steps below. Students practice all of the steps and demonstrate competency by using at least three of the steps:

1. Looking at the person
2. Smiling or having a pleasant expression
3. Waving, giving a high five, or handshake
4. Using a greeting, such as "Hi," "Hello," or "Good morning"...
5. Saying something friendly

Teaching Materials

School Materials
- Puppet of your choice
- Colors
- Loose-leaf binder rings (one per student)

SMART Materials
- Unit 1 Poster
- *My SMART Book* Unit 1 Coloring Page
- SMART Greetings and Student Name Recognition Cards
- SMART Checkout Record
- Unit 1 Reproducibles: 1-1 Student Greeter Cards (Optional)

Teaching Tips ··············

Positive Interactions
Meet students at the door each day as part of your morning routine. Start each student's day with a positive interaction.

Respond warmly to student greetings.
What a nice smile. It's great to see you.

Positive Feedback and Reinforcement
Provide positive descriptive feedback.
That was a nice greeting. You smiled and gave me a warm "Hello."

Use SMART Recognition Cards to acknowledge student efforts.

Connections
Reference your Guidelines for Success. For example, Be respectful.
I saw and heard a lot of SMART Greetings this morning. That shows you respect each other.

·········· Intervention ··········

Make an overt effort to practice SMART Greetings with students who are less adept at social interactions.

Have these students join you in greeting others. Prompt and guide practice.

Optional: Make Student Greeter Cards.

**GREETINGS ARE ...
OH, SO IMPORTANT!**
- When students are greeted at the door, they begin their day with a positive interaction.
- By learning to give a warm greeting, students learn how to initiate their own positive interactions.

2

Lesson Planner

Lesson	Activities	Materials and Materials Preparation
1 ●●●	**SMART Greetings Daily Routine** **Introduce SMART Greetings** **Introduce Unit 1 Poster** **When and Where to Use SMART Greetings**	**Unit 1 Poster** Reproducible: Print the Unit 1 Poster (2 pages) and affix to 11″ x 17″ poster board. (Or order premade color posters.)
2 ▲▲▲	**Practice Unit 1 Poster** **SMART Greetings Description and Modeling** **SMART/Not-So-SMART Puppet Play**	• **Unit 1 Poster** • **A puppet**
3 ◆◆◆	**Practice Unit 1 Poster** **What SMART Greetings Look and Sound Like** **SMART/Not-So-SMART Puppet Play**	• **Unit 1 Poster** • **A puppet**
4 ■■■	**Practice Unit 1 Poster** **Reasons for Using SMART Greetings** **SMART Greetings Practice**	**Unit 1 Poster**
5 ★★★	**Practice SMART Greetings** ***My SMART Book* Unit 1 Coloring Page** **SMART Greetings Checkouts and Recognition**	• ***My SMART Book* Unit 1 Coloring Page** Reproducible: Copy and bind the entire *My SMART Book* for each student. • **Colors** • **SMART Greetings and Student Name Recognition Cards** Reproducible: On card stock, make several copies of the cards. Cut and hole punch each card. • **SMART Checkout Record** Reproducible (5 Teacher Resources > A Record Keeping > 1 F_SMART Checkout Record): Print one copy and fill in student names.

Student Greeter Cards (Optional)

Reproducibles 1-1: On card stock, copy the greeter cards. Cut and hole punch each card as indicated.

● ········ Lesson Outline ········ ●

**❶ SMART Greetings
Daily Routine**

Model SMART Greetings as students
enter your classroom in the morning.

❷ Introduce SMART Greetings

Describe and model SMART Greetings.

❸ Introduce Unit 1 Poster

Introduce Gregory Gopher and Ms.
Sasha Smart, then read and rehearse
the Social Story with gestures.

**❹ When and Where to Use
SMART Greetings**

Explain and discuss when and where
SMART Greetings should be used.

**❶ SMART Greetings
Daily Routine**

Model SMART Greetings as students enter
your classroom in the morning.

❷ Introduce SMART Greetings

Describe and model SMART Greetings.

• **Describe a SMART Greeting.
Say something like:**
Today, we're going to learn how
to greet someone.

This morning, I greeted each of
you at the door. That was fun.

A greeting shows others that you are
happy to see them.

Nod your head if you think I was happy to
see you this morning.
I made you feel welcome because I used a
SMART Greeting.

I looked at you and smiled.
I waved, gave you a high five, or maybe
shook your hand.

I said "Hi" and then I said something
friendly.

• **Model a SMART Greeting. Have a student
go to the door. Then greet the student
with a welcoming voice, warm expression,
and a wave or a handshake.
Say something like:**
Watch and listen to me give [Isabella] a
SMART Greeting.
Wave and say: Good morning, [Isabella].
It's so nice to see you today.

4

❸ Introduce Unit 1 Poster

Introduce Gregory Gopher and Ms. Sasha Smart, then read and rehearse the Social Story with gestures. Say something like:

I have a new poster for us that tells about a SMART Greeting. Look at the picture. Gregory Gopher is giving his teacher Ms. Sasha Smart a SMART Greeting. It says, "Gregory Gopher gives great greetings." What is Gregory doing? (giving a great greeting, waving hello . . .)

• **Read the Social Story to students.**

Listen to me read about SMART Greetings. "When I see people I know . . ."

• Next, have students repeat each line after you.

Point to your eyes. *
Point to your mouth.

Wave, show a high five, and a handshake.

Point to yourself.

★ • • • • • • • • SMART • • • • • • • • ★
Greetings

When I see people I know, I look at them and smile.
I wave, give a high five, or shake their hands.
I say "Hi."
They say "Hi."
I say something friendly.
I can give a warm greeting.

Gregory Gopher gives great greetings.

★ • ★
UNIT 1

• Then, read the poster using a cloze procedure. Start each line and have students complete the last word or words of each line.

When I see . . . people I know,
I look at them and . . . smile.
I wave, give a . . . high five, or . . . shake their hands.
I say . . . "Hi."
They say . . . "Hi."
I say something . . . friendly.
I can give a . . . warm greeting.

❹ When and Where to Use SMART Greetings

Explain and discuss when and where SMART Greetings should be used.
Say something like:

You can use a SMART Greeting when you see me tomorrow morning.
You can use a SMART Greeting when you see your classmates.

Who can tell me when you can use a SMART Greeting? (when we see you tomorrow, when we see our classmates)

Who can tell me some other times you could use SMART Greetings?
(when we see another teacher, the principal, our friends, our parents . . .)

* See "How to Teach the Program" for gestures and ASL.

Lesson 2
SMART GREETINGS

▲ ······ Lesson Outline ······· ▲

❶ Practice Unit 1 Poster

Have students practice the Social Story with gestures.

❷ SMART Greetings Description and Modeling

Describe and model SMART Greetings using the poster steps.

❸ SMART/Not-So-SMART Puppet Play

Use a puppet to show SMART and Not-So-SMART Greetings. Use the poster steps to help students determine whether the greeting was SMART or Not-So-SMART. Then have students practice SMART Greetings.

PACING AND SCRIPTING

The detailed scripting in each lesson provides a model for how to explicitly teach the lesson. Review the scripts before instruction. During instruction, use the lesson outline.

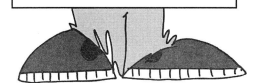

❶ Practice Unit 1 Poster

Have students practice the Social Story with gestures.

- Have students repeat each line after you.
- Then read the poster using a cloze procedure on the last word or words of each line.

★ · · · · · · · · · SMART · · · · · · · · · ★
Greetings

When I see people I know, I look at them and smile.
I wave, give a high five, or shake their hands.
I say "Hi."
They say "Hi."
I say something friendly.
I can give a warm greeting.

Gregory Gopher gives great greetings.

★ · ★
UNIT 1

❷ SMART Greetings Description and Modeling

Describe and model SMART Greetings using the poster steps. Say something like:

When you give someone a SMART Greeting, you use a SMART face and body.
That means you look at the person, smile and wave, give a high five, or shake hands.
You say "Hi" or "Good morning" and use the person's name.
Then you say something friendly, such as, "How are you?"

❸ SMART/Not-So-SMART Puppet Play

Use a puppet to show SMART and Not-So-SMART Greetings. Then have students practice SMART Greetings using the poster steps as a guide.

- **Have students watch the puppet use the steps for SMART Greetings.**

  First, have a student go to the door, pretend to enter the classroom, and then sit down.

  Have the puppet greet the student with a wave. In the puppet's voice, say:
  Hi, [Dejohn]. How are you this morning?

  Next, use the poster steps to help students evaluate whether it was a SMART Greeting. Ask students:
  Did the puppet look at [Dejohn]? (yes)
  I think the puppet also smiled.
  Did the puppet wave? (yes)
  What did the puppet say? (Hi, [Dejohn]. How are you this morning?)
  Did the puppet give a warm greeting? (yes)

  [Dejohn], did the puppet make you feel happy and welcome? (yes)

- **Have students watch the puppet use a Not-So-SMART Greeting.**
  Now let's look at a Not-So-SMART Greeting.

  **Have another self-assured student go to the door and pretend to enter the classroom and then sit down.
  Have the puppet barely look at the student.**

Did the puppet look at [Abrianna] and smile? (no)
Did the puppet wave or give a high five? (no)
Do you think the puppet made [Abrianna] feel happy and welcome? (no)
Do you think [Abrianna] feels like being the puppet's friend? (no)
I think we better try a SMART Greeting!

- **Guide students through a SMART Greeting. Have the same student enter the door again. Then say something like:**
  Let's make [Abrianna] feel welcome with a SMART Greeting.
  Everyone, smile, wave, and say "Hi, [Abrianna]." (Hi, [Abrianna].)
  Now say, "Come on in and join us." (Come on in and join us.)
  That shows you care.

UNIT 1

Lesson 3

SMART GREETINGS

◆ ······· Lesson Outline ······· ◆

❶ Practice Unit 1 Poster

Have students practice the Social Story with gestures.

❷ What SMART Greetings Look and Sound Like

Have students practice SMART Greetings, then share what SMART Greetings look and sound like.

❸ SMART/Not-So-SMART Puppet Play

Use a puppet to demonstrate SMART and Not-So-SMART Greetings. Use the poster steps to help students determine whether the greetings are SMART or Not-So-SMART. Then have students practice SMART Greetings.

---

❶ Practice Unit 1 Poster

Have students practice the Social Story with gestures.

- Have students repeat each line after you.
- Then read the poster using a cloze procedure on the last word or words of each line.

★ · · · · · · · · · · SMART · · · · · · · · · · ★
Greetings

When I see people I know, I look at them and smile.
I wave, give a high five, or shake their hands.
I say "Hi."
They say "Hi."
I say something friendly.
I can give a warm greeting.

Gregory Gopher gives great greetings.

★ · ★
UNIT 1

❷ What SMART Greetings Look and Sound Like

Have students practice SMART Greetings, then share what SMART Greetings look and sound like.

- Have students practice SMART Greetings. Say something like:

Let's all greet [Madison] and make [her] feel welcome.

[Madison], please go to the door.

Everyone, look at [Madison].
Smile and wave. Say "Hi, [Madison]."
(Hi, [Madison].)
Say "How are you doing?"
(How are you doing?)
[Madison], what will you say? (I'm fine.)
I like your smile, [Madison].

Have other individuals practice.

• **Have students share with partners what SMART Greetings look and sound like.**
We're going to tell our partners about SMART Greetings. For example, I might say, "A SMART Greeting includes a wave or a high five."
Partner 1, tell Partner 2 one thing about how to use a SMART Greeting.
Repeat with Partner 2.

[Malia], what did your partner say about how to use a SMART Greeting?
(Smile when you greet a person you know.)
That's right! Everyone, show me a smile.

What else do you do with a SMART Greeting? (wave, give a high five, shake hands . . .)

Then what do you do? (Say "Hi!" Say "Hello!" Say "Good morning!")
That's right. It's also nice to use the person's . . . name.

❸ **SMART/Not-So-SMART Puppet Play**

Use a puppet to demonstrate SMART and Not-So-SMART Greetings. Then have students practice SMART Greetings using the poster steps.

• **Review the steps for SMART Greetings.**
Remember, when you use SMART Greetings, you look and . . . smile.
You wave, give a high five, or . . . shake hands.
You say . . . "Hi!"
They say . . . "Hi!"
Then you can say something friendly.

• **Use the poster steps to help students determine whether the puppet is using SMART or Not-So-SMART Greetings. Have a student enter the room. Have the puppet look away from the student. Say something like:**
Thumbs up if that was a SMART Greeting.
Thumbs down if that was a Not-So-SMART Greeting.

Let's figure out why that was Not-So-SMART.
Did the puppet look and smile? (no)
Did the puppet say "Hi," "Hello," or "Good Morning"? (no)
Did the puppet wave, give a high five, or shake hands? (no)
Did the puppet show [Malia] that [he] cared about [her]? (no)
Do you think [Malia] wants the puppet to be [her] friend? (no)
What do we want to do in our classroom—SMART Greetings or Not-So-SMART Greetings? (SMART Greetings)

• **Have the puppet model a SMART Greeting. Use the poster to help students.**

Lesson 4

SMART GREETINGS

■ ······· Lesson Outline ······· ■

❶ Practice Unit 1 Poster

Have students practice the Social Story with gestures.

❷ Reasons for Using SMART Greetings

Discuss the reasons for using SMART Greetings.

❸ Practice SMART Greetings

Practice SMART Greetings with the group, with partners, and individually throughout the day.

❶ Practice Unit 1 Poster

Have students practice the Social Story with gestures.

- Have students repeat each line after you.
- Then read the poster using a cloze procedure on the last word or words of each line.

★ · · · · · · · · · · SMART · · · · · · · · · · ★
Greetings

When I see people I know, I look at them and smile.
I wave, give a high five, or shake their hands.
I say "Hi."
They say "Hi."
I say something friendly.
I can give a warm greeting.

Gregory Gopher gives great greetings.

★ · ★
UNIT 1

❷ Reasons for Using SMART Greetings

Discuss the reasons for using SMART Greetings. Say something like:

It's important to greet others.

When you use a SMART greeting, people will see that you are friendly.

People will be more likely to ask you to do fun things.

They may want to spend more time with you. What happens when you use a SMART Greeting? (People like you. You make new friends . . .)

If you don't greet people in a friendly way, people may think you don't want to be friends.
They may not want to get to know you.
They may leave you out.
It is hard to make friends if you don't know how to use a SMART Greeting.

❸ Practice SMART Greetings

Practice SMART Greetings with the group, with partners, and individually throughout the day.

- **Practice SMART Greetings with the group. Say something like:**
Everyone, pretend it's tomorrow morning and you see me. Show and tell me a SMART Greeting. (Hi, [Mrs. Mulkey].)
Great smiles! Nice waves!

If a child misses a step, tell the student what he or she did correctly. Gently guide a correction.
For example, if a child doesn't smile, provide positive feedback on what was correct.
[Connor], what a nice greeting. You said "Hi, [Mrs. Mulkey]."

Next, provide a correction.
Smile and say that again for me. (Hi [Mrs. Mulkey].)

When the child is successful, provide descriptive feedback. Say something like:
I liked that smile, [Connor]!

- **Practice SMART Greetings with partners. Say something like:**
Partner 1, turn to Partner 2 and give a SMART Greeting.
Partner 2, thumbs up if your partner gave you a SMART Greeting.

Repeat with Partner 2.

- **Celebrate each child's success. Review with individuals as needed. For example, when [Connor] enters the room after afternoon recess, say something like:**
Excellent, [Connor]. When you greeted me, you remembered to smile on your own. That made me feel like you were happy to see me. Remember to smile tomorrow when we greet each other in the morning.

PROMPT SMART GREETINGS
Provide prompts throughout the day. For example, when [Connor] enters the room after lunch, say something like:
Good to see you [Connor]. Remember to smile with your SMART Greeting.

11

★······· Lesson Outline ·······★

❶ Practice SMART Greetings

Get students' attention and acknowledge SMART Greetings during teacher-directed activities.

❷ My SMART Book Unit 1 Coloring Page

Have students color their SMART Greetings Coloring Pages for their SMART Books.

❸ SMART Greetings Checkouts and Recognition

Check out each student by having the student give you a greeting. Award SMART Greetings Recognition Cards as students demonstrate the skill.

CHAMPS
SMALL CELEBRATIONS

"Periodically reward both individuals and students with a celebration that acknowledges their progress and success in meeting behavioral and academic goals."

—Sprick, 2009, p. 293

Small Celebrations

❶ Practice SMART Greetings

Get students' attention and acknowledge SMART Greetings during teacher-directed activities. Say something like:

You've done a fantastic job learning about SMART Greetings.
I'm very proud of you all.
Everyone, look at [Caden] and [Ethan].
They were your Student Greeters this morning.
Did they look at you and smile? (yes)
Did they say "Hi"? (yes)
Wow, [Caden] and [Ethan] really know how to make SMART Greetings! Let's all give them a thumbs-up.

❷ My SMART Book Unit 1 Coloring Page

Have students color their SMART Greetings Coloring Pages for their SMART Books.
Say something like:
You can all make SMART Greetings.
You can all [be respectful and treat others like you want to be treated].

Because you all know how to make SMART Greetings, you've just earned the first page for your SMART Book! This is your My SMART Book. It's a very special book.

SMART Greetings

Gregory Gopher gives great greetings.

UNIT 1

★ ★
★ ★
★ ★

UNIT
1

Lesson 5
SMART GREETINGS

Every time you learn a new SMART skill you get to color a page in your book.
Put your name on the cover . . .

RECORD KEEPING

Use the SMART Checkout Record on the CD to keep track of student progress. See Intervention suggestions on the next page for students who need improvement.

❸ **SMART Greetings Checkouts and Recognition**

Check out each student by having the student give you a greeting. Award SMART Greetings Recognition Cards to individuals as they demonstrate the skill.

• **Tell students you will have each student give you a SMART Greeting while the class is coloring. Say something like:**
  While you are coloring your SMART Coloring Pages, I'm going to have each of you give me a SMART Greeting.

• **Show and explain the SMART Greetings Recognition Cards.**

  When you give me a SMART Greeting, you will get a binder ring, a Student Name Recognition Card, and a SMART Greetings Recognition Card. You can collect SMART Recognition Cards! On special occasions, I'll award you other SMART Recognition Cards that you can add to your ring.

• **While students are coloring, circulate and have each student give you a SMART Greeting. Model and guide as needed. Award SMART Recognition Cards, rings, Student Name Recognition Cards, and SMART Greetings Recognition Cards to each student, even if assistance is needed.**

Note: You can finish this informal assessment during your morning greeting with individual students, or during another independent work time. Keep track of students who would benefit from more guided practice.

End-of-Unit Tip

SMART GREETINGS

As you move forward, work on . . .

·············· Generalization ···············

Everyday Use: Have a Student Greeter help you or another adult welcome students each morning. Train all adults in SMART Greetings.

Continue to Encourage Efforts by:
- Responding warmly to student greetings.
- Providing positive descriptive feedback.
- Providing gentle corrections and guided practice as needed.
- Re-teaching periodically.
- Using SMART Greetings Recognition Cards to acknowledge student efforts.
- Referring to your Guidelines for Success.

·············· Intervention ···············

When a student or students have difficulty giving a warm greeting:

Add Practice
Give the student the job of Student Greeter and guide practice.

Scaffold Instruction
For some students, you may need to teach and reinforce one new step at a time.
- Start with the easiest step.
- Provide guided practice in small groups or one-to-one.
- When students master one step, add another.

For example, the social story says, "I look at them and smile." Students can practice looking at themselves in a mirror and smiling. Partners can practice looking and smiling at one another. Students can give the instructor a thumbs up or thumbs down. Once this is mastered, students can add a wave to their greeting.

**WEEKLY SMART JOB
Student Greeters**

Begin assigning the job of Student Greeter to one or two individuals. This is a great reward and reinforcer for a student who has just acquired this skill.

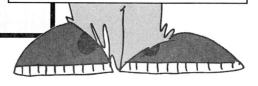

SMART Looking and Listening

Student Objectives

Targeted Objectives
I look and listen when someone is talking.

Review Objectives
I greet others with a smile and a "Hello."

UNIT 2 SMART LOOKING AND LISTENING
Overview

······· Teaching Objectives ·······

Students practice and demonstrate competency by using all of the steps below:

1. Sitting up
2. Smiling or having a pleasant expression
3. Looking
4. Listening
5. Mouth quiet
6. Hands and feet still

Teaching Materials

School Materials

- Puppet of your choice
- Colors

SMART Materials

- Units 1 and 2 Posters
- *My SMART Book* Unit 2 Coloring Page
- Recognition Cards for Greetings and Looking and Listening
- Unit 2 Reproducibles:
  2-2 Faces

SMART LOOKING AND LISTENING IS . . . OH, SO IMPORTANT!

- When students learn to look at and listen to teachers, they are also learning how to learn from adults.
- When students learn to look at and listen to peers, they are learning how to interact positively with others.

·············· Teaching Tips ··············

Positive Interactions

Respond warmly to students when they look and listen appropriately. Say things like:
I can tell you are ready to learn. You are using SMART Looking and Listening.

Positive Feedback and Reinforcement

Provide positive descriptive feedback.
Wow, everyone is looking at [Emma]. You have your mouth, hands, and feet quiet and you are ready for listening.

Use SMART Recognition Cards to acknowledge student efforts.

Connections

Reference your Guidelines for Success. For example, Be respectful. Always do your best.
I saw you using SMART Looking and Listening. It is a great way to be respectful. It also shows you are paying attention and doing your best.

·········· Intervention ··········

Make an overt effort to practice SMART Looking and Listening with students who have difficulty paying attention. Have these students model SMART Looking and Listening after prompting the group. Say something like:
We're going to use SMART Looking and Listening. Everyone, sit up. Look at [Berto]. He is sitting up.

Lesson Planner

Lesson	Activities	Materials and Materials Preparation
1 •••	**Introduce SMART Looking and Listening** **Introduce Unit 2 Poster** **When and Where to Use SMART Looking and Listening**	**Unit 2 Poster** Reproducible: Print the Unit 2 Poster (2 pages) and affix to 11"x 17" poster board. (Or order premade color posters.)
2 ▲▲▲	**Practice Unit 2 Poster** **SMART Looking and Listening Description and Modeling** **SMART/Not-So-SMART Puppet Play**	• **Unit 2 Poster** • **A puppet**
3 ♦♦♦	**Review Unit 1 Poster** **Review What SMART Greetings Look and Sound Like** **Review SMART Looking and Listening** **Pleasant and Not-So-Pleasant Faces**	• **Unit 1 Poster** • **Unit 2 Faces** Reproducible 2-2: Copy each of the six pleasant and not-so-pleasant faces on 8.5 x 11 inch card stock.
4 ■■■	**Practice Unit 2 Poster** **Reasons for Using SMART Looking and Listening** **Practice SMART Looking and Listening**	**Unit 2 Poster**
5 ★★★	**Practice SMART Looking and Listening** ***My SMART Book* Unit 2 Coloring Page** **SMART Looking and Listening Checkouts and Recognition**	• ***My SMART Book* Unit 2 Coloring Page** • **Colors** • **SMART Looking and Listening Recognition Cards** Reproducible: On card stock, make several copies of the cards. Cut and hole punch each card.

Lesson 1

SMART LOOKING AND LISTENING

● ········ Lesson Outline ········ ●

❶ Introduce SMART Looking and Listening

Model and explain SMART Looking and Listening during a sharing activity.

❷ Introduce Unit 2 Poster

Introduce Li Lizard, then read and rehearse the Social Story with gestures.

❸ When and Where to Use SMART Looking and Listening

Explain and discuss when and where SMART Looking and Listening should be used.

PACING AND SCRIPTING

Remember, scripting provides a model for how to teach explicitly. Use the scripts to prepare for instruction. Teach from the Lesson Outline.

❶ Introduce SMART Looking and Listening

Model and explain SMART Looking and Listening during a sharing activity.

- **Call on a student to share with the class. While the student is talking, tell students to watch you model SMART Looking and Listening. Say something like:**

  Sharing is an important time to be respectful of others. Watch me use SMART Looking and Listening while [Jabaar] shares.

  Use a friendly expression, and don't talk until the child finishes speaking.

- **When the student stops talking, say something like:**

  [Jabaar, your new snake book] looks interesting. [I can't wait to read it.]

- **Then, describe SMART Looking and Listening. Say something like:**

  I just used SMART Looking and Listening when [Jabaar] was talking.
  I sat up.
  My face was pleasant . . . I had a friendly expression.
  My eyes were looking at [Jabaar]. I listened and I didn't talk while [he] was talking.
  I showed respect by keeping my hands and feet still.
  Then I used [Jabaar]'s name and told [him] that [his snake book looked interesting].
  That's the way to do SMART Looking and Listening.

❷ Introduce Unit 2 Poster

Introduce Li Lizard, then read and rehearse the Social Story with gestures. Say something like:

Let's look at our SMART Looking and Listening Poster.
Gregory Gopher is sharing.
It says, "Li Lizard looks and listens."
What is Li Lizard doing? (looking and listening)
Right. He is being respectful.*

- **Read the Social Story to students.**
  Listen to me read about SMART Looking and Listening.
  "Someone is talking to the class . . ."

Sit up.**

Point to your eyes, then ears and mouth.

Point to your hands and feet.

Point to yourself.

★ · · · · · · · · · · SMART · · · · · · · · · · · ★
Looking and Listening

Someone is talking to the class.
I sit up.
My face is pleasant.
I look with my eyes.
I listen with my ears.
My mouth is quiet.
My hands and feet are still.
I can look and listen when someone is talking.

Li Lizard looks and listens.

★ · ★
UNIT 2   © 2010 The Mutley Company and Marilyn Sprick • Pacific Northwest Publishing

- Next, have students repeat each line after you.

- Then, read the poster using a cloze procedure on the last word or words of each line.
  Someone is talking . . . to the class.

❸ When and Where to Use SMART Looking and Listening

Explain and discuss when and where SMART Looking and Listening should be used. Say something like:

You can use SMART Looking and Listening at school when I'm talking to you or reading a story to you. You can use SMART Looking and Listening when your friends are talking to you.

Think of some other times you could use SMART Looking and Listening.
(when my mom is talking, during sharing . . .)

---

* "He is being respectful" models how to make reference to your Guidelines for Success.
** See "How to Teach the Program" for gestures and ASL.

▲ ······· Lesson Outline ······· ▲

❶ Practice Unit 2 Poster

Have students practice the Social Story with gestures.

❷ SMART Looking and Listening Description and Modeling

Describe and model SMART Looking and Listening using the poster steps.

❸ SMART/Not-So-SMART Puppet Play

Use a puppet to show SMART and Not-So-SMART Looking and Listening. Use the poster steps to guide instruction.

❶ Practice Unit 2 Poster

Have students practice the Social Story with gestures.

- Have students repeat each line after you.
- Then read the poster using a cloze procedure on the last word or words of each line.

★ · · · · · · · · · · SMART · · · · · · · · · · ★
Looking and Listening

Someone is talking to the class.

I sit up.

My face is pleasant.

I look with my eyes.

I listen with my ears.

My mouth is quiet.

My hands and feet are still.

I can look and listen when someone is talking.

Li Lizard looks and listens.

★ · ★
UNIT 2

❷ SMART Looking and Listening Description and Modeling

Describe and model SMART Looking and Listening using the poster steps. Say something like:

When you use SMART Looking and Listening, you:

- sit up.
- have a pleasant face.
- look at the person who is speaking.

When you use SMART Looking and Listening, you always keep your mouth quiet and let the speaker finish.

Then you might nod your head and say something like "I understand" or "That was interesting."

❸ **SMART/Not-So-SMART Puppet Play**

Use a puppet to show SMART and Not-So-SMART Looking and Listening. Use the poster steps to guide instruction.

- **Have students watch the puppet use the steps for SMART Looking and Listening. First, have a student tell you something he or she had for breakfast.**
  (I had toast and yogurt.)

Have the puppet look at the speaker, listen, and then say, "Oh, that sounds like a great breakfast."

Next ask students:
Was the puppet sitting up or standing up straight? (yes)
Did the puppet have a pleasant face? (yes)
Did the puppet look and listen? (yes)
Did the puppet talk while [Xiang] was talking? (no)

Partners, tell each other how the puppet showed that [he] was listening.

[Logan], what did you and your partner discuss? (The puppet nodded his head and said, "Oh, that sounds like a great breakfast.")
That's right! The puppet was doing a SMART job Looking and Listening.

- **Have students watch the puppet use Not-So-SMART Looking and Listening.**
  Now let's look at Not-So-SMART Looking and Listening.

Have another student tell you something he or she had for breakfast, something about his or her family, etc.
Have the puppet slouch, look away from the speaker, and interrupt the speaker.
Did the puppet sit up? (no)
Did the puppet look at [Xiang]? (no)
Did the puppet talk while [Xiang] was talking? (yes)
Did the puppet show [Xiang] that [he] cared about [her]? (no)
Do you think the puppet made [Xiang] feel like what [she] said was important? (no)
Do you think [Xiang] wants the puppet to be [her] friend? (probably not)

What do we want to use in our classroom—SMART Looking and Listening or Not-So-SMART Looking and Listening? (SMART Looking and Listening)
Yes, SMART Looking and Listening shows that we respect each other.

Lesson 3

SMART LOOKING AND LISTENING

◆ ········ Lesson Outline ········ ◆

❶ Review Unit 1 Poster

Have students practice the Social Story with gestures.

❷ Review What SMART Greetings Look and Sound Like

Have partners share what SMART Greetings look and sound like.

❸ Review SMART Looking and Listening

Review the poster steps for SMART Looking and Listening using a cloze procedure.

❹ Pleasant and Not-So-Pleasant Faces

Describe and show a pleasant and not-so-pleasant face. Then have students identify which of Li Lizard, Gregory Gopher, and Ms. Smart's faces are pleasant and not-so-pleasant.

❶ Review Unit 1 Poster

Have students practice the Social Story with gestures.

- Have students repeat each line after you.
- Then read the poster using a cloze procedure on the last word or words of each line.

★ ·········· SMART ·········· ★
Greetings

When I see people I know, I look at them and smile.
I wave, give a high five, or shake their hands.
I say "Hi."
They say "Hi."
I say something friendly.
I can give a warm greeting.

Gregory Gopher gives great greetings.

★ ·································· ★
UNIT 1

❷ Review What SMART Greetings Look and Sound Like

Have partners share what SMART Greetings look and sound like. Say something like:

Partner 1, tell Partner 2 one thing about how to use a SMART Greeting.

Repeat with Partner 2.

[Sophia], what did your partner say about how to use a SMART Greeting?

Excellent, everyone show me a smile.
What else do you do with a SMART greeting?
(You say SMART Greetings like "Hi," "Hello," or
"Good morning"...)

What do you do with the person's name?
(Use it.)

❸ Review SMART Looking and Listening

Review the poster steps for SMART Looking
and Listening. Say something like:
Remember, when you use SMART Looking
and Listening, you sit . . . (up).
Your face is . . . (pleasant).
You look with your . . . (eyes).
You listen with your . . . (ears).
Your mouth is . . . (quiet).
Your hands and feet are . . . (still).
You look and . . . (listen when someone is
talking).

❹ Pleasant and Not-So-Pleasant Faces

- Describe a pleasant face. Then show a
  pleasant and not-so-pleasant face. Say
  something like:
  People like others who look and listen with
  a pleasant face.
  Grin. This is a pleasant face.
  Frown and pout. This is a not-so-pleasant
  face.

- Hold up each face poster and have students
  identify whether the character has a
  pleasant or not-so-pleasant expression.
  Look at Li Lizard. Everyone, is this a
  pleasant face or a not-so-pleasant face?

Repeat with each Li Lizard, Gregory Gopher, and Ms. Smart face.

- **Have students show you a pleasant and not-so-pleasant face.**

- **Discuss which expression students would like to see when they are talking with friends or to the class.**
  Look at Li Lizard. Everyone, is this a
  pleasant face or a not-so-pleasant face?
  (not-so-pleasant)
  Would you like Li Lizard to listen to you
  with this face? (no)
  Why not? (He looks mad. He looks like he
  doesn't like what he hears . . .)

  Look at Li Lizard's other face. Is it pleasant
  or not-so-pleasant? (pleasant)
  Would you like Li Lizard to listen to you
  with this face? (yes)
  Why? (He looks interested. He looks like he
  likes what he hears . . .)

Lesson 4

SMART LOOKING AND LISTENING

■ ········· Lesson Outline ········· ■

❶ **Practice Unit 2 Poster**

Have students practice the Social Story with gestures.

❷ **Reasons for Using SMART Looking and Listening**

Discuss the reasons for using SMART Looking and Listening.

❸ **Practice SMART Looking and Listening**

Practice SMART Looking and Listening before and during sharing.

---

❶ **Practice Unit 2 Poster**

Have students practice the Social Story with gestures.

- Have students repeat each line after you.
- Then, read the poster using a cloze procedure on the last word or words of each line.

★ ＊ ＊ ＊ ＊ ＊ ＊ ＊ ＊ ＊ SMART ＊ ＊ ＊ ＊ ＊ ＊ ＊ ＊ ＊ ★
Looking and Listening

Someone is talking to the class.
I sit up.
My face is pleasant.
I look with my eyes.
I listen with my ears.
My mouth is quiet.
My hands and feet are still.
I can look and listen when someone is talking.

Li Lizard looks and listens.

UNIT 2

❷ **Reasons for Using SMART Looking and Listening**

Discuss the reasons for using SMART Looking and Listening. Say something like:

When you use SMART Looking and Listening, you are following a Guideline for Success—[treating others like you want to be treated].

When you are talking, do you want people to:

- listen to you or talk while you are talking? (to listen to me)

• look at you or away from you?
(to look at me)

When you use SMART Looking and Listening:
• people will know you care about them.
• people will want to be your friend.
• people will treat you in a nice way.

❸ Practice SMART Looking and Listening

Practice SMART Looking and Listening before and during sharing.

• **Have students review the steps for SMART Looking and Listening. Use the poster steps as a guide.**
  Say something like:
  We're going to review SMART Looking and Listening.
  Remember, when you use SMART Looking and Listening, you sit . . . (up).
  Your face is . . . (pleasant).
  You look with your . . . (eyes).
  You listen with your . . . (ears).
  Your hands and feet are . . . (still).
  You look and . . . (listen when someone is talking).

• **Have the student who is sharing and two other students go to the front of the sharing circle. Give the student who is sharing two SMART Looking and Listening Recognition Cards to award.**
  Say something like:
  It's [Dakota]'s turn to share something about [his pet snake].
  [Emma and Dimitre], it's your turn to be [Dakota]'s special SMART Looking and Listening buddies.

After [Dakota] has shared, prompt the students to make a nice comment.
[Emma], tell [Dakota] something nice about [his] sharing.
Start with "I thought it was interesting . . ."
([Dakota], I thought it was interesting to hear about your pet snake.)

Provide descriptive feedback.
[Emma], that was excellent.
You told [Dakota] what was interesting, and you used [his] name!
[Dimitre], what would you like to say to [Dakota]?

Have students describe students' efforts to use SMART Looking and Listening.
Everyone, thumbs up if [Dimitre and Emma] showed us SMART Looking and Listening.
What did [Dimitre and Emma] do while [Dakota] was talking?
(They looked at him. They listened. They waited until he finished talking. They said something nice.)

Have the student who shared award the SMART Looking and Listening Recognition Cards. Say something like:
[Dakota], did [Emma and Dimitre] say something nice about your sharing? (yes)
You can give them each a SMART Looking and Listening Recognition Card.

UNIT 2

Lesson 5

SMART LOOKING AND LISTENING

★······ Lesson Outline ·······★

❶ Practice SMART Looking and Listening

Get students' attention and acknowledge SMART Looking and Listening during teacher-directed activities.

❷ My SMART Book Unit 2 Coloring Page

Have students color their SMART Looking and Listening Coloring Pages for their My SMART Books.

❸ SMART Looking and Listening Checkouts and Recognition

Read a poster to a few students at a time and check out each student's looking and listening skills. Award SMART Looking and Listening Recognition Cards as students demonstrate the skill.

 CHAMPS EXPECTATIONS

"Define clear and consistent expectations for all regularly scheduled instructional activities . . . "

—Sprick, 2009, p. 151

By teaching SMART Looking and Listening, you have clarified behavioral expectations for paying attention during whole class and small group instruction and discussion.

Small Celebrations

❶ Practice SMART Looking and Listening

Get students' attention and acknowledge SMART Looking and Listening during teacher-directed activities.

Say something like:

You've done a great job learning about SMART Looking and Listening.

I'm proud of you all.

Everyone, look at [Xavier].

Is [his] mouth quiet? (yes)

Now, look at [Cailey].

Is [she] looking at me? (yes)

Look at [Dejohn].

Are [his] hands and feet still? (yes)

❷ My SMART Book Unit 2 Coloring Page

Have students color their SMART Looking and Listening Coloring Pages.

Say something like:

You can all use SMART Looking and Listening. You can [treat others like you want to be treated].

You've earned another page for your My SMART Book!

SMART Looking and Listening

Li Lizard looks and listens.

★ ★
★ ★
★ ★

UNIT
2

Lesson 5

SMART LOOKING AND LISTENING

INTERVENTION AND EXTRA PRACTICE

Watch the Intervention suggestions in the End-of--Unit Tips and keep teaching. Social skills will develop over time with your enduring patience, encouragement, teaching, and positive focus.

❸ **SMART Looking and Listening Checkouts and Recognition**

Read a poster to a few students at a time and check out each student's looking and listening skills. Award SMART Looking and Listening Recognition Cards to individuals as they demonstrate the skill.

Say something like:

While you are coloring your SMART Coloring Page, I'm going to read one of our posters to you and you can show me SMART Looking and Listening.

Show students the SMART Looking and Listening Recognition Cards.

When you show me SMART Looking and Listening, you will get a Recognition Card. Remember, you can collect SMART Recognition Cards! On special occasions, I'll award you other SMART Recognition Cards that you can add to your ring.

While students are coloring, circulate and have students show you SMART Looking and Listening while you read a poster. Model and guide as needed. Award SMART Recognition Cards, even if assistance is needed.

Note: If needed, finish this informal assessment during another independent work time or whole class activity. Keep track of students who would benefit from more guided practice.

End-of-Unit Tip

SMART LOOKING AND LISTENING

As you move forward, work on . . .

················· Generalization ·················

Everyday Use: During all whole class and small group lessons, have students use their looking and listening skills.

Continue to Encourage Efforts by:
- Responding warmly to students who are looking and listening.
- Providing positive descriptive feedback—especially to those for whom the skill is new or difficult.

  Wow! [Madison] is looking at [Emma] and ready to listen. [She] has [her] mouth, hands, and feet quiet.

- Providing gentle corrections and guided practice as needed.
- Re-teaching periodically.
- Using SMART Recognition Cards to acknowledge student efforts.
- Referring to your Guidelines for Success.

················· Intervention ·················

When a student or students have difficulty using SMART Looking and Listening Skills during instruction:

Prompt Practice
Prompt a difficult step in SMART Looking and Listening. Have a less skillful student serve as a model. Say something like:

Everyone, what's the first step in SMART Looking and Listening? (sitting up)
Everyone, sit up. Look at [Caden].
[He] is sitting up and ready to learn. Everyone, clap for [Caden].

Target Instruction and Add Practice
For some students, you may need to teach and reinforce specific steps. For example, if a student slouches, lies on his or her desk, and/or fidgets, have the student:
- Practice sitting up and looking in a mirror.
- Identify whether you are sitting up with a thumbs up or thumbs down.

Once this is mastered, the student can work on another targeted skill—such as listening with a pleasant face.

SHARING

SMART Looking and Listening is taught before and during normal sharing activities in Lessons 1 and 4. We suggest the following:
- Students all share on a weekly topic.
- 1/5 of the class shares each day in one or two short sessions.
- Each student is assigned a regular weekly sharing day.

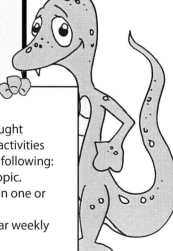

SMART Following Directions

Student Objectives

Targeted Objectives
I follow directions right away.

Review Objectives
I look and listen when someone is talking.

I greet others with a smile and a "Hello."

★ ★ ★ ★ ★ ★ ★ ★ ★

SMART FOLLOWING DIRECTIONS
Overview

····· Teaching Objectives ·······

Students practice all the steps below and demonstrate competency by using Steps 2, 3, and 5.

1. Looking at the teacher
2. Having a pleasant expression
3. Mouth quiet
4. Nodding or saying "OK"
5. Following directions right away

Teaching Materials
School Materials
- Puppet of your choice
- Colors

SMART Materials
- Units 2 and 3 Posters
- *My SMART Book* Unit 3 Coloring Page
- Recognition Cards for Following Directions and previous units

SMART FOLLOWING DIRECTIONS IS ... OH, SO IMPORTANT!

When students learn to follow directions, they are learning to cooperate—a skill that is critical to school success and the ability to maintain a job later in life.

 Teaching Tips ··············

Positive Interactions

Respond warmly to students when they follow directions. Say things like:

Thank you for following directions. Now, we can get started learning about [some of the biggest mammals that ever walked Earth]!

Positive Feedback and Reinforcement

Provide positive descriptive feedback.

Wow, everyone followed directions happily and right away.

Use SMART Recognition Cards to acknowledge student efforts.

Connections

Reference your Guidelines for Success. For example, Always do your best.

I saw you using SMART Following Directions. It is a great way to show you are ready to do your best.

··········· Intervention ···········

Make an overt effort to practice SMART Following Directions with students who have difficulty with compliance. If possible, have these students model SMART Following Directions early in the day.

Lesson Planner

Lesson	Activities	Materials and Materials Preparation
1 ●●●	**Introduce SMART Following Directions** **Reasons for Using SMART Following Directions** **Introduce Unit 3 Poster** **When and Where to Use SMART Following Directions**	**Unit 3 Poster** Reproducible: Print the Unit 3 Poster (2 pages) and affix to 11"x 17" poster board. (Or order premade color posters.)
2 ▲▲▲	**Practice Unit 3 Poster** **SMART Following Directions Description and Modeling** **SMART/Not-So-SMART Puppet Play**	• **Unit 3 Poster** • **A puppet**
3 ◆◆◆	**Review Unit 2 Poster** **Review What SMART Looking and Listening Looks and Sounds Like** **Practice SMART Following Directions**	**Unit 2 Poster**
4 ■■■	**Practice Unit 3 Poster** **More Reasons for Using SMART Following Directions** **Practice SMART Following Directions**	**Unit 3 Poster**
5 ★★★	**Practice SMART Following Directions** *My SMART Book* **Unit 3 Coloring Page** **SMART Following Directions Checkouts and Recognition**	• *My SMART Book* **Unit 3 Coloring Page** • **Colors** • **SMART Following Directions Recognition Cards** Reproducible: On card stock, make several copies of the cards. Then cut and hole punch each card.

> **········ Lesson Outline ········**
>
> **❶ Introduce SMART Following Directions**
>
> Model and explain SMART Following Directions at the beginning of a whole class activity.
>
> **❷ Reasons for Using SMART Following Directions**
>
> Discuss the reasons for using SMART Following Directions.
>
> **❸ Introduce Unit 3 Poster**
>
> Introduce Felicia Frog, then read and rehearse the Social Story with gestures.
>
> **❹ When and Where to Use SMART Following Directions**
>
> Explain and discuss when and where SMART Following Directions should be used.

❶ Introduce SMART Following Directions

Model and explain SMART Following Directions at the beginning of a whole class activity. Give students a direction. Say:

Walk quietly to the rug and sit down [on your pockets].

- **Provide positive feedback to students who are following the direction quickly and efficiently.**

  [Riley] and [Jabaar] just showed us how to follow directions in a SMART way.

- **Describe SMART Following Directions. Say something like:**

  They used a SMART face and body.
  They followed the direction right away.
  They walked quietly to the rug and sat [on their pockets].

❷ Reasons for Using SMART Following Directions

Discuss the reasons for using SMART Following Directions. Say something like:

It's important to follow directions when teachers ask you to do something. When we use SMART Following Directions, we learn a lot. Nod your head if you can follow directions.

When we use SMART Following Directions, we also get things done quickly so we can do other fun things. Put one hand on your head if you can follow directions.

When you follow directions, you are showing me you are on the job and [responsible]. Thumbs up if you can follow directions.

❸ Introduce Unit 3 Poster

Introduce Felicia Frog, then read and rehearse the Social Story with gestures.
Say something like:

Let's look at our SMART Following Directions Poster. It says, "Felicia Frog follows directions." What is Felicia Frog doing?
(following directions)

Listen to me read about SMART Following Directions.
"My teacher gives a direction . . ."

Next, have students repeat each line after you.

Then, read the poster using a cloze procedure on the last word or words of each line.

My teacher gives a . . . direction.

❹ When and Where to Use SMART Following Directions

Explain and discuss when and where SMART Following Directions should be used.
Say something like:

You can use SMART Following Directions at school when I ask you to do something in our classroom or outside our classroom.

Think of some other times you could use SMART Following Directions.
(at home when my dad asks me to do something, during recess . . .)

There is a time when you should never follow a direction. You should never follow a direction from a stranger who might tell you to get in his or her car. Should you follow a direction from a stranger? (no)

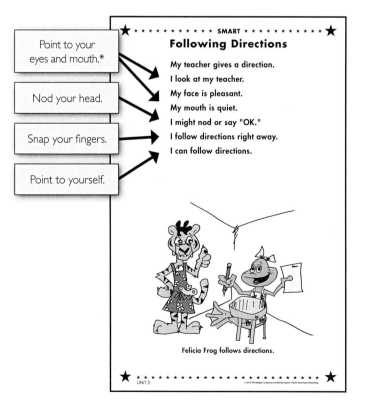

Point to your eyes and mouth.*

Nod your head.

Snap your fingers.

Point to yourself.

★ ＊＊＊＊＊＊＊＊＊ SMART ＊＊＊＊＊＊＊＊＊ ★
Following Directions

My teacher gives a direction.
I look at my teacher.
My face is pleasant.
My mouth is quiet.
I might nod or say "OK."
I follow directions right away.
I can follow directions.

Felicia Frog follows directions.

* See "How to Teach the Program" for gestures and ASL.

33

UNIT

3

▲▲▲▲▲▲▲▲▲▲▲▲▲▲▲▲▲▲▲▲▲▲▲▲▲▲▲▲▲▲▲▲▲▲▲
▲▲▲▲▲▲▲▲▲▲▲▲▲▲▲▲▲▲▲▲▲▲▲▲▲▲▲▲▲▲▲▲▲▲
▲▲▲▲▲▲▲▲▲▲▲▲▲▲▲▲▲▲▲▲▲▲▲▲▲▲▲▲▲▲▲▲▲▲▲

Lesson 2

SMART FOLLOWING DIRECTIONS

▲ ······· Lesson Outline ······· ▲

❶ Practice Unit 3 Poster

Have students practice the Social Story with gestures.

❷ SMART Following Directions Description and Modeling

Describe and have a student model SMART Following Directions using the poster steps.

❸ SMART/Not-So-SMART Puppet Play

Use a puppet to show SMART and Not-So-SMART Following Directions. Use the poster steps to guide instruction.

❶ Practice Unit 3 Poster

Have students practice the Social Story with gestures.

- Have students repeat each line after you.
- Then read the poster using a cloze procedure on the last word or words of each line.

★ ·········· SMART ·········· ★
Following Directions

My teacher gives a direction.
I look at my teacher.
My face is pleasant.
My mouth is quiet.
I might nod or say "OK."
I follow directions right away.
I can follow directions.

Felicia Frog follows directions.

★ ★★★★★★★★★★★★★★★★★★★★★★★ ★
UNIT 3

❷ SMART Following Directions Description and Modeling

Describe and have a student model SMART Following Directions using the poster steps.
Say something like:
When you use SMART Following Directions, you use a SMART face and body.
Let's watch [Malia] follow directions.
[Malia], please touch your head.
[Malia] looked at me with a pleasant face.

[Her] mouth was quiet and [she] followed directions right away. That's SMART Following Directions.

Watch [Connor]. [Connor], please stand up.
Did [Connor] look at me? (yes)
Does [he] have a pleasant face? (yes)
Was [his] mouth quiet? (yes)
Did [he] stand up right away? (yes)
Clap for [Connor]. [He] can follow directions right away.

❸ SMART/Not-So-SMART Puppet Play

Use a puppet to show SMART and Not-So-SMART Following Directions. Use the poster steps to guide instruction.

- **Have students watch a puppet use SMART Following Directions.**
  Say something like:
  I'm going to give a direction. Watch the puppet. Please go to the chalkboard and write "Hi" on the board.

  Have the puppet look at you, listen, and then go to the chalkboard and write "Hi."
  Next, ask students:
  Did the puppet look at me? (yes)
  Did the puppet have a pleasant face? (yes)
  Did [she] talk while I gave the direction? (no)
  Did the puppet write "Hi" right away? (yes)

  That's right! The puppet was doing a great job! [She] used SMART Following Directions.

- **Have students watch the puppet use Not-So-SMART Following Directions.**
  Now let's look at Not-So-SMART Following Directions.

  Tell the puppet to go to the chalkboard and wait quietly. Have the puppet look away from you, and say something like: "I will in just a second."
  What did the puppet do?
  ([She] didn't look at you.)
  Did [she] follow the direction quickly and quietly? (no)
  Was the puppet being responsible? (no)
  Was the puppet being respectful? (no)
  Do you think I will want to give [her] another job soon? (probably not)
  We can use SMART Following Directions in our classroom and on the playground because you are SMART Kids. You are responsible kids, and you are respectful kids.

Lesson 3

SMART FOLLOWING DIRECTIONS

♦ ········ Lesson Outline ········ ♦

❶ Review Unit 2 Poster

Have students practice the Social Story with gestures.

❷ Review What SMART Looking and Listening Looks and Sounds Like

Have partners share what SMART Looking and Listening looks and sounds like.

❸ Practice SMART Following Directions

Have students review and then practice the poster steps for SMART Following Directions.

---

❶ Review Unit 2 Poster

Have students practice the Social Story with gestures.

- Have students repeat each line after you.
- Then read the poster using a cloze procedure on the last word or words of each line.

★ · · · · · · · · · · SMART · · · · · · · · · · ★
Looking and Listening

Someone is talking to the class.

I sit up.

My face is pleasant.

I look with my eyes.

I listen with my ears.

My mouth is quiet.

My hands and feet are still.

I can look and listen when someone is talking.

Li Lizard looks and listens.

❷ Review What SMART Looking and Listening Looks and Sounds Like

Have partners share what SMART Looking and Listening looks and sounds like.

Say something like:

Partner 1, tell Partner 2 one thing about SMART Looking and Listening.

Repeat with Partner 2.
[Dimitre], what did your partner say about
SMART Looking and Listening?
Wonderful, everyone show me SMART
Looking and Listening.

What else does SMART Looking and Listening
look and sound like? (mouth is quiet, hands
and feet are still, look with eyes, listen with
ears . . .)

❸ **Practice SMART
Following Directions**

**Have students review and then practice
the poster steps for SMART Following
Directions.**

- **Review the steps. Say something like:**
  Remember, when you use SMART
  Following Directions, you look at your . . .
  teacher.
  Your face is . . . pleasant.
  Your mouth is . . . quiet.
  You might nod or say . . . OK.
  You do it . . . right away.
  You can . . . follow directions.

- **Have students practice the steps for
  SMART Following Directions.**
  Now I want everyone to show me SMART
  Following Directions.
  I am going to tell you something that I
  want you to do and then you will show me
  that you can do it.

**Tell students something like, "Please touch
your head," and watch for each of the steps.**
Good job! While I was giving the direction,
I saw everyone looking at me, using good
posture, and not talking.
Then I saw everyone do it quickly and
quietly.
That was SMART Following Directions.

**Repeat with other simple actions. Mix
group and individual turns.**

UNIT 3

Lesson 4

SMART FOLLOWING DIRECTIONS

■ ······· Lesson Outline ······· ■

❶ Practice Unit 3 Poster

Have students practice the Social Story with gestures.

❷ More Reasons for Using SMART Following Directions

Discuss the reasons for using SMART Following Directions.

❸ Practice SMART Following Directions

Review and practice SMART Following Directions. Use the poster steps to guide instruction.

---

❶ Practice Unit 3 Poster

Have students practice the Social Story with gestures.

- Have students repeat each line after you.
- Then read the poster using a cloze procedure on the last word or words of each line.

★ · · · · · · · · · · SMART · · · · · · · · · · ★
Following Directions

My teacher gives a direction.
I look at my teacher.
My face is pleasant.
My mouth is quiet.
I might nod or say "OK."
I follow directions right away.
I can follow directions.

Felicia Frog follows directions.

★ · ★
UNIT 3

❷ More Reasons for Using SMART Following Directions

Discuss the reasons for using SMART Following Directions. Say something like:

It's important to follow directions when teachers ask you to do something. When we use SMART Following Directions, we learn a lot.

Clap your hands two times if you can follow directions.

Excellent. When you use SMART Following Directions, you are showing me that you are on the job.
You are being [responsible] and [respectful].

Clap your hands three times if you can follow directions.

Ask students:
What do you think would happen if I said, "Class, please put your things away and line up for lunch," but half of you didn't follow my directions? (We wouldn't get to go to lunch.)
That's right. How would you feel if you didn't get to go to lunch? (unhappy, hungry, upset . . .)

What do you think would happen if I said, "Class, please put your things away and line up to go home," but half of you didn't follow my directions? (We might miss our bus . . .)

That's right. It's very important to follow my directions right away.

❸ Practice SMART Following Directions

Review and practice SMART Following Directions. Use the poster steps to guide instruction.

- **Have students review the steps for SMART Following Directions. Say something like:**
  Remember, when you use SMART Following Directions, you look at your . . . teacher.
  Your face is . . . pleasant.
  Your mouth is . . . quiet.
  You might nod or say . . . OK.
  You do it . . . right away.

You can . . . follow directions.

- **Have students practice SMART Following Directions. Practice with simple actions. If a child misses a step, provide a gentle correction. Say something like:**
  Everyone, watch [Isabella]. [Isabella], turn to [Dakota] and shake [his] hand.
  [Isabella], I liked how you looked at me and then followed my directions right away.

  [Xavier], what did [Isabella] do?
  [She] looked . . . (at you).
  That's right. Everyone, did [she] shake [Dakota]'s hand right away? (yes)

  Everyone, watch [Xavier]. [He]'s going to show us how to follow directions.
  [Xavier], touch your toes.
  Did [Xavier] look at me and listen? (yes)
  Did [Xavier] follow my directions right away? (yes)

  When the child is successful, say something like:
  [Xavier] and [Isabella] are both great at SMART Following Directions. They remembered to look at me, listen, and follow directions right away.

- **Provide prompts throughout the day.**

- **Provide ongoing positive descriptive feedback to acknowledge success. Say things like:**
  Wow! That was SMART Following Directions. You can be proud of yourself. You helped us learn [our new rules].

- **Practice SMART Following Directions with the group, then with partners.**

Lesson 5

SMART FOLLOWING DIRECTIONS

★········ Lesson Outline ········★

❶ Practice SMART Following Directions

Get students' attention and acknowledge SMART Following Directions during teacher-directed activities.

❷ My SMART Book Unit 3 Coloring Page

Have students color their SMART Following Directions Coloring Pages for their *My SMART Books*.

❸ SMART Following Directions Checkouts and Recognition

Check out each student by giving a simple direction. Award SMART Following Directions Recognition to individuals as they demonstrate the skill.

CHAMPS
INSTRUCTION

"When you teach students how to behave responsibly during the first month of school, you dramatically increase their chances of having a productive year."

—Sprick, 2009, p. 191

By teaching young children how to follow directions, they learn a set of behaviors that demonstrate responsible behavior. Though best taught early in the year, any time you teach this skill, you will reinforce and enhance student responsibility.

Small Celebrations

❶ Practice SMART Following Directions

Get students' attention and acknowledge SMART Following Directions during teacher-directed activities. Say something like:

You've done a great job learning the SMART way to follow directions. I'm proud of you.

Let's practice following directions. Everyone, stand up quickly and quietly.

Now, stretch your arms as high as you can.

Now, sit down quickly and quietly.

Did you look at me when I gave directions? (yes)
Did you have a pleasant face? (yes)
Was your mouth quiet? (yes)
Yes, you looked at me and you were quiet.
Yes, you were respectful!

Did you follow directions right away? (yes)
Yes, you are fast at following directions.
You are very responsible students.

❷ *My SMART Book* Unit 3 Coloring Page

Have students color their SMART Following Directions Coloring Pages.
Say something like:
You can all use SMART Following Directions. You can [be responsible] and [do your best].
You get to color another page in your *My SMART Book*!
It shows Felicia Frog. What is she doing? (following directions)

❸ SMART Following Directions Checkouts and Recognition

Check out each student by giving a simple direction. Award SMART Following Directions Recognition Cards to individuals as they demonstrate the skill.

- **While students are coloring, circulate and have individuals show you SMART Following Directions. Say something like:**

[Ethan], I'm going to give you a direction. Remember to use SMART Following Directions.
[Ethan], please touch your nose.

If the student forgets part of SMART Following Directions—forgets to: look at you with a pleasant expression, listen to you, and/or follow directions right away— gently correct by guiding practice. Say something like:
Let's try that again. You almost had it. You looked, listened, and followed directions right away. This time remember to use a pleasant face. Show me a pleasant face. Here's a new direction. Please write your name on your paper.

When the student demonstrates SMART Following Directions, award the Recognition Card, even if assistance is needed.

Notes:

- Keep track of students who would benefit from more guided practice.
- If needed, finish this informal assessment any time during the day. You can even assess some students during whole class activities. Observe students when you give an instruction and acknowledge their use of the skill. Say things like:
Class, when I asked you to line up, I saw [Dejohn] look at me, listen, and then follow directions right away. [Dejohn], here is your Recognition Card.

End-of-Unit Tip

SMART FOLLOWING DIRECTIONS

As you move forward, work on . . .

·············· **Generalization** ···············

Everyday Use: Have students practice SMART Following Directions as a part of all classroom activities.

Continue to Encourage Efforts by:
- **Providing positive descriptive feedback.**
  [Caden] got [his] crayon box and went to work right away.
- **Providing gentle corrections and guided practice as needed.**
  [Berto], you can show the class how you can get your crayons out right away.
- **Re-teaching periodically.**
- **Using SMART Recognition Cards to acknowledge student efforts.**
- **Referring to your Guidelines for Success.**
  [Abrianna] showed us how to use SMART Following Directions. [She] showed us a way to follow our school guidelines to be responsible and respectful.

·············· **Intervention** ············

When a student or students have difficulty following directions:

Prompt Correct Practice
- **Periodically, ask and have the class help you identify an important step for following directions.**
  Everyone, when do you follow a direction? (right away)
- **Have the intervention student(s) model the response.**
  [Malia], when do you follow directions? (right away)
- **Have the intervention student(s) demonstrate the behavior.**
  [Malia], you get to be the first one to follow this direction. Please pick up your pencil.
- **Reinforce the behavior with positive descriptive feedback.**
  [Malia], that was excellent. You looked at me with a pleasant face and followed directions right away.

STUDENT TRACKER CARD Intervention

Away from other students, give each intervention student a Student Tracker (5 Teacher Resources > B Intervention Tools > 1 Student Tracker). Tell students you are going to watch for their special efforts to follow directions right away. When you catch a student using SMART Following Directions, punch the Student Tracker and provide positive descriptive feedback.

SMART Review

Student Objectives

Review Objectives

I follow directions right away.

I look and listen when someone is talking.

I greet others with a smile and a "Hello."

★ ★ ★ ★ ★ ★ ★ ★ ★ ★

Let's Review!

······· Teaching Objectives ·······

1. SMART Greetings
2. SMART Looking and Listening
3. SMART Following Directions

Teaching Materials

School Materials

- Puppet of your choice
- Colors, scissors, glue for each student
- Two craft sticks for each student
- Small box
- Read Aloud book of your choice (See Lesson 2 for suggested titles.)

SMART Materials

- Units 1–3 Posters
- Recognition Cards for Units 1–3
- Unit 4 Reproducibles:
  - 4-1 Greetings Stick Puppets
  - 4-3 Treasure Hunt
  - 4-5a SMART/Not-So-SMART Cards
  - 4-5b *Sharing Book 1*

REVIEW IS . . . OH, SO IMPORTANT! EVERY DAY IS A DAY TO REVIEW

SMART Looking and Listening and Following Directions are critical to each child's success in school and eventually at work. Prompt students to use these skills everyday, in every classroom activity. Provide positive attention and descriptive feedback to help maintain these skills.

······· Teaching Tips ··············

Positive Interactions

Student Greeters welcome other students with a SMART Greeting.

Respond warmly to students when they use SMART Looking and Listening and SMART Following Directions.

Positive Feedback and Reinforcement

Provide positive descriptive feedback.
Wow! That was SMART Following Directions. I appreciate the way you all lined up right away . . .

Use SMART Recognition Cards to intermittently (unpredictably) acknowledge SMART Greetings, Looking and Listening, and Following Directions.

Connections

Reference your Guidelines for Success.
That was SMART Looking and Listening. It shows you want to do your best.

·········· Intervention ··········

Make an overt effort to prompt and practice SMART Greetings, Looking and Listening, and Following Directions with students who are just learning these skills.
Prompt. Everyone, let's practice SMART Looking and Listening. Remember to sit . . . (up). Show me a pleasant . . .
Use the student as a model. Everyone, look at [Emma]. Is she using SMART Looking and Listening? (yes)
Reinforce with positive descriptive feedback.

Lesson Planner

Lesson	Activities	Materials and Materials Preparation

1	**SMART Greetings Daily Routine**
	
	SMART Greetings Stick Puppets
	
	Review Unit 1 Poster
		• **SMART Greetings Recognition Cards**
		  Reproducible: Make additional cards as needed.
		• **SMART Greetings Stick Puppets**
		  Reproducible 4-1: Copy one SMART Greetings Stick Puppets page per student on 8.5 x 11 inch card stock. Make a sample of each puppet.
		• **Colors, scissors, and glue for each student**
		• **Two craft sticks for each student**
		• **Unit 1 Poster**

2	**Review Unit 2 Poster** **SMART Looking and Listening Read Aloud**	• **Unit 2 Poster** • **Read Aloud book of your choice** See Lesson 2 for suggested titles.

3	**Review Unit 3 Poster**
	
	SMART Following Directions Treasure Hunt
		• **Unit 3 Poster**
		• **Unit 4 Treasure Hunt**
		  Reproducible 4-3: See Special Preparation Note, p. 50.
		• **Small box**
		• **SMART Following Directions Recognition Cards**
		  Reproducible: Make additional cards as needed.

4	**Review Unit 2 Poster** **Review Unit 3 Poster** **Simon Says the SMART Way**	**Units 2 and 3 Posters**

5	**SMART/Not-So-SMART Cards**
	
	I'm a SMART Kid Sharing Book 1
	
	SMART Review Checkout
		• **Unit 4 SMART/Not-So-SMART Cards**
		  Reproducible 4-5a: Make one copy of each card.
		• ***Sharing Book 1***
		  Reproducible 4-5b: Copy one book per student on 8.5 x 11 inch paper.
		• **Colors**
		• **SMART Recognition Cards**
		  Reproducible: Make additional Greetings, Looking and Listening, and Following Directions Cards as needed.

Lesson Outline

❶ SMART Greetings Daily Routine

Have SMART Student Greeters at the door giving each student a SMART Greeting as they enter the classroom in the morning. Award SMART Greeting Recognition Cards to Student Greeters.

❷ SMART Greetings Stick Puppets

Have students make stick puppets of Ms. Sasha Smart and Gregory Gopher.

❸ Review Unit 1 Poster

Have students use their stick puppets to act out the SMART Greetings Poster.

❶ SMART Greetings Daily Routine

Have SMART Student Greeters at the door giving each student a SMART Greeting as they enter the classroom in the morning.

- Encourage Student Greeters to use a friendly expression, a welcoming voice, and a wave or a high five. Guide practice as needed.
- Award SMART Greeting Recognition Cards to Student Greeters.

❷ SMART Greetings Stick Puppets

Have students make stick puppets of Ms. Sasha Smart and Gregory Gopher.

- Show students your samples of completed SMART Greetings Stick Puppets.
- Give each student a copy of the SMART Greetings Stick Puppet reproducible and two craft sticks.
- Have students color the puppets, cut them out, and glue each puppet to a craft stick.

MANAGEMENT TIP

If time is limited, have puppets already cut out. Students will only need to color and glue them to their sticks.

❸ Review Unit 1 Poster

Have students use their stick puppets to act out the SMART Greetings Poster.

- **Tell students what their puppets are going to do. Say something like:**

  We're going to practice the Smart Greeting Social Story with your puppets.

  Everyone, hold up Ms. Sasha Smart.

  Now hold up Gregory Gopher.

  Gregory Gopher is going to give Ms. Smart a SMART Greeting.

- **Read the Social Story to students using a cloze procedure. Have students act out the social story with their puppets.**

  Everyone, hold up Gregory.

  He says:

  When I see . . . people I know,
  I look at them and . . . smile.

Everyone, wave Gregory's hand very carefully. Gregory says:

I wave, give a . . . high five . . . or shake their . . . hands.

I say . . . "Hi."

Now hold up Ms. Smart.
Wave Ms. Smart's hand very carefully.
They say . . . "Hi."

Now have Gregory say something friendly.
"It's nice to see you." (It's nice to see you.)
I can give a . . . warm greeting.

★ ･ ･ ･ ･ ･ ･ ･ ･ ･ ･ SMART ･ ･ ･ ･ ･ ･ ･ ･ ･ ･ ★

Greetings

When I see people I know, I look at them and smile.

I wave, give a high five, or shake their hands.

I say "Hi."

They say "Hi."

I say something friendly.

I can give a warm greeting.

Gregory Gopher gives great greetings.

★ ･ ★
UNIT 1

▲ ······· Lesson Outline ········ ▲

❶ Review Unit 2 Poster

Have students practice the Social Story.

❷ SMART Looking and Listening Read Aloud

Read aloud to students a picture book that has strong visuals and onomatopoeia (e.g., words that make sounds—buzz, buzz; rat-a-tat-tat; cluck, cluck, cluck).

Special Preparation Note ···········
Read Alouds

For this lesson, select a favorite Read Aloud from your library. Choose a book that has pictures that pop and noisy words that are fun to hear and repeat.

Suggestions:

THUMP, THUMP, Rat-a-Tat-Tat
by Gene Baer, illustrated by Lois Ehlert

It's a marching band full of pounding drums and squawking horns. It's a marching band full of festive colors and flashing brass. Baer and Ehlert join together to provide a bold, bright, and joyous picture book, a must for SMART Looking and Listening.

Barnyard Banter
by Denise Fleming

This Read Aloud is full of moos and clucks, and squeaks and shrieks as a colorful collage of farm animals asks, "But where's the goose?" Author and illustrator Denise Fleming's award winning picture book is perfect for SMART Looking and Listening.

Good-night Owl!
by Pat Hutchins

It was day and an owl was trying to sleep, but the bees buzzed, buzz, buzz, buzz. Poor owl! All day long he tried to sleep, but the world was full of noises. Hutchins has written and illustrated another wonderful picture book full of sounds and sights, also just right for SMART Looking and Listening.

❶ Review Unit 2 Poster

Have students practice the Social Story.

- Have students repeat each line after you.
- Then read the poster using a cloze procedure on the last word or words of each line.

★ • • • • • • • • SMART • • • • • • • • • ★
Looking and Listening

Someone is talking to the class.
I sit up.
My face is pleasant.
I look with my eyes.
I listen with my ears.
My mouth is quiet.
My hands and feet are still.
I can look and listen when someone is talking.

Li Lizard looks and listens.

★ • ★
UNIT 2

❷ SMART Looking and Listening Read Aloud

Read aloud to students a picture book that has strong visuals and onomatopoeia (e.g., words that make sounds—buzz, buzz; rat-a-tat-tat; cluck, cluck, cluck).

- **Before reading, review SMART Looking and Listening. Use the poster steps as a guide. Say something like:**
  You can use SMART Looking and Listening when I read to you.

You sit . . . up.
You look at the book with your . . . eyes.
You listen with your . . . ears.
Your mouth is . . . quiet.
Your hands and feet are . . . still.
You can do SMART Looking and Listening when I read to you.

- **Introduce the book. Say something like:**
  You can use SMART Listening and Looking when I read a story to you. Today, we're going to read *Thump, Thump, Rat-a-Tat-Tat* by Gene Baer. Gene Baer is the author. His story is a lot of fun. Many of the words he wrote make sounds.
  Listen to the title and then say it with me.
  THUMP, THUMP, Rat-a-Tat-Tat
  THUMP, THUMP, Rat-a-Tat-Tat
  Excellent! You did SMART listening.

  Now look at the picture on the cover.
  What do you see? (a band . . . drummers)
  Excellent. You did SMART looking.

  You did SMART Looking and Listening.

- **Throughout your read aloud, ask questions that prompt SMART Looking and Listening. Ask:**
  What do you see?
  What did you hear?

  Provide positive descriptive feedback.
  You could tell me what you saw and heard because your mouths were quiet.
  Your hands and feet were . . . still.
  You looked at the book and you listened with your . . . ears.
  Great SMART Looking and Listening.

♦ ········ Lesson Outline ········ ♦

❶ Review Unit 3 Poster

Have students practice the Social Story.

❷ SMART Following Directions Treasure Hunt

Have partners use SMART Following Directions (and SMART Looking and Listening) while going on a Treasure Hunt.

Special Preparation Note ··········

Treasure Hunt: Treasure Box and Clues

Print the Unit 4 Treasure Hunt reproducible and cut out the treasure box graphic and Clue Cards.

- **Affix the treasure box graphic to a small box.**
- **Fill the box with a SMART Following Directions Recognition Card for each student.**
- **When students are out of the room, hide the treasure box and Clue Cards 2–5 (see below for where to hide Clue Cards).**

Then, the hunt is on! Read each Clue Card to students until they find the treasure.

Clue Card 1: Keep Card 1 to start the game.
- If you're wearing blue, stand up. If you're wearing blue, sit down.
- Clue 2 is under the SMART Following Directions Poster.

Clue Card 2: Hide Card 2 under the SMART Following Directions Poster.
You are SMART Kids! Rub your tummy. Now pat your head. Clue 3 is under my desk.

Clue Card 3: Hide Card 3 under your desk.
You are SMART kids. Yes, you are. To Find Clue 4, think of a place that rhymes with "four."

Clue Card 4: Hide Card 4 on the back of the door.
That's right. "Four" rhymes with "door." Clue 5 is under something we use for waste.

Clue Card 5: Hide Card 5 under a wastebasket.
You are SMART Kids! You can follow directions right away. Your treasure is waiting for you. (Tell students where you hid the treasure box.)

❶ Review Unit 3 Poster

Have students practice the Social Story.

- Read the poster using a cloze procedure on the last word or words of each line.

★ •••••••••• SMART •••••••••• ★
Following Directions

My teacher gives a direction.
I look at my teacher.
My face is pleasant.
My mouth is quiet.
I might nod or say "OK."
I follow directions right away.
I can follow directions.

Felicia Frog follows directions.

UNIT 3

❷ SMART Following Directions Treasure Hunt

Have partners use SMART Following Directions (and SMART Looking and Listening) while going on a Treasure Hunt.

- **Introduce the Treasure Hunt.**

  Today, we're going to have a Treasure Hunt. In a Treasure Hunt, you listen to clues and follow directions. If you use SMART Following Directions, you are going to find the treasure.

Read the first line of Clue Card 1.
If you're wearing blue, stand up.

Provide positive descriptive feedback.
That was SMART Following Directions!
Your mouths were closed.
Your hands and feet were . . . still.

Read the second line of Clue Card 1.
If you're wearing blue, sit down.

Read the third line of Clue Card 1.
Now Clue 1 says, "Clue 2 is under the SMART Following Directions Poster."
[Dejohn], please look under the SMART Following Directions Poster . . .

Provide positive descriptive feedback.
You all used SMART Following Directions!
You looked at me when I read the directions.
Your mouths were . . . quiet.
You listened and then you followed directions . . . right away.

Repeat with each Clue Card.

- Celebrate finding the treasure. Pass out a SMART Recognition Card for Following Directions to each child.

■ ······· Lesson Outline ······· ■

❶ Review Unit 2 Poster

Have students practice the Social Story.

❷ Review Unit 3 Poster

Have students practice the Social Story.

❸ Simon Says the SMART Way

Have students use SMART Looking and Listening and SMART Following Directions while playing Simon Says.

TEACHING TIP

When a student forgets how to look and listen, use lines from the Social Story to prompt the appropriate behavior:

[Cailey], remember our Social Story. When the teacher is giving a direction, your mouth . . . is quiet.
That's right. Say, "My mouth is quiet." (My mouth is quiet.)

❶ Review Unit 2 Poster

Have students practice the Social Story.

• Read the poster using a cloze procedure. Fade your support by starting each line with just a word or two. Then have students complete the last words.

Someone is . . . talking to the class.
I sit . . . up.
My face . . . is pleasant.
I look . . . with my eyes.
I listen . . . with my ears.
My mouth . . . is quiet.
My hands . . . and feet are still.
I can . . . look and listen
When someone is . . . talking.

★ ·········· SMART ·········· ★
Looking and Listening

Someone is talking to the class.
I sit up.
My face is pleasant.
I look with my eyes.
I listen with my ears.
My mouth is quiet.
My hands and feet are still.
I can look and listen when someone is talking.

Li Lizard looks and listens.

★ ·········· ★
UNIT 2

• **Repeat, guiding only as needed. Say something like:**

Say the SMART Looking and Listening Social Story one more time. I think you can say it by yourself. I'll help out when you need me.

❷ Review Unit 3 Poster

Have students practice the Social Story.

- **Read the poster using a cloze procedure. Fade your support by starting each line with just a word or two. Then have students complete the last words.**

- **Repeat, guiding only as needed. Say something like:**

Say the SMART Following Directions Social Story one more time. I think you can say it by yourself. I'll help out when you need me.

★ ·········· SMART ·········· ★
Following Directions

My teacher gives a direction.
I look at my teacher.
My face is pleasant.
My mouth is quiet.
I might nod or say "OK."
I follow directions right away.
I can follow directions.

Felicia Frog follows directions.

★ ·········· ★
UNIT 3

❸ Simon Says the SMART Way

Have the class use SMART Looking and Listening and SMART Following Directions while playing Simon Says.

- **Show and explain how to play the game.**

You can use SMART Looking and Listening and SMART Following Directions while we play Simon Says.

Let's review how to play the game.

If I say "Simon says," your job is to follow the direction.
Let's try it. "Simon says touch your ear."
That's great. You followed directions.
Here's the hard part. If I don't say "Simon says," don't follow the direction.
You really have to use your SMART Looking and Listening skills.
Let's try it. Listen: Touch your ear.
Good! [Connor], why didn't you touch your ear? (You didn't say "Simon says.")

[Connor], help me show everyone what to do. Simon says put one hand on your head.
Everyone, did I say "Simon says"? (yes)
Did [Connor] follow the direction? (yes)
Right. [Connor] used SMART Looking and Listening and SMART Following Directions. Everyone, clap for [Connor].

Repeat with another student.

- **Have the class play the game.**

OK everyone! Let's all play the game!

Use positive descriptive feedback when students are successful. Use lines from the Social Story to reinforce the skill students have learned.

Lesson 5

SMART REVIEW

★········ Lesson Outline ········★

❶ SMART/Not-So-SMART Cards

Using the Unit 4 SMART and Not-So-SMART Cards, have students identify whether a character is being SMART or Not-So-SMART.

❷ *I'm a SMART Kid Sharing Book 1*

Have students complete an *I'm a SMART Kid Sharing Book 1*.

❸ SMART Review Checkout

Recheck each student's SMART Skills. Focus on students who are less socially adept. Award Recognition Cards as appropriate.

CHAMPS
SHARING WITH FAMILIES

"Making the effort to communicate with your students' families sends a powerful message that you want to include them in what happens at school."

—Sprick, 2009, p. 51

In this unit, students make an *I'm a SMART Kid Sharing Book*. Send these books home for students to share with their families.

❶ SMART/Not-So-SMART Cards

Using the Unit 4 SMART/Not-So-SMART Cards, have students identify whether a character is being SMART or Not-So-SMART. Say something like:

We all make mistakes. Mistakes are an opportunity to learn.

Let's decide whether Ms. Smart's kids were being SMART or Not-So-SMART.

Read each SMART Card. (Card text shown here.)

SMART CARD 1

An old friend of Li's dad comes for a visit. When he arrives, Li's dad says, "Li, meet my old friend Lou." Li is so busy playing in his sand pit he doesn't even look up.

Thumbs up if Li remembered to give a warm greeting. Thumbs down if Li was Not-So-SMART.

What should Li do?

READ SMART CARD 1 — Greetings

An old friend of Li's dad comes for a visit. When he arrives, Li's dad says, "Li, meet my old friend Lou." Li is so busy playing in his sand pit he doesn't even look up.

Thumbs up if Li remembered to give a SMART Greeting.
Thumbs down if Li was Not-So-SMART.

What should Li do?

READ SMART CARD 2 — Following Directions

Ms. Smart hears the fire alarm and tells the class to line up. Everyone stops, then walks quickly and quietly to the door. No one talks.

Thumbs up if Ms. Smart's class remembered how to follow directions.
Thumbs down if Ms. Smart's class was Not-So-SMART.

What did Ms. Smart's class do that was smart?

READ SMART CARD 3 — Looking & Listening

During recess, Gregory Gopher and Carlos Cougar get in a big argument. They are still angry when it's time to go in.

After the kids are seated, Ms. Smart introduces the fire chief. While the chief talks, most of the kids sit up. Their faces are pleasant and they look and listen without talking. Gregory and Carlos are still angry. They scowl and frown while the chief talks.

Thumbs up or thumbs down. Did most of the class remember their SMART Looking and Listening Skills? Were Gregory and Carlos smart?

What should Gregory and Carlos have done while the chief was talking?

READ SMART CARD 4 — Greetings

One day, Ms. Smart is sick. The kids are very unhappy. When Li sees the substitute at the door, he snarls, "Why are you here? Where is Ms. Smart?"

Thumbs up if Li remembered a SMART Greeting. Thumbs down if Li was Not-So-SMART.

How do you think the substitute felt?
What should Li have done to give the substitute a SMART Greeting?

READ SMART CARD 5 — Looking & Listening

Ms. Smart's kids get to go on a field trip to the fire station. At the fire station, the kids listen carefully as the firefighters explain and show how to use the equipment. At the end of the visit, the firefighters are so impressed with Ms. Smart's class that they take the kids for a ride in the fire engine.

Thumbs up if you think Ms. Smart's class used SMART Looking and Listening.
Thumbs down if you think Ms. Smart's class was Not-So-SMART.

Would you like to be in Ms. Smart's class? Why or why not?

Small Celebrations

❷ I'm a SMART Kid Sharing Book 1

Have students complete the *I'm a SMART Kid Sharing Book 1*.

- Guide students through the book.
- Demonstrate how to trace the "I" statements.

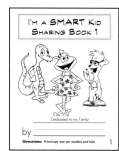

- Have students complete their books by coloring each picture. Have students use at least three colors.
- Have students take their books home to share with their families.

❸ Recheck Students' SMART Skills

Recheck each student's SMART Skills. Focus on students who are less socially adept. Award Recognition Cards as appropriate.

End-of-Unit Tip

SMART REVIEW

As you move forward, work on . . .

·············· Generalization ···············

Everyday Use: Have students practice SMART Greetings, Looking and Listening, and Following Directions everyday. These skills should become part of your daily routine.

Continue to Encourage Efforts by:
- Providing positive descriptive feedback.
- Providing gentle corrections and guided practice as needed.
- Re-teaching periodically.
- Using SMART Recognition Cards to acknowledge student efforts.
- Referring to your Guidelines for Success.

·············· Intervention ···············

When a student or students have difficulty with any of the three skills learned to date:
   Target one or two skills—Greetings, Looking and Listening, or Following Directions.

Scaffold Practice
For the targeted social skill, identify the easiest step of the social skill for the student. Practice and reinforce this step. Once the step is mastered, add another step. Practice and reinforce both steps. When the student masters these steps, add another.

Prompt Correct Practice
- Periodically, ask and have the class identify an important step in a social skill.
- Have the intervention student(s) say the step.
- Have the intervention student(s) demonstrate the behavior.
- Reinforce the behavior with positive descriptive feedback.

NEVER GIVE UP!
Use Student Trackers (see Intervention Tools in Teacher Resources on the CD) and Recognition Cards when you catch intervention students using SMART Greetings, Looking and Listening, and Following Directions. These skills can be difficult for some students. Gradually, teach and shape the desired behaviors. Then celebrate each small step towards routine use.

SMART Polite Requests

Student Objectives

Targeted Objectives
I say "Please" when I want something and "Thank you" when I get it.

Review Objectives
I follow directions right away.

I look and listen when someone is talking.

I greet others with a smile and a "Hello."

★ ★ ★ ★ ★ ★ ★ ★

SMART POLITE REQUESTS
Overview

······· Teaching Objectives ·······

Students practice all the steps below and demonstrate competency by using Steps 4, 5, and 6.

1. Body quiet
2. Having a pleasant expression
3. Looking at the person
4. Using a calm voice
5. Saying "Please"
6. Saying "Thank you" or "OK"

Teaching Materials

School Materials

- Puppet of your choice
- Colors

SMART Materials

- Units 3 and 5 Posters
- *My SMART Book* Unit 5 Coloring Page
- Recognition Cards for Polite Requests and previous units
- Unit 5 Reproducibles:
  - 5-4a Practice Cards
  - 5-4b Help Cards (suggested)

SMART POLITE REQUESTS ARE . . . OH, SO IMPORTANT!

When students learn to make requests calmly and politely, people listen and respond calmly and politely. SMART Polite Requests help students learn to create positive interactions in multiple contexts.

············· Teaching Tips ·············

Positive Interactions

Respond warmly to students when they use SMART Polite Requests—even if the answer is "No." Say things like:

That was a SMART Polite Request. It was very polite. I'm sorry to say . . .

Positive Feedback and Reinforcement

Provide positive descriptive feedback.

I am very proud of the way this class makes requests. You say "Please" and "Thank you." Your voice and body are calm and quiet.

Use SMART Recognition Cards to acknowledge student efforts.

Connections

Reference your Guidelines for Success. For example, Be respectful.

I heard a SMART Polite Request. That's a great way to show respect.

·········· Intervention ··········

Make an overt effort to practice SMART Polite Requests with students who need additional practice.

Prompt "Please" and "Thank you" whenever appropriate.

Lesson Planner

Lesson	Activities	Materials and Materials Preparation
1	**Model and Explain SMART Polite Requests** **Introduce Unit 5 Poster** **Discuss When and Where to Use SMART Polite Requests**	**Unit 5 Poster** Reproducible: Print the Unit 5 Poster (2 pages) and affix to 11" x 17" poster board. (Or order premade color posters.)
2	**Practice Unit 5 Poster** **SMART Polite Requests Description** **SMART/Not-So-SMART Puppet Play**	• **Unit 5 Poster** • **A puppet**
3	**Review Unit 3 Poster** **Review What SMART Following Directions Looks and Sounds Like** **Practice SMART Polite Requests**	**Unit 3 Poster**
4	**Practice Unit 5 Poster** **Reasons for Using SMART Polite Requests** **SMART Practice Cards**	• **Unit 5 Poster** • **Unit 5 Practice Cards** Reproducible 5-4a: Make one copy of each card. • **Help Cards (suggested)** Reproducible 5-4b: Copy one card per student.
5	**Practice SMART Polite Requests** *My SMART Book* **Unit 5 Coloring Page** **SMART Polite Requests Checkouts and Recognition**	• *My SMART Book* **Unit 5 Coloring Page** • **Colors** • **SMART Polite Requests Recognition Cards** Reproducible: On card stock, make several copies of the cards. Then cut and hole punch each card.

Lesson Outline

❶ Model and Explain SMART Polite Requests

Model and explain SMART Polite Requests with a class demonstration.

❷ Introduce Unit 5 Poster

Introduce Penelope Parrot, then read and rehearse the Social Story with gestures.

❸ Discuss When and Where to Use SMART Polite Requests

Explain and discuss when and where SMART Polite Requests should be used.

Please?

❶ Model and Explain SMART Polite Requests

Model and explain SMART Polite Requests with a class demonstration.

- Have a student helper ask you for something (such as permission to sharpen a pencil, get materials, a toy, etc.). Prior to the demonstration, tell the student helper to use the word "Please."
  Say something like:
  Class, today we're going to learn how to make a SMART Polite Request. [Madison] is my student helper. [She] is going to help me. Everyone, use SMART Looking and Listening.

- Have your student helper ask you if [she could please play with the big class bear].
  [Ms. Santana], may I please [play with the class bear]?
  Okay, [Madison], you may [play with him for five minutes].
  Thank you, [Ms. Santana].

- Describe a SMART Polite Request.
  Say something like:
  [Madison] just made a SMART Polite Request. [She] used a SMART body and face. [Her] body was quiet. That means her hands were relaxed. She looked calm. She had a pleasant look. She looked at me and remembered to say "Please" when [she] asked. When I told [her] "Yes," [she] even remembered to say "Thank you."

  I think [Madison] knows that [she] is more likely to get a "Yes" when [she] says "Please" and "Thank you."

❷ Introduce Unit 5 Poster

Introduce Penelope Parrot, then read and rehearse the Social Story with gestures.

- **Have students give a SMART Greeting to Penelope Parrot. Say something like:**
  Let's look at our Polite Requests Poster.
  Let's greet our new character.
  "Hello, Penelope." (Hello, Penelope.)
  That was a great SMART Greeting.
  The Poster says, "Penelope Parrot says 'Please' and 'Thank you.'"
  Let's look at the first part of the picture.
  What do you think Penelope wants?
  (the soccer ball)
  So, what do you think she said? (Please)
  Yes, I think she said, "Gregory, please may I have the soccer ball?" After Gregory gave Penelope the ball, she said . . . Thank you.

- **Read the SMART Social Story using the suggested gestures and sign language.**
  Listen to me read about a SMART Request.
  "When I want or need something . . ."

- **Next, have students repeat each line after you.**

- **Then, read the poster using a cloze procedure on the last word or words of each line.**
  When I want or need . . . something . . .

❸ Discuss When and Where to Use SMART Polite Requests

Explain and discuss when and where SMART Polite Requests should be used.
Say something like:
You can use a SMART Polite Request at school when you want to ask me something.
If you want to ask to borrow a pencil, what would you say? (Please may I borrow a pencil?)
If you want to ask to pass out papers, what would you say? (Please may I pass out the papers?)
If you want to go to the restroom, what would you say? (Please may I go to the restroom?)

Think of some other times you could use a SMART Request with a friend.
(when I want to ask my friend if I can play with [him] . . .)

Point to yourself.

Sign for "please."*

Point to your ear, nod, and then sign for "Thank you."*

Point to your ear, shake your head, and then sign for "OK."*

Point to yourself.

★ • • • • • • • • • • SMART • • • • • • • • • • ★
Polite Requests

When I want or need something, I can ask.
My body is quiet.
My face is pleasant.
I look at the person.
I use a calm voice and say, "Please . . . "
If I hear "Yes," I can say "Thank you."
If I hear "No," I can say "OK."
I know how to say "Please" and "Thank you," too.

Please?   Thank you!

Penelope Parrot makes polite requests.

★ • ★
UNIT 5   © 2010 The Mailey Company and Marilyn Sprick - Pacific Northwest Publishing

* See "How to Teach the Program" for gestures and ASL.

Lesson 2

SMART POLITE REQUESTS

▲ ······· Lesson Outline ······· ▲

❶ Practice Unit 5 Poster

Have students practice the Social Story with gestures.

❷ SMART Polite Requests Description

Describe a SMART Polite Request using the poster steps.

❸ SMART/Not-So-SMART Puppet Play

Use a puppet and a student to model a SMART and a Not-So-SMART Polite Request. Use the poster steps to guide instruction.

---

❶ Practice Unit 5 Poster

Have students practice the Social Story with gestures.

- Have students repeat each line after you.
- Then read the poster using a cloze procedure on the last word or words of each line.

★ ········· SMART ········· ★
Polite Requests

When I want or need something, I can ask.
My body is quiet.
My face is pleasant.
I look at the person.
I use a calm voice and say, "Please . . . "
If I hear "Yes," I can say "Thank you."
If I hear "No," I can say "OK."
I know how to say "Please" and "Thank you," too.

Please? Thank you!

Penelope Parrot makes polite requests.

★ ★ UNIT 5 ★ ★

❷ SMART Polite Requests Description

Describe a SMART Polite Request using the poster steps. Say something like:

When you make a SMART Polite Request, use a SMART face, voice, and body. When you ask for something, your body is quiet. Your face is pleasant. Show me a pleasant face. You look at the person and it's important to use a SMART voice.

That means you say "Please" in a calm and friendly voice like I'm using right now.

Then if the person tells you "Yes," you say "Thank you."

If the person says "No," you say "OK."

❸ SMART/Not-So-SMART Puppet Play

Use a puppet and a student to model a SMART and a Not-So-SMART Polite Request. Use the poster steps to guide instruction.

- **Before the lesson, role play how to say "Please" and "Thank you" with a student and the puppet.**

  The puppet asks:

  [Ethan], may I use your red crayon, please?

  The student replies: Yes.

  The puppet then says:

  Thank you, [Ethan].

- **Have your students watch the puppet model a SMART Polite Request with the student.**

  Then, ask students:

  Did the puppet have a pleasant face? (yes)

  What did the puppet do?

  (The puppet looked at [Ethan].)

  What did the puppet ask?

  (May I use your crayon, please?)

  Did the puppet use a nice, calm, friendly voice? (yes)

  What did the puppet say when [Ethan] said "Yes"? (The puppet said "Thank you, [Ethan]" in a nice voice.)

  That's right, and I think the puppet smiled too. The puppet was doing a SMART job saying "Please" and "Thank you"!

- **Have students watch the puppet model a Not-So-SMART Polite Request.**

  Now let's look at a Not-So-SMART Polite Request.

  Have the puppet ask another student for the crayon, but this time, have the puppet say "Give me your red crayon" in a loud bossy voice. Have the puppet look away from the student.

  Then discuss the role play.

  Say something like:

  Let's stop and talk about what happened.

  What did the puppet say?

  (Give me your red crayon!)

  Describe the puppet's tone of voice.

  (It was loud and bossy.)

  Did the puppet say "Please"? (no)

  Do you think [Xavier] would say "Yes" and let the puppet use [his] crayon? (no)

  I think we better make SMART Polite Requests in our classroom and on the playground!

Lesson 3

SMART POLITE REQUESTS

♦ ········ Lesson Outline ········ ♦

❶ Review Unit 3 Poster

Have students practice the Social Story with gestures.

❷ Review What SMART Following Directions Looks and Sounds Like

Have partners share what SMART Following Directions looks and sounds like.

❸ Practice SMART Polite Requests

Have students review and then practice the poster steps for SMART Polite Requests.

❶ Review Unit 3 Poster

Have students practice the Social Story with gestures.

- Have students repeat each line after you.
- Then read the poster using a cloze procedure on the last word or words of each line.

★ ··········· **SMART** ··········· ★
Following Directions

My teacher gives a direction.
I look at my teacher.
My face is pleasant.
My mouth is quiet.
I might nod or say "OK."
I follow directions right away.
I can follow directions.

Felicia Frog follows directions.

★ ·············· UNIT 3 ·············· ★

❷ Review What SMART Following Directions Looks and Sounds Like

Have partners share what SMART Following Directions looks and sounds like.

Say something like:

Partner 1, tell Partner 2 one thing about SMART Following Directions.

Repeat with Partner 2.

[Isabella], what did your partner say about SMART Following Directions?
Great. Your mouths are . . . quiet.
And your face is . . . pleasant.

What else do you do with SMART Following Directions? (look at the teacher and follow directions)
Yes, and when do you follow directions? (right away)

❸ **Practice SMART Polite Requests**

Have students review and then practice the poster steps for SMART Polite Requests.

• **Review the steps for SMART Polite Requests. Say something like:**
Remember, when you make SMART Polite Requests, your body is . . . quiet.
Your face is . . . pleasant.
You look at the person and in a calm voice you say . . . "Please."
If you hear "Yes," you can say . . . "Thank you."
If you hear "No," you can say . . . "OK."
You know how to say . . . "Please" and "Thank you" too.

• **Have students practice the steps for a SMART Polite Request.**
Now I want everybody to show me a SMART Polite Request.
We are going to pretend that you want to have story time.
Everyone ask: "May we have story time, please?" (May we have story time, please?)

Then, say something like:
Wow, good job! I saw everyone looking at me, using good posture, a SMART voice, and the word "Please." That was a SMART Polite Request!
Even if you say "Please," sometimes the answer isn't "Yes."
We have other things to do before we can have story time.
So, you will need to say "OK."
What will you say? (OK)

Have individuals or small groups practice SMART Polite Requests with "Yes" for an answer and "No" for an answer.

Lesson 4

SMART POLITE REQUESTS

■ ········ Lesson Outline ········ ■

❶ Practice Unit 5 Poster

Have students practice the Social Story with gestures.

❷ Reasons for Using SMART Polite Requests

Discuss the reasons for using SMART Polite Requests.

❸ SMART Practice Cards

Using the Unit 5 Practice Cards, have students practice SMART Polite Requests.

HELP CARDS

Make Help Cards for each student's desk. Tell students to stand their card up on their desk when they need something. When you see a Help Card, say something like: Remember to use a Polite Request. Start with "May I please . . ." (May I please go to the restroom?)

Provide positive descriptive feedback. Excellent, you used a pleasant voice and said, "May I please go to the restroom?" When I said "Yes," you remembered to say "Thank you."

HELP CARD

I can make a polite request. I'm a SMART Kid.

---

❶ Practice Unit 5 Poster

Have students practice the Social Story with gestures.

- Have students repeat each line after you.
- Then, read poster using a cloze procedure on the last word or words of each line.

★ · · · · · · · · · · · SMART · · · · · · · · · · · ★
Polite Requests

When I want or need something, I can ask.
My body is quiet.
My face is pleasant.
I look at the person.
I use a calm voice and say, "Please . . ."
If I hear "Yes," I can say "Thank you."
If I hear "No," I can say "OK."
I know how to say "Please" and "Thank you," too.

Please? Thank you!

Penelope Parrot makes polite requests.

★ ★ · ★
UNIT 5

❷ Reasons for Using SMART Polite Requests

Discuss the reasons for using SMART Polite Requests. Say something like:

It's important to use SMART Polite Requests when you *want* something. They are also important when you want to *do* something.

When you SMART Polite Requests, other people will be more likely to treat you in a nice way. SMART Polite Requests will also help you follow our Guideline for Success. [Be respectful.]

What happens if you say something like, "You have to play with me" in a bossy voice?
Will other kids want to play with you? (no)
Will others want to be your friend? (no)
That's right. Other kids don't like people who aren't respectful.

What happens if you say something like, "Would you like to play with me? Please come play soccer with me."
Will other kids want to play with you? (yes)
Will others want to be your friend? (yes)
That's right. Other kids like people who are respectful and use SMART Polite Requests.

Let's see if we can figure out three reasons for using SMART Polite Requests. Here's one idea. You are more likely to hear a "Yes."

What's another idea? (It is more respectful. People like SMART Polite Requests more than Not-So-SMART Polite Requests. It sounds better . . .)

That's right, and SMART Polite Requests show good manners!

❸ SMART Practice Cards
Using the Unit 5 Practice Cards, have students practice SMART Polite Requests.
- **Read Practice Card 1. Then have partners practice making a request.**

READ PRACTICE CARD 1

You've finished your work and want to use the computer. Make a SMART Polite Request.

Start with "May I . . . "

If a child misses a step, say:
[Xiang], I liked how you looked at me when you asked if you could use the computer.

Let's try that again with "Please."
Ask, "Please may I use the computer?"

When the child is successful, say:
I liked the way you remembered to say "Please" and "Thank you." That showed good manners and respect!

- **Repeat with Practice Cards 2–7.**

READ PRACTICE CARD 2

You need help on your math. Make a SMART Polite Request.

Start with "I need some help. Would you please . . . "

READ PRACTICE CARD 3

You and your friends want to play soccer at recess. You will need a soccer ball. Make a SMART Polite Request.

Start with "We want to play soccer during recess. Could we . . . "

READ PRACTICE CARD 4

You want to watch your favorite TV show. Make a SMART Polite Request.

Start with "My TV show is on soon. Please . . . "

READ PRACTICE CARD 5

You are proud of your work and want to take a note home to your family. Make a SMART Polite Request.

Start with "I'm proud of my [picture]. Would you . . . "

READ PRACTICE CARD 6

You are hungry and would like to eat a snack. Make a SMART Polite Request.

Start with "I'm feeling very hungry. May I . . . "

READ PRACTICE CARD 7

You don't feel well. Your head hurts and your face feels hot. Make a SMART Polite Request.

Start with "I don't feel good. My head hurts and my face feels hot. May I . . . "

Lesson 5

SMART POLITE REQUESTS

★⋯⋯⋯ Lesson Outline ⋯⋯⋯★

❶ Practice SMART Polite Requests

Get students' attention and acknowledge SMART Polite Requests during teacher-directed activities.

❷ My SMART Book Unit 5 Coloring Page

Have students color their SMART Polite Requests Coloring Pages for their SMART Books.

❸ SMART Polite Requests Checkouts and Recognition

Check out each student by having the student make a request. Award SMART Polite Requests Recognition Cards to individuals as they demonstrate the skill.

CHAMPS
GETTING ASSISTANCE

"Develop a specific system that enables students to ask questions and get help during independent work periods."

—Sprick, 2009, p. 103

When doing independent work, students need a way to get your attention so they can make polite requests for help. The Help Card system supports students' efforts to use Polite Requests in this classroom context.

Small Celebrations

❶ Practice SMART Polite Requests

Get students' attention and acknowledge SMART Polite Requests during teacher-directed activities. Say something like:

You've all done an awesome job learning about SMART Polite Requests. I'm very proud of you. Everyone, look at [Jabaar].

When [he] needed a [pencil], [he] looked at me and asked in a calm voice, "May I borrow a [pencil], please?"

When I said "OK," [he] remembered to say "Thank you."

Does [Jabaar] know how to make a SMART Polite Request? (yes)

❷ My SMART Book Unit 5 Coloring Page

Have students color their SMART Polite Requests Coloring Pages. Say something like: You can all use SMART Polite Requests. You can [treat others like you want to be treated].

Because you all know how to make SMART Polite Requests, you get to color another page in your *My SMART Book*! It says, "Penelope Parrot says 'Please' and 'Thank you.'"

SMART Polite Requests

Please? *Thank you!*

Penelope Parrot makes polite requests.

❹ UNIT 5

★ ★
★ ★
★ ★

UNIT

5

Lesson 5

SMART POLITE REQUESTS

❸ SMART Polite Requests Checkouts and Recognition

Check out each student by having the student make a simple request. Award SMART Polite Requests Recognition Cards to individuals as they demonstrate the skill.

Say something like:

While you are coloring your SMART Coloring Pages, I'm going to listen to your give me a SMART Polite Request so you can earn your SMART Polite Requests Recognition Card.

End-of-Unit Tip

SMART POLITE REQUESTS

As you move forward, work on . . .

·············· Generalization ···············

Everyday Use: Have students practice SMART Polite Requests when they need something.

Continue to Encourage Efforts by:
- **Providing positive descriptive feedback.**
  Thank you for asking if we could take a break in a calm voice.
- **Providing gentle corrections and guided practice as needed.**
  [Logan], you made a Polite Request. Please use a calm voice.
  Say, "May I please take a break?"
- **Re-teaching periodically.**
- **Using SMART Recognition Cards to acknowledge student efforts.**
- **Referring to your Guidelines for Success.**
  [Riley] showed us how to use a SMART Polite Request. [She] looked at me with a pleasant face, used a calm voice, and said "Please." That's a great way to follow our school guideline about being respectful.

·············· Intervention ··············

When a student or students have difficulty making Polite Requests:

Prompt Correct Practice
- **Periodically, ask and have the class help you identify an important step for Polite Requests.**
  Everyone, when you need something, what do you say?
  (please)
- **Have the intervention student(s) model the response.**
  [Lee], what do you say when you need something? (please)
- **Have the intervention student(s) demonstrate the behavior.**
  [Lee], use a Polite Request and ask if we can go to recess early.
  (May we please go to recess early?)
- **Reinforce the behavior with positive descriptive feedback.**
  [Lee], that was excellent. Everyone, give [Lee] a thumbs up. The answer is "Yes," we can go to recess five minutes early. Everyone, say . . . (thank you).

SPECIAL CELEBRATION
Stage a juice party for students who can benefit from practicing Polite Requests. Model and have students practice making Polite Requests while drinking juice and eating cookies. Have fun!

SMART Compliments

Student Objectives

Targeted Objectives
I give compliments to others.

Review Objectives
I say "Please" when I want something and "Thank you" when I get it.

I follow directions right away.

I look and listen when someone is talking.

I greet others with a smile and a "Hello."

★ ★ ★ ★ ★ ★ ★ ★ ★ ★

SMART COMPLIMENTS
Overview

···· Teaching Objectives ······

Students practice all the steps below and demonstrate competency by using Steps 1–4.

1. Having a pleasant face
2. Looking at the person
3. Saying something nice that I mean
4. Using a happy voice

Teaching Materials

School Materials

- Puppet of your choice
- Colors
- One can (e.g., coffee can)

SMART Materials

- Units 5 and 6 Posters
- *My SMART Book* Unit 6 Coloring Page
- Recognition Cards for Compliments and previous units
- Unit 6 Reproducibles:
  6-4 Can of Compliments

SMART COMPLIMENTS ARE ... OH, SO IMPORTANT!

SMART compliments help young children learn to be positive with those around them. SMART Compliments also help children develop a positive focus as they learn to observe and articulate what they like.

······ Teaching Tips ·············

Positive Interactions

Compliment individuals—especially for efforts and improvements on skills that might be difficult for them. Say things like:

I noticed you gave [Jabaar] a SMART Greeting. Nice job!

Positive Feedback and Reinforcement

Provide positive descriptive feedback.

Wow! That was a SMART Compliment. You smiled at [Xavier], noticed his new boots, and said, "Those are nice boots!" [Xavier] was happy that you noticed.

Use SMART Recognition Cards to acknowledge student efforts.

Connections

Reference your Guidelines for Success. For example, Be respectful.

I heard a SMART Compliment. That's a great way to show you respect [Ethan].

·········· Intervention ··········

Make an overt effort to practice SMART Compliments with students who do not know how to build positive relationships with others. Model and prompt practice.

Lesson	Activities	Materials and Materials Preparation
1	**Model and Explain SMART Compliments** **Introduce Unit 6 Poster** **When to Give SMART Compliments**	**Unit 6 Poster** Reproducible: Print the Unit 6 Poster (2 pages) and affix to 11"x 17" poster board. (Or order premade color posters.)
2	**Practice Unit 6 Poster** **SMART Compliments Description and Modeling** **SMART/Not-So-SMART Teacher Role Playing**	**Unit 6 Poster**
3	**Review Unit 5 Poster** **SMART Polite Requests Role Playing** **Practice SMART Compliments**	**Unit 5 Poster**
4	**Practice Unit 6 Poster** **Reasons for Using SMART Compliments** **SMART Can of Compliments**	• **Unit 6 Poster** • **One can (e.g., coffee can)** • **Unit 6 Can of Compliments** Reproducible 6-4: See Special Preparation Note, p. 80.
5	**Practice SMART Compliments** ***My SMART Book* Unit 6 Coloring Page** **SMART Compliments Checkouts and Recognition**	• ***My SMART Book* Unit 6 Coloring Page** • **Colors** • **SMART Compliments Recognition Cards** Reproducible: On card stock, make several copies of the cards. Then cut and hole punch each card.

Lesson 1

SMART COMPLIMENTS

```
• ········· Lesson Outline ········· •
```

❶ Model and Explain SMART Compliments

Model and explain SMART Compliments with the whole class (e.g., during a Read Aloud).

❷ Introduce Unit 6 Poster

Introduce Carlos Cougar, then read and rehearse the Social Story with gestures.

❸ When to Give SMART Compliments

Explain and discuss when SMART Compliments can be given.

❶ Model and Explain SMART Compliments

Model and explain SMART Compliments with the whole class (e.g., during a Read Aloud).

- **Compliment your students during a Read Aloud session when they are all using SMART Looking and Listening. Say something like:**
  Everyone used SMART Looking and Listening while I read our story.
  I'd like to compliment you all.
  You are doing a great job looking and listening!

- **Describe SMART Compliments. Say something like:**
  When you say something nice about a person or something they've done, it's called a compliment. Everyone, what is a nice comment called? (a compliment)

  Today, I gave everybody a compliment because you used SMART Looking and Listening while I was reading our story. I said, "You are doing a great job looking and listening." That was a nice comment about something important.

  Sometimes I tell you that you are great kids. That's also giving a compliment because I am saying something that is nice. It makes you feel good. It's a . . . compliment.

❷ SMART Compliments Poster

Introduce Carlos Cougar, then read and rehearse the Social Story with gestures.

• **Give a SMART Greeting to Carlos Cougar. Say something like:**

Let's look at our SMART Compliments Poster and greet our new character. This is Carlos Cougar. Everyone, wave and say "Hello, Carlos." (Hello, Carlos.)

Who else is in the picture? (Penelope Parrot)

Let's greet Penelope. (Hello, Penelope.)

That was a great SMART Greeting.

The Poster says, "Carlos Cougar gives cool compliments."

Carlos is looking at Penelope's picture.

What do you think Carlos said to Penelope? (Nice picture! Great picture! I like the mountain and sun . . .)

Point to your eyes.

Sign for "say."*

Sign for "happy."*

Point to yourself.

★ • • • • • • • • • • • SMART • • • • • • • • • • • ★
Compliments

I can give a compliment when I notice something nice.

My face is pleasant.

I look at the person.

I say something nice—something that I really mean with a happy voice.

I can help someone feel happy and important.

I can give a compliment.

Carlos Cougar gives cool compliments.

★ • ★
UNIT 6

* See "How to Teach the Program" for gestures and ASL.

When you say something nice, it's a compliment. Those are all great compliments.

How do you think Penelope feels? (happy, proud, good)

Do you think Penelope feels like Carlos is a friend? (yes)

• **Read the SMART Social Story using the suggested gestures and sign language.**

Listen to me read about a SMART Compliment. "I can give a compliment . . . "

• **Next, have students repeat each line after you.**

• **Then, read the poster using a cloze procedure on the last word or words of each line.**

I can give a . . . compliment.

❸ When to Give SMART Compliments

Explain and discuss when SMART Compliments can be given. Say something like:

You can give SMART Compliments when someone does something nice for you.

You can give compliments when you notice something nice about someone else. For example, you might say "nice haircut" or "I like your new shoes."

You can give compliments when you notice someone doing a good job. A compliment tells people you care about them. It makes me feel good when someone says, "That was a great story. I liked it." It makes me feel good because it's a . . . compliment.

Lesson 2
SMART COMPLIMENTS

▲······· Lesson Outline ·······▲

❶ Practice Unit 6 Poster

Have students practice the Social Story with gestures.

❷ SMART Compliments Description and Modeling

Describe and model SMART Compliments using the poster steps.

❸ SMART/Not-So-SMART Teacher Role Playing

Demonstrate and then have students identify with a thumbs-up or thumbs-down whether your comments are SMART Compliments or not. Use the poster steps to guide instruction.

❶ Practice Unit 6 Poster

Have students practice the Social Story with gestures.

- Have students repeat each line after you.
- Then read the poster using a cloze procedure on the last word or words of each line.

★ ········· SMART ········· ★
Compliments

I can give a compliment when I notice something nice.

My face is pleasant.

I look at the person.

I say something nice—something that I really mean with a happy voice.

I can help someone feel happy and important.

I can give a compliment.

Carlos Cougar gives cool compliments.

❷ SMART Compliments Description and Modeling

Describe and model SMART Compliments using the poster steps.

Say something like:

When you give a SMART Compliment, you use a SMART face and voice.

That means your face is . . . pleasant.

You look at the person and say

something . . . nice . . . with a happy . . . voice.

Before you give a SMART Compliment, notice something nice. Think about something special about the person.

Make sure what you say is honest—something you really mean. I might say to [Abrianna], "I enjoy your friendly smile." I really do like [Abrianna]'s smile, so it's something I mean. It's a nice comment. It's a . . . compliment.

A compliment can be anything nice about a person or what someone has done. You could say, "[Caden], I like your painting."
You could say, "[Oksana], nice job reading with expression" or you could say something like, "[Logan], I like the shark you brought for sharing."
Those comments are all . . . compliments.

❸ **SMART/Not-So-SMART Teacher Role Playing**

Demonstrate and then have students identify with a thumbs-up or thumbs-down whether your compliments are SMART Compliments or not. Use the poster steps to guide instruction.

- **Have students watch you use the steps for SMART Compliments. Say something like:**
  [Cailey], you are a nice friend to everyone.

  Next, ask students:
  Did I smile and look at [Cailey]? (yes)
  Did I notice something special and say something nice? (yes)
  What did I say? ([Cailey], you are a nice friend to everyone.)
  [Cailey], did my compliment make you feel

happy and important? (yes)
Thumbs up if that was a SMART Compliment. Thumbs down if it wasn't a SMART Compliment.

- **Have students watch and listen as you make a comment that is not a compliment. Look and smile at the same student and say something nice that isn't true. Say something like:**
  Now let's think about a comment that isn't a compliment.
  Listen: [Cailey], I love your curly hair!

  Next, ask students:
  Did I look at [Cailey] and smile? (yes)
  Yes, I had a pleasant face.
  Did I say something nice? (yes)
  What did I say? ([Cailey], I love your curly hair.)
  Did I really mean what I said? (no)
  Was it honest? (no)
  How do you know? ([Cailey] doesn't have curly hair.)
  That's right. I didn't really mean it.
  Thumbs up if that was a SMART Compliment. Thumbs down if it wasn't a SMART Compliment.
  Let me try again. [Cailey], you have beautiful straight hair.

  Repeat as time allows with other role plays:
  [Berto], I like the way you are doing SMART Looking and Listening.
  [Dakota], your new jacket is great. [Dimitre], I enjoyed listening to you read. You read with expression!

Lesson 3

SMART COMPLIMENTS

♦ ······· Lesson Outline ······· ♦

❶ Review Unit 5 Poster

Have students practice the Social Story with gestures.

❷ SMART Polite Requests Role Playing

Have partners practice SMART Polite Requests.

❸ Practice SMART Compliments

Have students review and then practice the poster steps for SMART Compliments.

---

❶ Review Unit 5 Poster

Have students practice the Social Story with gestures.

- Have students repeat each line after you.
- Then read the poster using a cloze procedure on the last word or words of each line.

★ · · · · · · · · · · · SMART · · · · · · · · · · · ★
Polite Requests

When I want or need something, I can ask.
My body is quiet.
My face is pleasant.
I look at the person.
I use a calm voice and say, "Please . . . "
If I hear "Yes," I can say "Thank you."
If I hear "No," I can say "OK."
I know how to say "Please" and "Thank you," too.

Penelope Parrot makes polite requests.

❷ SMART Polite Requests Role Playing

Have partners practice SMART Polite Requests. Say something like:

Partner 1, we're going to practice SMART Polite Requests. Pretend you want someone to listen to you read. Make a SMART Polite Request that starts with "May I . . ." Partner 2, answer "Yes."

Partner 2, did your partner say "Please"? (yes)
Partner 2, did your partner use your name? (yes)
Partner 2, did your partner say "Thank you"? (yes)

Rotate turns. Repeat role playing with requests such as:

- A partner giving the other partner a ball, jump rope, etc.
- A partner inviting the other to eat lunch with him or her
- A partner sharing a box of crayons

❸ **Practice SMART Compliments**

Have students review and then practice the poster steps for SMART Compliments.

- **Review the steps for SMART Compliments. Say something like:**

  Remember, when you give a SMART Compliment, your face is ... pleasant.
  You look at the ... person.
  You say ... something nice ...
  Something that you really ... mean.
  You use a happy ... voice.

- **Have students practice the steps for SMART Compliments.**

  Now I want everybody to get ready to give me a SMART Compliment.
  Everyone, say, "[Mrs. Mulkey], you are a good teacher!"
  ([Mrs. Mulkey], you are a good teacher.)

Give the students positive descriptive feedback.

Wow, everyone looked at me, smiled, and used a nice voice. Your compliment made me feel great. And, you even remembered to use my name.

Have individuals or the group practice as time permits. Use prompts and sentence starters. Say something like:

Let's give [Sophia] a compliment about [her] great handwriting. Say, "[Sophia], you have great ... handwriting."
What else could you say?

Model and guide practice as needed.

Lesson 4

SMART COMPLIMENTS

■ ······· Lesson Outline ······· ■

❶ Practice Unit 6 Poster

Have students practice the Social Story with gestures.

❷ Reasons for Using SMART Compliments

Discuss the reasons for using SMART Compliments.

❸ SMART Can of Compliments

Have students review how to give a SMART Compliment. Then, draw (take out) premade compliments about each student from a can. Using the child's first initial and a prewritten compliment, have students guess who the compliment is about.

Special Preparation Note ··········
Can of Compliments

Print the Unit 6 Can of Compliments reproducible and cut out the label and the Compliment Cards. Print additional pages so you have one Compliment Card per student.

- Affix the label to a can.
- Write a compliment for each student and put the cards in the can.

Examples of compliments:

COMPLIMENT CARD

This __girl__'s name begins with the letter __S__.
She __has__ beautiful red hair

I like the __way she reads with expression__

Who is it?

COMPLIMENT CARD

This __boy__'s name begins with the letter __D__.
He __has__ has a big smile and a new front tooth
I like the __great purple mountain he painted__

Who is it?

❶ Practice Unit 6 Poster

Have students practice the Social Story with gestures.

- Have students repeat each line after you.
- Then read the poster using a cloze procedure on the last word or words of each line.

★ • • • • • • • • • SMART • • • • • • • • • ★
Compliments

I can give a compliment when I notice
    something nice.

My face is pleasant.

I look at the person.

I say something nice—something that I
    really mean with a happy voice.

I can help someone feel happy and important.

I can give a compliment.

Carlos Cougar gives cool compliments.

★ • ★
UNIT 6

❷ Reasons for Using SMART Compliments

Discuss the reasons for using SMART Compliments. Say something like:
It's important to give compliments!
Our Social Story tells us why. Compliments
help us feel . . . happy and important.

Giving compliments shows that you care.
Compliments encourage people to try harder
and keep up the good work. Do you think
your teachers like compliments? (yes)
I love compliments. They make me feel happy.

Do friends give each other compliments? (yes)
Yes, friends encourage each other.
Friends give . . . compliments.

❸ SMART Can of Compliments

Have students review how to give a SMART Compliment. Then, draw (take out) premade compliments about each student from the Can of Compliments. Have students guess who the compliment is about.

Note: This activity should be spread across a day or two. If the activity is started in the morning, tell students you will read cards for a few kids after lunch, before recess . . . until everyone has heard their special Compliment Card.

- **First, have students review the poster steps for SMART Compliments. Say:**
  Remember, when you give a SMART
  Compliment, you smile and . . . look at
  the person.
  You say . . . something nice . . .
  Something that you really . . . mean.
  You use a happy . . . voice.

- **Draw compliments from a can. Read the Compliment Card. Then have students guess who the compliment is about.**

  Reread the Compliment Card. Then have individuals practice giving the first part of the compliment. Say something like:
  [Connor], please give [Malia] the first part
  of the compliment. Say [Malia]'s name.
  Then start with "You have . . ." ([Malia], you
  have a great smile.)

  Next, reread the compliment and have individuals practice giving the next part of the compliment.

UNIT 6

Lesson 5

SMART COMPLIMENTS

★········ Lesson Outline ········★

❶ **Practice SMART Compliments**

Get students' attention and acknowledge SMART Compliments during teacher-directed activities.

❷ ***My SMART Book* Unit 6 Coloring Page**

Have students color their SMART Compliments Coloring Pages for their *My SMART Books*.

❸ **SMART Compliments Checkouts and Recognition**

Check out each student's SMART Compliments by listening to them pretend to give Penelope Parrot a compliment. Award SMART Compliments Recognition Cards to individuals as they demonstrate the skill.

 CHAMPS CONTINGENT FEEDBACK

"Contingent feedback has been shown to successfully increase academic and social behaviors . . ."

—*Sprick, 2009, p. 286*

By teaching students to give others compliments (that they really mean), you are teaching them how to give *contingent* feedback. When students give compliments, they reinforce and motivate one another.

EVERYDAY USE

Prompt students at appropriate times during the day to use the SMART Skills they've learned: SMART Greetings, Looking and Listening, Following Directions, Requests, and Compliments.

❶ **Practice SMART Compliments**

Get students' attention and acknowledge SMART Compliments during teacher-directed activities. Say something like:

You've all done a fabulous job learning about SMART Compliments.

You should be so proud of yourselves! Everyone, look at [Riley].

[She] gave [Dejohn] a compliment earlier today.

[She] smiled. Then [she] looked at [Dejohn] and told [him] [she] liked [his] story. [Riley] gave [Dejohn] a compliment that [she] really meant. That made [him] feel very happy. [Her] voice was happy too.

Does [Riley] know how to give a SMART Compliment? (yes)

82

★ ★

UNIT
6

Lesson 5

SMART COMPLIMENTS

Small Celebrations

❷ *My SMART Book* Unit 6 Coloring Page

Have students color their SMART Compliments Coloring Pages. Say something like:

You all know how to give SMART Compliments. You can [treat others like you want to be treated].

You've earned another page for your *My SMART Book!*

❸ SMART Compliments Checkouts and Recognition

Check out each student's SMART Compliments by listening to them pretend to give Penelope Parrot a compliment. Award SMART Compliments Recognition Cards to individuals as they demonstrate the skill. Say something like:

While you are coloring your SMART Coloring Pages, I'm going to listen to each of you give a SMART Compliment to Penelope Parrot. You will earn a SMART Compliments Recognition Card.

[Xiang], it's your turn to give Penelope Parrot a compliment.

What would you like to say to her?

If a student has difficulty or leaves out a step, model and then have the student try again.

That was a great compliment. You said, "I like your painting. It has a lot of colors."

Try it one more time, but this time use a happier voice and Penelope's name. Say, "Penelope, I like your painting. It has a lot of colors!" (Penelope, I like your painting. It has a lot of colors.)

Note: When you model, do not exaggerate. Use a pleasant natural voice.

Celebrate each child's success. Say something like:

You are getting good at giving SMART Compliments in a nice tone of voice. You can be proud of yourself. Compliments make people feel good about themselves.

End-of-Unit Tip

SMART COMPLIMENTS

As you move forward, work on . . .

····················· Generalization ···················

Everyday Use: Model giving compliments by providing frequent positive feedback when your students meet expectations.

Continue to Encourage Efforts by:
- Prompting the use of compliments.
- Providing positive descriptive feedback when you hear students giving compliments.
- Re-teaching periodically.
- Using SMART Recognition Cards to acknowledge student efforts.
- Referring to your Guidelines for Success.

···················· Intervention ····

INCREASING POSITIVE INTERACTIONS

Knowing how to give an honest compliment will help your students learn how to encourage other students and initiate positive interactions with adults—including staff and coworkers.

When a student or students have difficulty giving compliments:

Prompt Correct Practice
- Before an activity, such as art, writing, sharing, etc., have intervention students practice SMART Compliments. Model and guide practice.

  Today, we're going to be drawing self-portraits. You and I get to give the other kids SMART Compliments.
  Will your face be pleasant or not-so-pleasant? (pleasant)
  Who will you look at?
  Will you say something nice or not-so-nice?
  What kind of voice will you use?
  Let's practice some things we might say.
  You could say, "I really like the smile you drew." Try that.
  What else could you say?

- Reinforce SMART Compliments with positive descriptive feedback.

SMART Taking Turns

Student Objectives

Targeted Objectives
I can take turns.

Review Objectives
I give compliments to others.

I say "Please" when I want something and "Thank you" when I get it.

I follow directions right away.

I look and listen when someone is talking.

I greet others with a smile and a "Hello."

UNIT 7 — SMART TAKING TURNS
Overview

······· Teaching Objectives ·······

Students practice and demonstrate competency on all the steps below:

1. Waiting with a pleasant face
2. Watching and listening
3. Keeping hands and feet still

Teaching Materials

School Materials

- Colors
- Five sacks, toothpaste, soap, cell phone, key, sponge, paper, marker, small book, stapler, blunt-end scissors
- Music player and music (of your choice)
- Can or box
- Craft sticks (one per student)
- Six nested boxes
- Wrapping paper—or butcher paper, newspaper, brown paper sack, etc.
- Optional: Edible treat or school supply (one per student)

SMART Materials

- Units 1–7 Posters
- Unit 2 Faces
- Awards: Kid Badges
- *My SMART Book* Unit 7 Coloring Page
- Recognition Cards for Units 1–3 and 5–7
- Unit 7 Reproducibles:
  7-1 and 7-2 *Pass the Sack*
  7-4 SMART/Not-So-SMART Cards

 ············· Teaching Tips ·············

Positive Interactions

Prompt SMART Taking Turns whenever appropriate. This skill helps students build positive interactions and relationships with one another.

Positive Feedback and Reinforcement

Provide positive descriptive feedback to explain why taking turns is important.

[Isabella], you waited patiently for your turn. That helped [Sophia] feel important.

Use SMART Recognition Cards.

Connections

Pair positive feedback with your Guidelines.

·········· Intervention ··········

Before a task that requires turn taking, verbally prompt SMART Taking Turns. Ask questions like:

If you are using SMART Taking Turns, will you be tapping your foot? (no)

If you are using SMART Taking Turns, what will you be doing? (following in my book, watching and listening . . .)

Award Recognition Cards when you catch students taking turns on their own.

SMART TAKING TURNS IS . . . OH, SO IMPORTANT!

Taking turns is a difficult skill. SMART Taking Turns helps students learn how to behave with maturity and social grace. Taking turns is a skill that helps children keep friends and work with others.

Lesson Planner

Lesson	Activities	Materials and Materials Preparation
1 • • •	**When and Where to Use SMART Taking Turns** **Introduce Unit 7 Poster** **Introduce SMART Taking Turns With *Pass the Sack***	• **Unit 7 Poster** • Reproducible: Print the Unit 7 Poster (2 pages) and affix to 11"x 17" poster board. (Or order premade color posters.) • **Five sacks, toothpaste, soap, cell phone, key, sponge** See *Pass the Sack* Special Preparation Note, p. 88. • **Music player and music (of your choice)** • **Unit 7 *Pass the Sack* (Clue Cards 1–5)** Reproducible 7-1: Make one copy of each card.
2 ▲ ▲ ▲	**Practice Unit 7 Poster** **Review Pleasant and Not-So-Pleasant Faces** **Practice SMART Taking Turns With *Pass the Sack***	• **Unit 7 Poster** • **Unit 2 Faces** • **Five sacks, paper, marker, one small book, stapler, blunt-end scissors** See *Pass the Sack* Special Preparation Note, p. 90. • **Music player and music (of your choice)** • **Unit 7 *Pass the Sack* (Clue Cards 6–10)** Reproducible 7-2: Make one copy of each card.
3 ♦ ♦ ♦	**Review What SMART Compliments Look and Sound Like** **Review SMART Posters for Units 1–3 and 5–7**	• **Units 1–7 Posters** • **Can or box** • **Craft sticks (one per student)** Write each student's name on a craft stick.
4 ■ ■ ■	**Practice Unit 7 Poster** **SMART/Not-So-SMART Cards**	• **Unit 7 Poster** • **Unit 7 SMART/Not-So-SMART Cards** Reproducible 7-4: Make one copy of each card.
5 ★ ★ ★	**Practice and Check Out SMART Taking Turns With *Pass the Package*** ***My SMART Book* Unit 7 Coloring Page**	• **Awards: Kid Badges (see Teacher Resources on CD)** Reproducible: Copy one badge per student. Optional Alternative: Provide an edible treat or school supply for each student instead. • **Six Nested Boxes and Wrapping Materials** See *Pass the Package* Special Preparation Note, p. 96. • ***My SMART Book* Unit 7 Coloring Page** • **Colors** • **SMART Taking Turns Recognition Cards** Reproducible: On card stock, make several copies of the cards. Then cut and hole punch each card.

UNIT 7

Lesson 1

SMART TAKING TURNS

● · · · · · · · Lesson Outline · · · · · · · ●

❶ When and Where to Use SMART Taking Turns

Explain and discuss when and where SMART Taking Turns should be used.

❷ Introduce Unit 7 Poster

Introduce Tony Turtle, then read and rehearse the Social Story with gestures.

❸ Introduce SMART Taking Turns With *Pass the Sack*

Introduce the game *Pass the Sack*. Use student modeling of SMART Taking Turns. Reinforce SMART Taking Turns with positive descriptive feedback.

Special Preparation Note · · · · · · · · · · ·

Pass the Sack

Put the following objects in sacks. Fold the tops of the sacks.

- Sack 1: Toothpaste
- Sack 2: Soap
- Sack 3: Cell phone
- Sack 4: Key
- Sack 5: Sponge

Make Clue Cards 1–5 from the reproducible.

❶ When and Where to Use SMART Taking Turns

Explain and discuss when and where SMART Taking Turns should be used.
Say something like:
You know a lot about SMART Taking Turns. You take turns being Student Greeters. You take turns during reading group. When else do you take turns in our classroom? (during sharing, being a messenger, using the computer . . .)

When do you take turns at recess? (on the swings, playing with the ball . . .)

When do you take turns at home? (picking a TV show, playing with mom, using the computer . . .)

Lesson 1

SMART TAKING TURNS

❷ Introduce Unit 7 Poster

Introduce Tony Turtle, then read and rehearse the Social Story with gestures.
Say something like:
Look at our SMART Taking Turns Poster. It says, "Tony Turtle takes turns." What are Tony and his friends doing? (playing four square) That's right. It isn't Tony's turn yet. He is standing in line, waiting patiently. I think Tony Turtle knows how to take turns.

- **Read the Social Story with gestures.**

- **Next, have students repeat each line after you.**

- **Then, read poster using a cloze procedure on the last word or words of each line.**

Sign for "take turns."*	★ ★ ★ ★ ★ ★ ★ ★ ★ SMART ★ ★ ★ ★ ★ ★ ★ ★ ★ ★ **Taking Turns**
Point to your face.	When I'm playing with friends, I can take turns.
	Sometimes, it's my turn first. Sometimes, last. And sometimes, not at all.
Point to your eyes, then your ears.	When it's someone else's turn, I wait with a pleasant face.
	I watch and listen.
	I keep my hands and feet still.
Point to your hands, then your feet.	I wait patiently.
	I can take turns.
Sign for "take turns."*	

Tony Turtle takes turns.

★ ★
UNIT 7   © 2010 The Mailey Company and Marilyn Sprick · Pacific Northwest Publishing

* See "How to Teach the Program" for gestures and ASL.

❸ Introduce SMART Taking Turns With *Pass the Sack*

- **Seat students in a circle. Provide positive descriptive feedback for following directions right away.**

- **Show students the five sacks and the Clue Cards. Tell students you will read a clue and they will guess what's in each sack.**

- **Read the first clue card. Write guesses on the board.**

- **Once three to five guesses have been made, students will pass the sack to music. When the music stops, the student with the sack gets a turn to gently shake the sack and declare what he or she thinks is in the sack.**

- **Repeat three more times. On the last turn, the student with the sack opens it and reveals the object. Students pat themselves on their backs if they guessed correctly.**

- **Throughout the game, prompt SMART Taking Turns—waiting patiently with a pleasant face, by watching and listening, and keeping hands and feet still.**

Repeat until the contents of each sack have been revealed or as time permits.

When it's someone's turn to guess what's in the sack, point out student models of SMART Taking Turns. Use positive descriptive feedback.
[Berto] is using watching and listening while [Malia] shakes the sack. Nice job, [Berto].

Lesson 2

SMART TAKING TURNS

▲ ······· Lesson Outline ······· ▲

❶ Practice Unit 7 Poster

Have students practice the Social Story with gestures.

❷ Review Pleasant and Not-So-Pleasant Faces

Use the Unit 2 Faces. Have students identify and then practice making pleasant and not-so-pleasant faces.

❸ Practice SMART Taking Turns With *Pass the Sack*

Play *Pass the Sack* with Clue Cards 6–10.

Special Preparation Note ···········
Pass the Sack

Put the following objects in sacks. Fold the tops of the sacks.

- Sack 6: Paper
- Sack 7: Marker
- Sack 8: Small book
- Sack 9: Stapler
- Sack 10: Blunt-end scissors

Make Clue Cards 6–10 from the reproducibles.

---

❶ Practice Unit 7 Poster

Have students practice the Social Story with gestures.

★ ·········· SMART ·········· ★
Taking Turns

When I'm playing with friends, I can take turns.

Sometimes, it's my turn first. Sometimes, last. And sometimes, not at all.

When it's someone else's turn, I wait with a pleasant face.

I watch and listen.

I keep my hands and feet still.

I wait patiently.

I can take turns.

Tony Turtle takes turns.

★ ★★★★★★★★★★★★★★★★★★★★ ★
UNIT 7

- Have students repeat each line after you.
- Then read the poster using a cloze procedure on the last word or words of each line.

❷ Review Pleasant and Not-So-Pleasant Faces

Use the Unit 2 Pleasant and Not-So-Pleasant Faces. Have students identify and then practice making pleasant and not-so-pleasant faces.

- Show students the Unit 2 Pleasant and Not-So-Pleasant Faces for Ms. Smart. Say something like:

When you use SMART Taking Turns, you wait for your turn patiently.
That means you have a pleasant face.
You watch and listen, and you keep your hands and feet still.

Let's review what a pleasant face looks like.
Look at Ms. Smart. Does she have a pleasant or a not-so-pleasant face?
(pleasant face)
Show me your pleasant face.

Now look at Ms. Smart.
Does she have a pleasant or a not-so-pleasant face? (not-so-pleasant)

Which face would you like to see if it's your turn? (the pleasant face)

- Repeat with Gregory Gopher and Li Lizard.

❸ Practice Smart Taking Turns With *Pass the Sack*

- Seat students in a circle. Provide positive descriptive feedback for following directions right away.

- Read Clue Card 6. Write guesses on the board.

- Once three to five guesses have been made, have students pass the sack to music. When the music stops, the student with the sack gets a turn to gently shake the sack and declare what he or she thinks is in the sack.

- Repeat three more times. On the last turn, the student with the sack opens it and reveals the object. Have students who guessed correctly put their thumbs up.

- Throughout the game, prompt SMART Taking Turns—waiting patiently with a pleasant face, watching and listening, and keeping hands and feet still.

Repeat until the contents of each sack have been revealed, or as time permits.

When it's someone's turn to guess what's in the sack, point out student models of SMART Taking Turns. Use positive descriptive feedback.
[Jabaar]'s hands and feet are still and [he] is watching and listening politely. I am very proud of all of you. You know how to take turns!

♦ ⋯⋯⋯ Lesson Outline ⋯⋯⋯ ♦

❶ Review What SMART Compliments Look and Sound Like

Have students review what SMART Compliments look and sound like.

❷ Review SMART Posters for Units 1–3 and 5–7

Have students practice the Social Stories. Select a name from a box or can to determine who gets a turn as the "teacher." Have the student select a poster and help you guide practice. Use the poster steps to guide instruction.

Have students practice giving the student helper or "teacher" SMART Compliments.

Special Preparation Note ⋯⋯⋯

- Before reviewing the posters, write each student's name on a craft stick.
- Put the craft sticks in a can.

To determine whose turn it is to lead poster practice, you or a student will pick a name out of the can. Turns will be based on an element of chance, so students can review the concept "I may be first. I may be last, or I may not get a turn at all."

❶ Review What SMART Compliments Look and Sound Like

Have students review what SMART Compliments look and sound like.

- **Give examples of SMART Compliments you've heard from students.**
  I've heard a lot of SMART Compliments. I heard [Caden] tell [Logan] that [he] ran a great race. I heard [Riley] tell . . . Compliments show you respect and encourage each other.

- **Review the steps in a SMART Compliment by following the steps in the Social Story.**

- **Review having a pleasant face.**
  Show me a pleasant face.
  Now show me an angry face.
  Now, show the face you will use when giving a compliment.

- **Review looking at the person.**
  Pretend you are giving me a compliment.
  Show me where you should look.

- **Review giving a compliment with a pleasant voice.**
  Listen to me compliment [Oksana].
  (Use a sarcastic tone of voice.)
  Well, aren't those the coolest shoes ever . . .
  Thumbs up if that was a nice compliment.
  Thumbs down if it wasn't so nice.
  Why did you think it wasn't so nice. (It sounded like you were saying, "Yuck" . . .)
  (Use a pleasant tone of voice.)
  Listen again. [Oksana], those are the coolest shoes. I really like them.
  Thumbs up if that was a nice compliment.
  Thumbs down if it wasn't so nice.

- **Have students review how a SMART Compliment makes them feel.**
  [Oksana], how did my last compliment make you feel? (happy, proud . . .)

❷ **Review SMART Posters for Units 1–3 and 5–7**

Have students practice the Social Stories with a student. Use the poster steps to guide instruction.

- **Tell students you are going to select a name from the can to determine who gets to be the "teacher." Explain that the "teacher" will get to select a poster and help review the Social Story. Review the steps in SMART Taking Turns.**
  Say something like:
  Today, six of you will get to be the teacher while we practice our posters.

Will you pout and say "Not fair" if your name doesn't get picked? (no)
Will you run away? (no)
Will you scream and shout? (no)
Will you talk to your friend? (no)
Nice job. You are Smart Kids. You will wait for a turn by showing us a pleasant . . . face, watching and . . . listening, keeping your hands . . . and feet still.

- **Select a name. Have the selected student choose a poster and hold up it for the class.**

- **Read the poster using a cloze procedure.**

- **Model a compliment. Say something like:**
  [Dejohn], you were a great teacher. You held the poster high so we could all see.

- **Have the student shake the can, then pick a name.**

  Repeat with the remaining posters. Prompt and compliment SMART Taking Turns.
  I'm proud of the way you can take turns.
  Remember, you may be . . . first,
  you may be . . . last,
  or you may not get . . . a turn at all.
  Will you pout if your name doesn't get picked? (no)
  No, you are SMART Kids!
  You can wait patiently for a turn.

UNIT 7

Lesson 4

SMART TAKING TURNS

■ ······· Lesson Outline ······· ■

❶ Practice Unit 7 Poster

Have students practice the Social Story with gestures.

❷ SMART/Not-So-SMART Cards

Using the Unit 7 SMART/Not-So-SMART Cards, have students identify whether characters are being SMART or Not-So-SMART. Then, discuss the reasons for using SMART Taking Turns.

❶ Practice Unit 7 Poster

Have students practice the Social Story with gestures.

- Have students repeat each line after you.
- Then read the poster using a cloze procedure on the last word or words of each line.

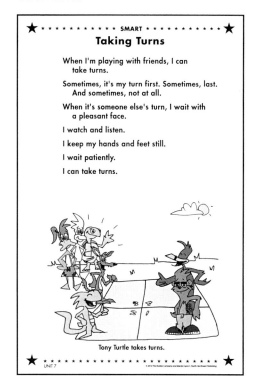

★ · · · · · · · · · · SMART · · · · · · · · · · ★

Taking Turns

When I'm playing with friends, I can take turns.

Sometimes, it's my turn first. Sometimes, last. And sometimes, not at all.

When it's someone else's turn, I wait with a pleasant face.

I watch and listen.

I keep my hands and feet still.

I wait patiently.

I can take turns.

Tony Turtle takes turns.

★ · ★
UNIT 7

❷ SMART/Not-So-SMART Cards

Using the Unit 7 SMART/Not-So-SMART Cards, have students identify whether characters are being SMART or Not-So-SMART. Then, discuss the reasons for using SMART Taking Turns. Say something like:

Mistakes are an opportunity to learn. We're going to decide whether Ms. Smart's kids were being SMART or Not-So-SMART.

Read each SMART Card. (Card text and sample student responses are shown here.)

READ SMART CARD 1

Some of the kids are playing jump rope games at recess. Jada Jackrabbit is in the middle of the line, but she is tired of waiting for her turn. Jada pushes her way to the front of the line.

Was Jada's behavior SMART or Not-So-SMART? What do you think the other kids think about Jada's behavior? (She goofed. She was being babyish. She was being selfish . . .)

Do you think the other kids will want Jada to play with them? (no)

We like Jada! What do you think she needs to do? (remember to take turns, apologize, go to the back of the line . . .)

Why? (The kids won't want to play with her.)

READ SMART CARD 2

During reading group, it's Li Lizard's turn to read. Felicia Frog gets so excited about the story that she begins reading with Li.

Was Felicia's behavior SMART or Not-So-SMART? (Not-So-SMART)

How do you think Li feels about Felicia helping him with his turn? (He probably doesn't like it. He probably thinks Felicia is being rude . . .)

Why is it important to use SMART Taking Turns? (The other kids don't like it when someone takes their turn . . .)

READ SMART CARD 3

During reading group, it's Carlos Cougar's turn to read. All the other kids watch, listen, and follow along. When Carlos finishes reading, Ms. Smart asks the kids questions about the story.

The kids take turns sharing their ideas. Then Ms. Smart says, "I am so proud of you. You are smart and creative! You listened to Carlos read and are making great predictions."

Was Ms. Smart's reading group SMART or Not-So-SMART? (SMART)

READ SMART CARD 3 (Cont.)

How do you think the kids in Carlos's reading group felt? (smart, respectful, grown up . . .)

What did the kids do that made Ms. Smart so proud? (They used SMART Taking Turns. They looked and listened. They were respectful. They were responsible. They did their best.)

READ SMART CARD 4

Ms. Smart's class has just gotten back from a field day. They had fun but they are hot and tired. Penelope Parrot and Tony Turtle rush across the classroom to the drinking fountain, pushing Carlos out of the way. Tony, Penelope, and Carlos end up on the floor.

Were Penelope and Tony being SMART or Not-So-SMART? (Not-So-SMART)

How do you think Carlos feels? (angry, upset . . .)

Tony was supposed to stay over night with Carlos. What do you think will happen next?

Why is SMART Taking Turns important?

READ SMART CARD 5

After Tony and Penelope crashed into Carlos, Tony and Penelope felt bad. They told Carlos they were sorry. They said it wouldn't happen again.

After school, Tony lets Carlos take turns riding his new bike. Carlos and Tony have a great time.

Was Tony being SMART or Not-So-SMART? (SMART)

How do you think Carlos feels? (happy)

Are Tony and Carlos still friends? (yes)
Why? (Tony let Carlos take turns riding his bike. Tony said he would never push Carlos again . . .)

Lesson 5

SMART TAKING TURNS

★ ······ Lesson Outline ······· ★

❶ Practice and Check Out SMART Taking Turns With *Pass the Package*

Introduce *Pass the Package.* While students are playing the game, check out each student's SMART Taking Turns Skills. Award SMART Taking Turns Recognition Cards between rounds of *Pass the Package.*

❷ *My SMART Book* Unit 7 Coloring Page

Have students color their SMART Taking Turns Coloring Pages for their *My SMART Books.*

 CHAMPS
HIGH EXPECTATIONS

"To be an effective teacher, you must have and convey high expectations for all your students in regard to both academic achievement and their ability to behave responsibly."

—Sprick, 2009, p. 40

Taking turns is difficult for young children, but they can do it when taught.

Special Preparation Note ···········
Pass the Package

- Before playing *Pass the Package*, collect six boxes that nest one inside the other.
- In the smallest box, place a surprise. Consider an edible treat for each child, a school supply such as a few sticky notes, or make Kid Badges (see Skill Awards and Notes in Teacher Resources on the CD).
- Wrap the smallest box like a present and place it in the next to smallest box. Continue wrapping each box and placing it in the next one until all the boxes have been wrapped.

Note: You may wish to wrap all but the smallest box in butcher paper, newspaper, a brown paper sack, brown paper, paper towels, etc.

Small Celebrations

❶ Practice and Check Out SMART Taking Turns

- Seat students in a circle. Provide positive descriptive feedback for following directions right away.

- Show students the package. Tell them they are going to play a fun game that's similar to *Pass the Sack.* They will pass the package to music. When the music stops, whoever has the package will get a turn to unwrap one layer of paper (one box).

Tell students there's a surprise inside the last box, but there are several boxes to unwrap.

- Remind students to use SMART Taking Turns—waiting patiently with a pleasant face, watching and listening, and keeping hands and feet still when it isn't their turn. Tell students you will be checking out their ability to take turns while they are playing the game.

- Once the game is in play, check out student's SMART Taking Turns. Award Recognition Cards after each round of the game.

Nice job! While you were played the game and [Emma] unwrapped the first box, I saw [Xiang], [Dakota], [Dimitre], and [Cailey] waiting patiently for a turn. While [Connor] had a turn opening the package, they watched and listened, and kept their hands and feet still.

During the game, keep the suspense going. Say things like:
Nice job unwrapping the blue box. What was inside the blue box? (a red box)
Hmmm . . . I wonder how many boxes there are. I wonder what's in the last box.

Repeat until the last layer of wrapping has been removed. Then celebrate with the surprise!

❷ *My SMART Book* **Unit 7 Coloring Page**

Have students color their SMART Taking Turns Coloring Pages. Say something like:
You can all use SMART Taking Turns.
You can wait patiently with a pleasant face.
You can watch and listen.
You can keep your hands and feet still.
And, you can wait patiently even when your turn is last or you don't get a turn at all. You've earned another page for your *My SMART Book!*

97

End-of-Unit Tip

SMART TAKING TURNS

As you move forward, work on . . .

·············· Generalization ··············

Everyday Use: Students practice taking turns in multiple contexts throughout the school day during sharing, discussions, reading groups, and recess games . . .

Continue to Encourage Efforts by:
- Providing positive descriptive feedback.
- Providing gentle corrections and guided practice as needed.
- Re-teaching periodically.
- Using SMART Recognition Cards to acknowledge student efforts.
- Referring to your Guidelines for Success.

·············· Intervention ··············

When a student or students have difficulty taking turns:

Prompt Correct Practice
- Before taking turns is required, have the class or student help you identify the steps in SMART Taking Turns.
  Everyone, when it isn't your turn, what will your face look like: pleasant or not-so-pleasant?
  Will you watch what's going on or do something else?
  Will your hands and feet be busy or still?

- Catch the intervention student(s) taking turns appropriately. Have these students serve as student models.

- Reinforce the behavior with positive descriptive feedback.
  [Madison], I noticed you standing in the jump rope line—waiting for your turn. You looked like you were having fun counting how many times [Abrianna] jumped rope.

PRACTICE IN MULTIPLE SETTINGS

Knowing how to take turns appropriately is a complex social skill. Intervention students will benefit from positive practice and coaching in multiple contexts.

SMART Review

Student Objectives

Review Objectives

I can take turns.

I give compliments to others.

I say "Please" when I want something and "Thank you" when I get it.

I follow directions right away.

I look and listen when someone is talking.

I greet others with a smile and a "Hello."

★ ★ ★ ★ ★ ★ ★ ★ ★

Let's Review!

Teaching Objectives

1. SMART Greetings
2. SMART Looking and Listening
3. SMART Following Directions
4. SMART Polite Requests
5. SMART Compliments
6. SMART Taking Turns

Teaching Materials

School Materials

- Read Aloud book of your choice (See Lesson 1 for suggested titles.)
- Colors, scissors, glue for each student
- Two craft sticks for each student
- Craft sticks with student names from Unit 7 (or cards with student names) and a can
- Edible treat or school supply (one per student)

SMART Materials

- Units 1–3 and 5–7 Posters
- Recognition Cards for Units 1–3 and 5–7
- Treasure box from Unit 4 (or Reproducible 4-3 Treasure Hunt and a box)
- Awards: Kid Badges
- Unit 8 Reproducibles:
  - 8-2 Treasure Hunt Clue Cards
  - 8-3 Polite Requests Stick Puppets
  - 8-5a SMART/Not-So-SMART Cards
  - 8-5b *Sharing Book 2*

Teaching Tips

Positive Interactions

Student Greeters welcome other students with a SMART Greeting.

Model the use of SMART Compliments when students use SMART Skills.

Positive Feedback and Reinforcement

Provide positive descriptive feedback to the class and individuals.

Use SMART Recognition Cards to intermittently (unpredictably) acknowledge all six SMART Skills—Greetings, Looking and Listening, Following Directions, Compliments, Polite Requests, and Taking Turns as appropriate.

Connections

Reference your Guidelines for Success.

Intervention

Make an overt effort to prompt and practice targeted skills with students who have difficulty using them habitually.

Catch individuals using SMART Skills. Then, use the student as a model.

Reinforce with positive descriptive feedback. Set up positive practice in small groups or individually.

REVIEW IS OH, SO IMPORTANT! REVIEW EVERYDAY.

Your students have learned SMART Skills that are critical to their success at school and at work.

Skills that promote positive interactions with others include: Greetings, Compliments, Polite Requests, and Taking Turns. Skills that promote strong work habits include: Looking and Listening, Following Directions, and Taking Turns. Prompt and reinforce students for using these skills daily, in every classroom activity.

Lesson	Activities	Materials and Materials Preparation
1 ●●●	**SMART Greetings Daily Routine** **Review Unit 2 Poster** **Read Aloud Book of Your Choice**	• **SMART Greetings Recognition Cards** Reproducible: Make additional cards as needed. • **Unit 2 Poster** • **Read Aloud book of your choice** See Lesson 1 for suggested titles.
2 ▲▲▲	**SMART Greetings Daily Routine** **Review Unit 3 Poster** **SMART Treasure Hunt**	• **SMART Greetings Recognition Cards** Reproducible: Make additional cards as needed. • **Unit 3 Poster** • **Treasure box (from Unit 4) and Unit 8 Treasure Hunt Clue Cards** See Special Preparation Note, p. 104. • **Awards (one per student): edible treat, school supply, or Kid Badge (see Teacher Resources)**
3 ◆◆◆	**SMART Greetings Daily Routine** **SMART Polite Requests Stick Puppets** **Review Unit 5 Poster**	• **SMART Greetings Recognition Cards** Reproducible: Make additional cards as needed. • **SMART Polite Requests Stick Puppets** Reproducible 8-3: Copy one SMART Polite Requests Stick Puppets page per student on 8.5 x 11 inch card stock. Make a sample of each puppet. • **Colors, scissors, and glue for each student** • **Two craft sticks for each student** • **Unit 5 Poster**
4 ■■■	**Review SMART Posters 1–3 and 4–7**	• **Craft sticks with student names from Unit 7 and a can** Use the labeled craft sticks from Unit 7 or write each student's name on a card and put them in a can. • **Units 1–3 and 4–7 Posters**
5 ★★★	**SMART/Not-So-SMART Cards** *I'm a SMART Kid Sharing Book 2* **SMART Skills Recheck and Recognition**	• **Unit 8 SMART/Not-So-SMART Cards** Reproducible 8-5a: Make one copy of each card. • ***Sharing Book 2*** Reproducible 8-5b: Copy one book per student on 8.5 x 11 inch paper. • **SMART Recognition Cards** Reproducible: Make additional Greeting, Looking and Listening, Following Directions, Polite Requests, Compliments, and Taking Turns Cards as needed.

Lesson 1

SMART REVIEW

● ······· Lesson Outline ······· ●

❶ SMART Greetings Daily Routine

Have SMART Student Greeters at the door giving morning greetings. Award SMART Greeting Recognition Cards to Student Greeters.

❷ Review Unit 2 Poster

Have students practice the Social Story.

❸ Read Aloud Book of Your Choice

Have students practice SMART Looking and Listening while you read aloud a picture book that has strong visuals and onomatopoeia.

Special Preparation Note ··········
Read Alouds

For this lesson, select a favorite Read Aloud from your library. Choose a book that has lively pictures and noisy words.

Suggestions:

Crocodile Beat
by Gail Jorgensen, illustrated by Patricia Mullins

Down by the river . . . the crocodile sleeps and awaits his prey. Zzzzzzzzzzz . . . while the animals play. On each colorful spread, your students will look at interesting collages and listen to animals sing, swoop, and stomp their feet.

In the Small, Small Pond
by Denise Fleming

This Caldecott Honor book is full of the wiggles and jiggles, shivers and quivers, dabbles and dips found in a small pond.

Suggestions from Unit 2:

THUMP, THUMP, Rat-a-Tat-Tat
by Gene Baer, illustrated by Lois Ehlert

Barnyard Banter
by Denise Fleming

Good-night Owl!
by Pat Hutchins

❶ SMART Greetings Daily Routine

Have SMART Student Greeters at the door giving each student a SMART Greeting as they enter the classroom in the morning.

- Encourage Student Greeters to use a friendly expression, a welcoming voice, and a wave or a high five. Guide practice as needed.
- Award SMART Greeting Recognition Cards to Student Greeters.

❷ Review Unit 2 Poster

Have students practice the Social Story.

- Have students repeat each line after you.
- Then read the poster using a cloze procedure on the last word or words of each line.

★ • • • • • • • • • • SMART • • • • • • • • • • ★
Looking and Listening

Someone is talking to the class.
I sit up.
My face is pleasant.
I look with my eyes.
I listen with my ears.
My mouth is quiet.
My hands and feet are still.
I can look and listen when someone is talking.

Li Lizard looks and listens.

★ • ★
UNIT 2

❸ Read Aloud Book of Your Choice

Read aloud a picture book that has strong visuals and onomatopoeia (e.g., words that make sounds—splitter, splatter, SNAP!)

- **Review SMART Looking and Listening. Use the poster steps as a guide.**
  Remember to use SMART Looking and Listening when I read to you.
  Will you lie down or sit up? (sit up)
  Will your face be pleasant or not-so-pleasant? (pleasant)
  Will you look at the book and listen with your ears? (yes)
  Will you talk to your neighbor? (no)
  You can do SMART Looking and Listening!

- **Introduce the book. Say something like:**
  Listen to the title and then say it with me.

  Crocodile Beat Crocodile Beat

  This book is about a crocodile waiting to eat. The first page says "Down by the river . . ." What sound did you hear the crocodile make? (Zzzzzzzzzzz Zzzzzzzzzzz Zzzzzzzzzzz . . .)
  That means the crocodile is . . . asleep.
  What do you see? (a big crocodile sleeping in the sun, floating in the water)
  Tell me about his teeth. (They are sharp . . .)
  Tell me about his skin. (It's green. It's . . .)
  Nice job, looking and listening!

- **Throughout the book, ask questions that prompt SMART Looking and Listening.**

- **Model SMART Compliments with positive descriptive feedback.**

Lesson 2

SMART REVIEW

▲ ······· Lesson Outline ······· ▲

❶ **SMART Greetings Daily Routine**

Have SMART Student Greeters at the door giving morning greetings. Award SMART Greetings Recognition Cards to Student Greeters.

❷ **Review Unit 3 Poster**

Have students practice the Social Story.

❸ **SMART Treasure Hunt**

Have students use SMART Following Directions, SMART Looking and Listening, and SMART Taking Turns while going on their second Treasure Hunt.

Special Preparation Note ··········
Treasure Hunt: Treasure Box and Clues

Reuse the treasure box from Unit 4 or make a new one using the Unit 4 Treasure Hunt reproducible.

- Fill the box with an edible treat, a school supply, or a Kid Badge.
- Print and cut out the Unit 8 Clue Cards.
- When students are out of the room, hide the treasure box and Clue Cards 2–5 (see below).

Clue Card 1: Keep Card 1 to start the game.

- If you're wearing red, put one hand on your head. If you're wearing red, put your hands in your lap.
- To find Clue 2, think of something that rhymes with "rag" and has 50 stars.

Clue Card 2: Hide Card 2 behind your U.S. Flag.

- You are SMART Kids! Touch your toes. Now touch your nose.
- Clue 3 is taped to the bottom of my shoe.

Clue Card 3: Tape Card 3 to the sole of your shoe.

- You can follow directions. Put your hand up. Put your hand down.
- Now think about something that we use to keep our writing sharp and clear. You'll find Clue 4 near this thing.

Clue Card 4: Hide Card 4 near the pencil sharpener.

- You are SMART Kids. Give me a high five!
- Now, think of something that has the letters of the alphabet on it. You'll find Clue 5 there.

Clue Card 5: Hide Card 5 near the computer.

You are smart! You can look and listen and follow directions right away. Your treasure is waiting for you [under my coat].

❶ SMART Greetings Daily Routine

Have SMART Student Greeters at the door giving each student a SMART Greeting as they enter the classroom in the morning.

- Encourage Student Greeters to use a friendly expression, a welcoming voice, and a wave or a high five. Guide practice as needed.
- Award SMART Greetings Recognition Cards to Student Greeters.

❷ Review Unit 3 Poster

- Have students practice the Social Story.
- Read the poster using a cloze procedure on the last word or words of each line.

★ • • • • • • • • • SMART • • • • • • • • • ★
Following Directions

My teacher gives a direction.
I look at my teacher.
My face is pleasant.
My mouth is quiet.
I might nod or say "OK."
I follow directions right away.
I can follow directions.

Felicia Frog follows directions.

★ • ★
UNIT 3

❸ SMART Treasure Hunt

Have students use SMART Following Directions, Looking and Listening, and Taking Turns.

- **Introduce the Treasure Hunt.**
  We're going to do your second Treasure Hunt. If you use SMART Following Directions, you will find the treasure.
  Read the first line of Clue Card 1.
  "If you're wearing red, put one hand on your head. If you're wearing red, put your hands in your lap."

  Provide positive descriptive feedback.
  That was SMART Following Directions!
  Your mouths were closed.
  Your hands and feet were . . . still.

  Read the second bullet of Clue Card 1. Assist as needed.
  "To find Clue 2, think of something that rhymes with 'rag' and has 50 stars."
  Everybody think—what word rhymes with "rag"? (bag, hag, flag . . .)
  Watch me hold the flag out.
  What does it have on it? (stars)
  Help me count the stars. (one, two . . .)

  Provide positive descriptive feedback.
  [Connor], you looked and listened and followed directions right away.
  Your hands and feet were still.
  You looked and listened and then you followed directions right away. You get a turn to find the next clue. It's behind the flag.

- **Repeat with each Clue Card.**

- **Celebrate finding the treasure. Pass out a treat, school supply, or badge to each student.**

♦ ⋯⋯⋯ Lesson Outline ⋯⋯⋯ ♦

❶ SMART Greetings Daily Routine

Have SMART Student Greeters at the door each morning giving morning greetings. Award SMART Greetings Recognition Cards to Student Greeters.

❷ SMART Polite Requests Stick Puppets

Have students make stick puppets of Penelope Parrot and Li Lizard.

❸ Review Unit 5 Poster

Have students use their stick puppets to act out the SMART Polite Requests Poster steps and practice making SMART Polite Requests.

❶ SMART Greetings Daily Routine

Have SMART Student Greeters at the door each morning giving morning greetings. Award SMART Greetings Recognition Cards to Student Greeters.

❷ SMART Polite Requests Stick Puppets

Have students make stick puppets of Penelope Parrot and Li Lizard.

- Show students samples of completed SMART Polite Requests Stick Puppets.
- Give each student a copy of the SMART Requests Stick Puppet reproducible and two craft sticks.
- Have students color the puppets, cut them out, and glue each puppet to a craft stick.

MANAGEMENT TIP

If time is limited, have puppets already cut out. Students will only need to color and glue them on their sticks.

❸ Review Unit 5 Poster

Have students use their stick puppets to act out the SMART Polite Requests Poster steps and practice making SMART Polite Requests.

- **Tell students what their puppets are going to do. Say something like:**
  We're going to practice the Smart Polite Requests Social Story with your puppets.
  Everyone, hold up Penelope Parrot.
  Now hold up Li Lizard.
  Penelope Parrot is going make a SMART Polite Request. She is going to ask Li Lizard if she can play with his ball.

★ · · · · · · · · · · SMART · · · · · · · · · · ★
Polite Requests

When I want or need something, I can ask.
My body is quiet.
My face is pleasant.
I look at the person.
I use a calm voice and say, "Please . . . "
If I hear "Yes," I can say "Thank you."
If I hear "No," I can say "OK."
I know how to say "Please" and "Thank you," too.

Penelope Parrot makes polite requests.

★ · ★
UNIT 5

- **Read the Social Story to students using a cloze procedure. Have students act out the social story with their puppets.**
  Everyone, hold up Penelope Parrot and Li Lizard. They are going to practice the

poster steps with us. Get your puppets ready to help tell our social story.
When I want or need . . . something,
I can . . . ask.
My body is . . . quiet.
My face is . . . pleasant.
I look at the . . . person.
I use a calm voice and say . . . "Please."

- **Have students act out a SMART Polite Request with the puppets.**
  Everyone, have Penelope look at Li.
  Let's have Penelope ask Li if she can play with his ball. Start with "May I please."
  (May I please play with your ball?)

  Now hold up Li.
  Everyone, have Li say "Yes." (yes)

  Now hold up Penelope . . .
  What will Penelope say? (thank you)
  Have Penelope say "Thank you." (thank you)

- **Repeat with Li asking to borrow a pencil. Have Penelope say, "No, sorry, but you might ask the teacher." Have Li say "OK."**

- **Repeat with Penelope asking Li to play Checkers. Have Penelope say, "I'd like to play Checkers. Li, please . . . "**
  Have Li say, "Yes, that would be fun."
  Have Penelope say, "Great, thank . . . "

107

■ ·········· Lesson Outline ········· ■

❶ Review SMART Posters 1–3 and 4–7

Have students practice the Social Stories. Select a name from a can to determine who gets a turn as the "teacher." Have the "teacher" select a poster and help you guide practice using the poster steps.

Special Preparation Note ··········

- Use the craft sticks with student names from Unit 7 or write each student's name on a card.
- Put the craft sticks or cards in a can.

To determine whose turn it is to lead poster practice, you or a student will pick a name out of the can.

❶ Review SMART Posters for Units 1–3 and 5–7

Have students practice the Social Stories with a "teacher." Use the poster steps to guide instruction.

- Tell students six individuals will get to be the "teacher" today. You will select a name from the can to determine who gets the first turn to lead a social story review.

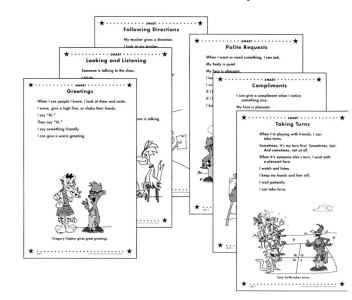

- **Review the poster steps in SMART Taking Turns. Say something like:**

  Today, six of you will get to be the teacher while we practice our posters.

  Show me a not-so-pleasant face.
  Will you use that face if your name isn't picked? (no)

  If it isn't your turn, will you talk to your friend? (no)
  Will you wiggle around? (no)

  Remember, you may be . . . first,
  you may be . . . last,
  or you may not get . . . a turn at all.

- **Select a name from the can.**

- **Have the selected student chose a poster.**

- **Have the teacher hold the poster.**

- **Read the poster using a cloze procedure.**

- **Have the student shake the can and pick another name.**

- **Repeat with each poster.**

Lesson 5

SMART REVIEW

★ ·········· Lesson Outline ········· ★

❶ **SMART/Not-So-SMART Cards**

Using the Unit 8 SMART/Not-So-SMART Cards, have students identify whether a character is being SMART or Not-So-SMART.

❷ ***I'm a SMART Kid Sharing Book 2***

Have students complete an *I'm a SMART Kid Sharing Book 2*.

❸ **SMART Skills Recheck and Recognition**

Recheck each student's SMART Skills. Focus on students who are less socially adept. Award Recognition Cards as appropriate.

CHAMPS
SUSTAINING SMART SKILLS

"Behaviors that are rewarded over time are maintained, while those that are not rewarded are typically extinguished."

—Sprick, 2009, p. 18

SMART Skills are reviewed within the context of the SMART Lessons. In between and moving forward, continue to reward use of these skills with your verbal acknowledgements, Recognition Cards, Home Notes, Kid Badges, and Postcards . . .

❶ **SMART/Not-So-SMART Cards**

SMART CARD 1

Carlos starts doing his math, but he runs into a problem that he can't do. Carlos puts his Help Card up on his desk and does the next problem. Ms. Smart goes to Carlos's desk. Carlos says, "I can't remember how to do this. Please help me."

Thumbs up or thumbs down? Did Carlos remember how to make a SMART Request?

What did Carlos do that was smart?

Using the Unit 8 SMART and Not-So-SMART Cards, have students identify whether a character is being SMART or Not-So-SMART. Say something like:

The kids in Ms. Smart's room usually remember their SMART Skills, but once in awhile someone forgets. Ms. Smart doesn't worry. She knows her kids will learn from their mistakes. Let's decide whether the kids are being SMART or Not-So-SMART.

Read each SMART Card. (Card text shown here.)

READ SMART CARD 1   Polite Requests

Carlos starts doing his math, but he runs into a problem that he can't do. Carlos puts his Help Card up on his desk and does the next problem. Ms. Smart goes to Carlos's desk. Carlos says, "I can't remember how to do this. Please help me."

Thumbs up or thumbs down? Did Carlos remember how to make a SMART Request?

What did Carlos do that was smart?

READ SMART CARD 2   Polite Requests

Penelope runs into a problem with her math, so she begins to mumble and pout. Then she jumps up and says, "I need help." Then Penelope goes to Ms. Smart and tugs on her apron.

Thumbs up or thumbs down? Did Penelope remember how to make a SMART Request?

What should Penelope do?

★ ★
★ ★
★ ★

UNIT

8

Lesson 5

SMART REVIEW

READ SMART CARD 3 — Taking Turns

Gregory Gopher is reading and gets to a hard word. While he's sounding it out, Felicia gets impatient and says the word for him. Ms. Smart says, "Felicia, please wait for your turn."

Next, it's Carlos's turn, but Felicia says, "I'll read."

Thumbs or thumbs down? Is Felicia remembering to use her SMART Skills?

How do you think the boys feel about Felicia?

Do you think they want to be her friend?
What should Felicia do during reading group?

READ SMART CARD 4 — Taking Turns

Felicia and Penelope are playing with a ball. Carlos and Tony want the ball, so they try to grab it from the girls.

Thumbs up or thumbs down? Are the boys remembering to use their SMART Skills?

What should the boys do?

READ SMART CARD 5 — Compliments

The kids are playing soccer. Tony kicks the ball and scores. Gregory pats Tony on the back and says, "Wow! That was a great kick. I'm sure glad you are on my team."

Thumbs up if you think Gregory gave Tony a SMART Compliment.

How do you think the compliment made Tony feel?

Do you think Tony wants Gregory to be his friend? Why or why not?

Small Celebrations

❷ I'm a SMART Kid Sharing Book 2

Have students complete an *I'm a SMART Kid Sharing Book 2*.

- Guide students through the book.
- Demonstrate how to trace the "I" statements.
- Have students complete their books by coloring each picture. Have students use at least three colors.
- Have students take their books home to share with their families.

I'M A SMART KID
SHARING BOOK 2

by _____
Dedicated to my family

Directions: Print/copy one per student and fold.   1

❸ SMART Skills Recheck and Recognition

Recheck each student's SMART Skills. Focus on students who are less socially adept. Award Recognition Cards as appropriate.

End-of-Unit Tip

SMART REVIEW

As you move forward, work on . . .

· · · · · · · · · · · · · · Generalization · · · · · · · · · · · · · ·

Everyday Use: Have students practice the six SMART Skills they've learned so far—Greetings, Looking and Listening, Following Directions, Polite Requests, Compliments, and Taking Turns. These skills are important to school success and should be part of your daily routine.

Continue to Encourage Efforts by:
- Providing positive descriptive feedback.
- Providing prompts (verbal reminders).
- Providing gentle corrections and guided practice as needed.
- Re-teaching periodically.
- Using SMART Recognition Cards to acknowledge student efforts.
- Referring to your Guidelines for Success.

· · · · · · · · · · · · · · Intervention · · · · · · · · · · · · · ·

When a student or students have difficulty with any of the six skills learned to date:
> Target one or two skills—Greetings, Looking and Listening, Following Directions, or Taking Turns.

Scaffold Practice
For the targeted social skill, identify the easiest step for the student. Practice and reinforce this step. Then add another step. Practice and reinforce both steps. Then add another step and practice in multiple contexts.

CATCH INTERVENTION KIDS USING SMART SKILLS!

Don't give up! Many adults haven't mastered SMART Skills. Use Student Trackers and Recognition Cards when you catch intervention kids using any of the SMART Skills you've taught. Gradually, teach and shape the skill. Celebrate each small step towards routine use.

SMART Including Others

Student Objectives

Targeted Objectives
I can include others and make new friends.

Review Objectives
I can take turns.

I give compliments to others.

I say "Please" when I want something and "Thank you" when I get it.

I follow directions right away.

I look and listen when someone is talking.

I greet others with a smile and a "Hello."

SMART INCLUDING OTHERS
Overview

····· Teaching Objectives ·······

Students practice and demonstrate competency on all the steps below:

1. Smiling at others
2. Saying things like "Hi! What's happening?" or "Hi! What do you like to play?"
3. Inviting others to play

Teaching Materials

School Materials
- Puppet of your choice
- Colors

SMART Materials
- Units 7 and 9 Posters
- Optional: Unit 7 craft sticks with student names (or cards with student names) and a can
- *My SMART Book* Unit 9 Coloring Page
- Recognition Cards for Including Others and previous units

SMART FRIENDSHIP SKILLS ARE . . . OH, SO IMPORTANT!

When students can initiate friendships by starting a conversation and inviting others to play, they are more likely to be accepted into social situations and to develop peer groups. Research indicates that a sense of group belonging is strongly related to mental health.

Teaching Tips ··············

Positive Feedback and Reinforcement

Provide positive descriptive feedback.
That was a nice way to invite someone to play. You smiled and greeted your friend. You know how to include others.

Use SMART Recognition Cards to acknowledge student efforts at initiating friendships.

Connections

Reference your Guidelines for Success. For example, treat others with care and concern. Encourage others.
This afternoon, I saw [Madison] and [Logan] inviting others to play in their four square game. They were including others.

·········· Intervention ··········

Prompt socially adept students to enlarge their circle of friends and invite others to play.

With less socially adept students, continue to work on Greetings, Compliments, Polite Requests (and thank yous), Looking and Listening, and Taking Turns.

Gradually work on initiating conversations and inviting others to play.

Lesson	Activities	Materials and Materials Preparation
1 •••	**Introduce a Friendship Circle** **Introduce the Song "Make New Friends but Keep the Old"** **Introduce Unit 9 Poster**	**Unit 9 Poster** Reproducible: Print the Unit 9 Poster (2 pages) and affix to 11" x 17" poster board. (Or order premade color posters.)
2 ▲▲▲	**Practice Positive Statements in a Friendship Circle** **Practice the Song "Make New Friends but Keep the Old"** **Practice Unit 9 Poster** **SMART Including Others Description, Modeling, and Practice**	**Unit 9 Poster**
3 ◆◆◆	**Review Unit 7 Poster** **Review SMART/Not-So-SMART Taking Turns With a Puppet** **Practice SMART Including Others** **SMART/Not-So-SMART Puppet Play**	• **Unit 7 Poster** • **A puppet** • **Unit 9 Poster**
4 ■■■	**Practice Positive Statements in a Friendship Circle** **Practice Unit 9 Poster** **Reasons for Using SMART Including Others** **Practice SMART Including Others in a Friendship Circle**	**Unit 9 Poster**
5 ★★★	**Sing "Make New Friends" in a Friendship Circle** **Practice SMART Including Others With Partners** *My SMART Book* **Unit 9 Coloring Page** **SMART Including Others Checkouts and Recognition**	• **Unit 9 Poster** • **Optional: Unit 7 craft sticks with student name and a can** • *My SMART Book* **Unit 9 Coloring Page** • **Colors** • **SMART Including Others Recognition Cards** Reproducible: On card stock, make several copies of the cards. Then cut and hole punch each card.

UNIT 9

Lesson 1

SMART INCLUDING OTHERS

○ ⋯⋯⋯ Lesson Outline ⋯⋯⋯ ○

❶ Introduce a Friendship Circle

Have students sit in a circle to form a friendship circle. Have students practice positive statements about their SMART Skills and interactions with others.

❷ Introduce the Song "Make New Friends but Keep the Old"

Teach students the classic song and discuss what it means.

❸ Introduce Unit 9 Poster

Introduce Izzy Iguana, then read and rehearse the Social Story with gestures.

Note: "Make New Friends but Keep the Old" is an old favorite—often sung around the campfire and at scout meetings. If you are unfamiliar with the song, search the Internet for a recording. This song is often sung as a round, but for young students, you may wish to just teach the first verse.

❶ Introduce a Friendship Circle

Start the day with a friendship circle. Have students practice positive statements about their SMART Skills and interactions with others.

- **Have students sit in a circle.**

- **Have students repeat positive statements about themselves and their social skills.**
  I'm very proud of this class.
  You greet one another. What do you do?
  (We greet one another.)
  You look at each other and listen.
  What do you do? (We look at each other and listen.)

  Repeat with making polite requests, complimenting each other, and taking turns.

- **Have students repeat positive statements about how they are following their Guidelines for Success.**
  Say, "We can be respectful."
  (We can be respectful.)
  Say, "We can encourage each other."
  (We can encourage each other.)

- **Help students make connections between your Guidelines for Success and doing what friends do. Say something like:**
  Friends treat each other with respect.
  Friends encourage each other.

Nod your head if you are a good friend to others in our class.

Yes, people in my class are good to each other. So, this is a friendship circle.

❷ Introduce the Song "Make New Friends but Keep the Old"

- **Tell students they are going to learn a song—an old favorite that people have sung for many years about new friends and old friends.**

- **Have students listen to you sing the song.** Listen to the song. "Make new friends but keep the old. One is silver and the other gold."

- **Repeat the first line. Then have students sing with you.** Listen to the first line. "Make new friends but keep the old." Now sing it with me . . .

- **Repeat the second line. Then have students sing with you.**

- **Repeat the whole song and have students sing along.**

- **Discuss what the song means. Say:** The song says that new friends are silver and old friends are gold. What do you think that means? (Friends are like a treasure . . . They are worth a lot . . .) Yes, the song tells us that new friends and old friends are very important.

❸ Introduce Unit 9 Poster

Introduce Izzy Iguana, then read and rehearse the Social Story with gestures. Say something like:

* See "How to Teach the Program" for gestures and ASL.

Our new poster talks about how to include others and make new friends. Izzy Iguana is inviting others to play. It's a great way to include others and make new friends. Our poster says, "Izzy Iguana includes others. Izzy Iguana makes new friends."

- **Read the Social Story to students.**

- **Next, have students repeat each line after you.**

- **Then, read poster using a cloze procedure.** I can include others and make new . . . friends.

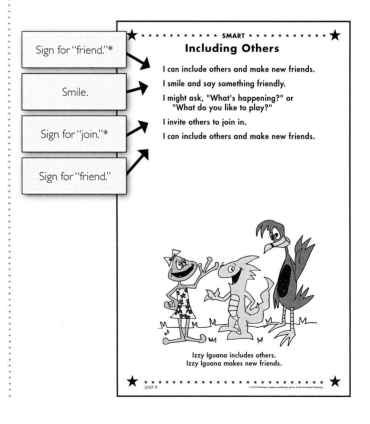

Sign for "friend."*

Smile.

Sign for "join."*

Sign for "friend."

★ ★ ★ ★ ★ ★ ★ ★ SMART ★ ★ ★ ★ ★ ★ ★ ★
Including Others

I can include others and make new friends.

I smile and say something friendly.

I might ask, "What's happening?" or "What do you like to play?"

I invite others to join in.

I can include others and make new friends.

Izzy Iguana includes others.
Izzy Iguana makes new friends.

UNIT 9

117

Lesson 2

SMART INCLUDING OTHERS

▲ ······· Lesson Outline ······· ▲

❶ Practice Positive Statements in a Friendship Circle

Have students gather in a friendship circle and practice positive statements about their interactions with others.

❷ Practice the Song "Make New Friends but Keep the Old"

Have students sing "Make new friends but keep the old. One is silver and the other gold."

❸ Practice Unit 9 Poster

Have students practice the Social Story with gestures.

❹ SMART Including Others Description, Modeling, and Practice

Describe, model, and practice SMART Including Others by following the steps on the poster.

❶ Practice Positive Statements in a Friendship Circle

Have students gather in a friendship circle and practice positive statements about their interactions with others.

❷ Practice the Song "Make New Friends but Keep the Old"

Have students sing "Make new friends but keep the old. One is silver and the other gold."

❸ Practice Unit 9 Poster

Have students practice the Social Story with gestures.

- Have students repeat each line after you.
- Then read the poster using a cloze procedure.

★ · · · · · · · · · · SMART · · · · · · · · · · ★
Including Others

I can include others and make new friends.
I smile and say something friendly.
I might ask, "What's happening?" or "What do you like to play?"
I invite others to join in.
I can include others and make new friends.

Izzy Iguana includes others.
Izzy Iguana makes new friends.

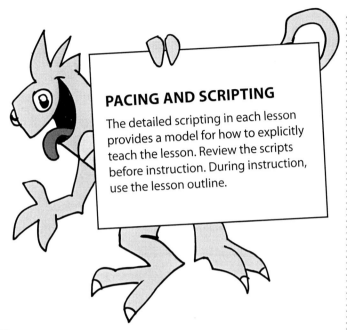

PACING AND SCRIPTING

The detailed scripting in each lesson provides a model for how to explicitly teach the lesson. Review the scripts before instruction. During instruction, use the lesson outline.

❹ SMART Including Others Description, Modeling, and Practice

Describe, model, and practice SMART Including Others by following the steps on the poster.

- **Use the Social Story and Izzy to guide students. Say something like:**

  Izzy can include others. When she sees someone on the playground, what does she do? (She smiles.)

  Show me a smile.

  Excellent. You can smile too.

  Then she says something friendly. What are some friendly things we could say and ask? (Hi! What's happening? What do you like to play? How's it going . . .)

  Izzy invites others to join in. She says things like, "Come on in. Do you want to join us?" What else do you think she might say? (Would you like to play?)

- **Model including a student.**

  Watch me being a SMART Friend. [Dimitre], will you help me? (sure)

  "Hi, [Dimitre]. What's happening?" (not much)

  Would you like to play something? (sure)

  What do you want to do? (I don't know.)

  Let's go play on the climbing tower.

  Did I have a pleasant face? (yes)

  Did I use a friendly voice? (yes)

  Do you think I was honest? Did I mean what I said? (yes)

  Yes! I can include others and have a good time.

- **Have partners practice SMART Including Others by following the steps on the poster.**

Lesson 3

SMART INCLUDING OTHERS

◆ · · · · · · · Lesson Outline · · · · · · · ◆

❶ Review Unit 7 Poster

Have students practice the Social Story with gestures.

❷ Review SMART/Not-So-SMART Taking Turns With a Puppet

Have a puppet act out pushing in line. Use the poster steps to help students determine whether the puppet used SMART Taking Turns. Then have students tell the puppet what it should do.

❸ Practice SMART Including Others

Have students review and practice SMART Including Others using the poster steps.

❹ SMART/Not-So-SMART Puppet Play

Use a puppet to demonstrate SMART/Not-So-SMART Including Others. Then use the steps on the poster to help students determine whether the puppet was SMART or Not-So-SMART.

❶ Review Unit 7 Poster

Have students practice the Social Story with gestures.

- Have students repeat each line after you.
- Then read poster using a cloze procedure.

★ · · · · · · · · · · SMART · · · · · · · · · · ★
Taking Turns

When I'm playing with friends, I can take turns.

Sometimes, it's my turn first. Sometimes, last. And sometimes, not at all.

When it's someone else's turn, I wait with a pleasant face.

I watch and listen.

I keep my hands and feet still.

I wait patiently.

I can take turns.

Tony Turtle takes turns.

★ · ★
UNIT 7

- Make a connection for students. Say something like:

When you invite someone to play, it's SMART to take turns. It's fun to play with people who take turns.

❷ Review SMART/Not-So-SMART Taking Turns With a Puppet

Have a puppet act out pushing in line. Use the poster steps to help students determine whether the puppet used SMART Taking Turns. Then have students tell the puppet what it should do.

- Have four students line up with the puppet. Have the other students watch the puppet gently push [his] way to the front of the line and say:
  It's my turn first.

- Next, use the poster to help students determine whether that was a SMART way to take turns. Ask students:
  Did the puppet watch and listen until it was [his] turn? (no)
  Did [he] keep [his] hands and feet to [himself]? (no)
  Did [he] wait patiently and take turns? (no)
  [Xiang], would you want to play with the puppet? (no)

  Let's tell the puppet how to use SMART Taking Turns. What should [he] do?
  ([He] should keep [his] hands and feet to [himself]. [He] should watch and listen . . .)

❸ **Practice SMART Including Others**

Review and Practice SMART Including Others using the poster steps.
- Review the steps for SMART Including Others.
- Have students practice the steps for SMART Including Others.

❹ **SMART/Not-So-SMART Puppet Play**

Use a puppet to demonstrate SMART/Not-So-SMART Including Others. Use the steps on the poster to help students determine whether the puppet was SMART or Not-So-SMART.

- Have the puppet loudly say something like:
  Go away. [Dakota] and I are playing with the blocks.

  Thumbs up or thumbs down. Was that SMART Including Others? (no)

  Let's figure out why that was Not-So-SMART. Did the puppet say "Hi"? (no)
  Did the puppet say or ask something nice like, "What's happening?" (no)
  Did the puppet use a friendly voice and invite [Dejohn] to play? (no)
  Do you think [Dejohn] would like to be friends with the puppet? (no)
  Why not? (The puppet used a loud voice. The puppet wasn't nice. The puppet didn't invite [Dejohn] to play . . .)
  What do we want to do in our classroom— SMART Including Others or Not-So-SMART Including Others? (SMART Including Others)

- **Make connections with your Guidelines for Success.**
  We want to use SMART Including Others because it shows we are kind. It shows we encourage others and respect each other. I will be proud of each of you when I see you using SMART Including Others.

- **As time permits, repeat with other SMART and Not-So-SMART examples.**

■ ········ Lesson Outline ········ ■

❶ Practice Positive Statements in a Friendship Circle

Have students gather in a friendship circle and practice positive statements about their interactions with others.

❷ Practice Unit 9 Poster

Have students practice the Social Story with gestures.

❸ Reasons for Using SMART Including Others

Discuss the reasons for using SMART Including Others.

❹ Practice SMART Including Others in a Friendship Circle

Have students practice inviting students to join the circle.

❶ Practice Positive Statements in a Friendship Circle

Have students gather in a friendship circle and practice positive statements about their interactions with others.

❷ Practice Unit 9 Poster

Have students practice the Social Story with gestures.

- Have students repeat each line after you.
- Then read the poster using a cloze procedure.

★ · · · · · · · · · · SMART · · · · · · · · · · ★
Including Others

I can include others and make new friends.

I smile and say something friendly.

I might ask, "What's happening?" or "What do you like to play?"

I invite others to join in.

I can include others and make new friends.

Izzy Iguana includes others.
Izzy Iguana makes new friends.

★ · ★
UNIT 9

❸ Reasons to Use SMART Including Others

Discuss the reasons for using SMART Including Others. Say something like:

It's important to use SMART Including Others.

People like others who are friendly and kind. When you include others, you will also be included. You will have a nice circle of friends.

❹ Practice SMART Including Others in a Friendship Circle

Have five or six students sit inside the circle. Have students practice inviting them to join the circle.

- **Tell students they are going to practice including others.**

- **Have students count off by five. Have the fifth student sit inside the circle. Repeat until you've gone around the circle.**

- **Have students practice inviting these students to join the friendship circle.**
  Let's include [Sophia] in our friendship circle. Everyone, smile and say, "Hi [Sophia]. What's happening?"
  (Hi [Sophia]. What's happening?)
  Sophia replies: (not much)

  [Cailey], ask [Sophia] to join our circle.
  (Would you like to join our circle?)
  That's great. [Sophia], please sit down in the circle with us. [Ethan], who should we include next?

- **Next, have individual students practice inviting students into the friendship circle.**

Note: If a child misses a step, tell the student what he or she did correctly. Gently guide a correction. For example, if a child forgets to invite the student to join the circle, say something like:

Positive Feedback:
[Caden], you smiled and said "Hi." You remembered to ask something friendly.
Correction:
Now invite [Berto] to join the friendship circle. You can say, "Great, come join us."

PROMPT SMART INCLUDING OTHERS

- Encourage all students to include others.

- Encourage socially adept students to invite others to play with them. For example, before free choice, say something like:
  [Emma], you are a great kid. You have many friends. You can help me today by inviting others to join you. During free choice, invite someone you don't usually play with to do something with you. Who could you invite to do something with you? What might you do together?

- Debrief with the student. Award a Recognition Card. Provide positive descriptive feedback.
  [Emma], I saw you reading with [Malia] today. How did it go? (Good. [Malia] is a great reader.)
  Did you give [her] a SMART Compliment? (Yes, and [she] told me I was a good reader too.)
  That's great. I hope you'll feel like inviting [Malia] to join you again. (We already decided to read together again tomorrow.)
  Wow! That's great. You've both made new friends.

123

Lesson 5

SMART INCLUDING OTHERS

★·········· Lesson Outline ········ ★

❶ **Sing "Make New Friends" in a Friendship Circle**

Sing "Make New Friends but Keep the Old."

❷ **Practice SMART Including Others With Partners**

Have students practice including others by following the steps in the poster.

❸ ***My SMART Book* Unit 9 Coloring Page**

Have students color their SMART Including Others Coloring Pages for their *My SMART Books*.

❹ **SMART Including Others Checkouts and Recognition**

Check out each student by having partners demonstrate inviting each other to play or sit together. Award SMART Including Others Recognition Cards to individuals as they demonstrate the skill.

CHAMPS
VALUING OTHERS

"Like all of us, students need to be noticed and valued. When they feel noticed and valued, they are more likely to be motivated to engage in appropriate behaviors."

—Sprick, 2009, p. 279

By teaching SMART Including Others, you are teaching students how to notice and value others. By teaching this skill, your students become contributors to a warm and invitational classroom environment.

Small Celebrations

❶ **Sing "Make New Friends" in a Friendship Circle**

Have students gather in a friendship circle and sing "Make New Friends but Keep the Old."

❷ **Practice SMART Including Others With Partners**

Have students practice the steps of including others by following the steps in the poster.

• Use the poster to quickly review the steps for including others before starting the activity.

• Have partners practice SMART Including Others. Remind students to smile and say or ask something friendly, then invite their partners to work or play.

- As time permits, call on two students or draw two names from your Unit 7 Names in a Can. Have Student 1 demonstrate how to include Student 2.

- Have students finger clap—index finger to index finger—for students as you provide positive descriptive feedback. **Say something like:**

[Abrianna] smiled and greeted [Oksana] and asked, "How's it going?"

Then [Oksana] said "Great." Next, [Abrianna] said, "Do you want to play checkers?"

Nod your head if you saw SMART Including Others.

Everyone, finger clap for [Abrianna] and [Oksana].

❸ *My SMART Book* Unit 9 Coloring Page

Have students color their SMART Including Others Coloring Pages. Say something like:

You have all shown that you know how to include others. You can invite others to play and make friends. Friends are important.

You have earned the next page for your *My SMART Book!*

SMART Including Others

Izzy Iguana includes others.

UNIT 9 ⓻

❹ SMART Including Others Checkouts and Recognition

Check out each student by having partners demonstrate inviting each other to play or sit together. Award SMART Including Others Recognition Cards to individuals who can demonstrate the skill. Say something like:

While you are coloring your SMART Coloring Page, I'm going to have partners show me SMART Including Others. When you and your partner show me SMART Including Others, you will earn a Recognition Card to add to your ring.

While students are coloring, circulate and have partners show you SMART Including Others. Model and guide as needed. Award SMART Recognition Cards to partners. Say something like:

[Riley], pretend it's time to go to recess. Show me how you would include [Abrianna].

[Connor], pretend it's time to go to lunch. Show me how you would include [Dimitre].

Note: If needed, finish this informal assessment during free time activities or partner activities. Keep track of students who would benefit from more guided practice. Observe students during choice time and recesses.

End-of-Unit Tip

SMART INCLUDING OTHERS

As you move forward, work on . . .

·············· Generalization ···············

Everyday Use: Periodically, have students form a friendship circle. Have students greet the person next to them and give them a compliment and/or invite them to play at recess.

Continue to Encourage Efforts by:

- Prompting socially adept students to include others. Say things like:

  [Xavier], I noticed [Jabaar] standing by [himself] at recess. You can be my special Friendship Builder by inviting [him] to play in the four square game. Can you do that?

- Catching and acknowledging the efforts of students when they make efforts to include others.

  [Connor], I noticed you invited [Logan] to join the soccer game. I saw [Logan] smile. You made [him] feel welcome.

- Re-teaching periodically.
- Using SMART Recognition Cards to acknowledge student efforts.
- Reminding students to use their SMART skills when a new student joins the class.
- Using Read Alouds to reinforce the importance of friends.
- Referring to your Guidelines for Success.

··············· Intervention ················

- Friendship Builder: Give a socially adept student the job of being a Friendship Builder—someone who watches out for others and includes them. Guide practice and provide positive descriptive feedback. Send the student a thank you note.
- Video Lesson: Pair a socially adept student with a less adept student to make a video of including others. Have students rehearse each step of the Social Story by looking at themselves in a mirror. Next, record the students. Play the video, providing positive descriptive feedback for each small step. Then rehearse and film again. Show the video to the class when re-teaching SMART Including Others.

SMART Friends

Student Objectives

Targeted Objectives
I join in, play nicely, and cheer my friends along.

Review Objectives
I can include others and make new friends.

I can take turns.

I give compliments to others.

I say "Please" when I want something and "Thank you" when I get it.

I follow directions right away.

I look and listen when someone is talking.

I greet others with a smile and a "Hello."

SMART FRIENDS
Overview

···· Teaching Objectives ·······

Students practice and demonstrate competency on at least four of the five steps below:

1. Asking to join in
2. Playing nicely with my friends
3. Taking turns and sharing
4. Cheering others along
5. Showing I care

Teaching Materials

School Materials

- Colors
- Puzzle, clay, and/or blocks
- Read Aloud book of your choice (See Lesson 4 for suggested titles.)

SMART Materials

- Units 9 and 10 Posters
- *My SMART Book* Unit 10 Coloring Page
- Recognition Cards for SMART Friends and previous units
- Unit 10 Reproducibles: 10-3 Practice Cards

SMART FRIENDSHIP SKILLS ARE . . . OH, SO IMPORTANT!

"Make new friends but keep the old. One is silver and the other gold." The lyrics of this classic round speak volumes. Research indicates that students who have positive peer relationships are less likely to experience emotional and behavioral problems. Knowing how to make and keep friends is a precious skill.

·········· Teaching Tips ·············

Positive Interactions

Students use the skills of SMART Friends throughout the day—before school and during recess and lunch. These skills should also be used during instruction, at centers, and during independent work. Positive peer interactions can occur anytime, in any setting.

Positive Feedback and Reinforcement

Provide positive descriptive feedback to explain why the steps in SMART Friends are important. Use SMART Recognition Cards to acknowledge student efforts.

Connections

Pair positive feedback with your Guidelines for Success.

·········· Intervention ··········

When a student or students have difficulty with the skills of SMART Friends:

Target Subskills

- Work on one or two steps in SMART Friends. Target subskills that will most help the students develop and maintain friends.

Prompt Correct Practice

- Prompt the student to use SMART Skills. If you are at the art center and [Logan] joins you, what will you do with the clay? (share it) How? (I can give [Logan] half of it.)
- Reinforce the behavior with positive descriptive feedback.

Lesson	Activities	Materials and Materials Preparation
1 ● ● ●	**Introduce SMART Friends in a Friendship Circle** **Introduce Unit 10 Poster** **When and Where to Use SMART Being a Friend**	**Unit 10 Poster** Reproducible: Print the Unit 10 Poster (2 pages) and affix to 11"x 17" poster board. (Or order premade color posters.)
2 ▲▲▲	**Practice Unit 10 Poster** **SMART Friends Description, Modeling, and Practice**	• **Unit 10 Poster** • **Puzzle of your choice**
3 ◆◆◆	**Review Unit 9 Poster** **SMART Practice Cards** **Practice Unit 10 Poster** **Brainstorm What Friends Do**	• **Unit 9 Poster** • **Unit 10 Practice Cards** Reproducible10-3: Make one copy of each card. • **Unit 10 Poster**
4 ■■■	**Practice Unit 10 Poster** **SMART Friends Read Aloud** **Reasons for SMART Friends**	• **Unit 10 Poster** • **Read Aloud book of your choice** See Lesson 4 for suggested titles.
5 ★★★	**Sing "Make New Friends but Keep the Old"** **Brainstorm What Friends Do** *My SMART Book* **Unit 10 Coloring Page** **SMART Friends Checkouts and Recognition**	• *My SMART Book* **Unit 10 Coloring Page** • **Colors** • **Materials for a Small Group activity of your choice (e.g., clay, puzzle, blocks, etc.)** • **SMART Friends Recognition Cards** Reproducible: On card stock, make several copies of the cards. Then cut and hole punch each card.

Lesson 1

SMART FRIENDS

Lesson Outline

❶ Introduce SMART Friends in a Friendship Circle

Have students make positive statements about their SMART Skills. Then make a connection between SMART Skills and SMART Friends.

❷ Introduce Unit 10 Poster

Introduce Jada Jackrabbit, then read and rehearse the Social Story with gestures.

❸ When and Where to Use SMART Being a Friend

Explain and discuss when and where the steps in SMART Friends should be used.

❶ Introduce SMART Friends in a Friendship Circle

Have students gather in their friendship circle.

- **Have students sit in a circle.**

- **Have students repeat positive statements about their social skills.**
  You greet one another. What do you do? (We greet one another.)
  You look at each other and listen. What do you do? (We look at each other and listen.)

  Repeat with making polite requests, complimenting each other, taking turns, and including others.

- **Help students make connections between their social skills and being a friend.**
  I think friends do all of those things!
  Do friends greet one another? (yes)
  Do friends look at each other and listen? (yes)

  Repeat with making polite requests, complimenting each other, taking turns, and including others.
  You already know a lot about being SMART Friends.

❷ Introduce Unit 10 Poster

Introduce Jada Jackrabbit, then read and rehearse the Social Story with gestures. Say something like:

Let's look at our SMART Friends Poster. Jada Jackrabbit is joining a soccer game with her friends. It says, "Jada Jackrabbit joins in and plays nicely. Jada is a good friend." What is Jada Jackrabbit doing? (joining in with others and playing nicely, being a good friend . . .)

- **Read the Social Story to students.**
- **Next, have students repeat each line after you.**
- **Then, read the poster using a cloze procedure on the last word or words of each line.**

Sign for "friend."*

Sign for "join."*

Sign for "take turns."*

Thumbs up.

Sign for "friend."*

★ ★ ★ ★ ★ ★ ★ ★ **SMART** ★ ★ ★ ★ ★ ★ ★ ★ ★
Friends

I can be a good friend.
I ask to join in.
I play nicely with my friends.
I take turns and share.
I cheer my friends along.
I show my friends I care.
I can be a good friend.

**Jada Jackrabbit joins in and plays nicely.
Jada Jackrabbit is a good friend.**

★ ★
UNIT 10   © 2010 The Mulkey Company and Marilyn Sprick • Pacific Northwest Publishing

❸ When and Where to Use SMART Being a Friend

Explain and discuss when and where the steps in SMART Friends should be used. Say something like:

You can use the steps in SMART Friends whenever you would like to be part of an activity. You can use SMART Friends any time you are working or playing with others.

- **Have students help identify where they would use SMART Friends.**
  Would you want to use the steps in SMART Friends on the playground? (yes)
  Where else? (at home, in the classroom, on the bus . . .)

- **Use examples and have students help identify the steps in SMART Friends.**
  Let's think about building a block tower during a rainy day recess.
  Would a friend ask to join in? (yes)

  Would a friend play nicely or get mad and pout? (play nicely)

  Would a friend take all the turns building the tower or take turns? (take turns)

  If the tower fell down accidentally, would a friend get mad or say, "Let's build it again"? (Let's build it again.)

  That's right. Friends have fun and cheer each other along.

* See "How to Teach the Program" for gestures and ASL.

Lesson 2
SMART FRIENDS

▲ ········ Lesson Outline ········ ▲

❶ Practice Unit 10 Poster

Have students practice the Social Story with gestures in their friendship circle.

❷ SMART Friends Description, Modeling, and Practice

Describe and model joining others for puzzle making. Have students practice. Use the poster steps to guide instruction.

❶ Practice Unit 10 Poster

Have students practice the Social Story with gestures.

- Have students sit in their friendship circle.
- Have students repeat each line after you.
- Then read the poster using a cloze procedure.

★ ⋆ ⋆ ⋆ ⋆ ⋆ ⋆ ⋆ ⋆ ⋆ ⋆ SMART ⋆ ⋆ ⋆ ⋆ ⋆ ⋆ ⋆ ⋆ ⋆ ★
Friends

I can be a good friend.
I ask to join in.
I play nicely with my friends.
I take turns and share.
I cheer my friends along.
I show my friends I care.
I can be a good friend.

Jada Jackrabbit joins in and plays nicely.
Jada Jackrabbit is a good friend.

★ ⋆ ★
UNIT 10

❷ SMART Friends Description, Modeling, and Practicing

Describe and model the steps in SMART Friends using the poster steps.

- Have two students sit in the center of your circle working on a puzzle. Describe what a friend looks and sounds like.

  When you use the steps in SMART Friends, you use a friendly face, a calm body, and a nice voice.

- **Model asking to join in.**

  If other kids are playing or doing something interesting, ask if you can join in. Watch me ask if I can join [Isabella] and [Emma].

  That looks like fun. Can I join you? (Sure.) Great, thanks!

- **Have three or four students practice asking to join in. Prompt what to say. Provide positive descriptive feedback and gentle corrections.**

  [Riley], ask us if you can join in. Remember to say something friendly like, "Wow, that puzzle looks hard" or "I like doing puzzles." Then ask if you can join in.

  [Riley]: (I like puzzles. Can I join you?)

  [Isabella] and [Emma]: (Sure.)

  Now [Riley], say "Thanks." (Thanks.)

  That was great. Your face was friendly. Your body was calm, and you used a pleasant voice.

- **Model accepting "No" and leaving the puzzle-making group.**

  Watch me ask if I can join the puzzle group again. This time they are going to say "No." Then they are going to show they care by explaining why.

  That looks like fun. [Isabella], can I join you too? (no)

  [Emma], say, "I'm sorry. There isn't enough room."

  (I'm sorry. There isn't enough room.)

  [Isabella], say, "You can try again tomorrow."

  (You can try again tomorrow.)

What do you think I should do next? (Say "OK.")

Excellent. Should I yell "OK"? (no)

That's right. My voice should be pleasant. Should I pout? (no)

That's right. I can have a pleasant face. Should I clench my fists? (no)

That's right. I can keep my body calm because it really is OK to find something else to do.

We can all be SMART Friends.

- **Review SMART Friends.**

  Smart Friends ask to join in. They play nicely—take turns and share. They cheer their friends along and show they care.

◆ ········ Lesson Outline ········ ◆

❶ Review Unit 9 Poster

Have students practice the Social Story with gestures.

❷ SMART Practice Cards

Using the Unit 10 Practice Cards, have partners practice SMART Including Others.

❸ Practice Unit 10 Poster

Have students practice the Social Story with gestures.

❹ Brainstorm What Friends Do

Using what they've learned from SMART Including Others and SMART Friends, have students generate a list of what friends do. Write responses on the board or a chart for use with a Read Aloud in Lesson 4.

❶ Review Unit 9 Poster

Have students practice the Social Story with gestures.

- Have students repeat each line after you.
- Then read the poster using a cloze procedure.

★ · · · · · · · · · · SMART · · · · · · · · · · ★

Including Others

I can include others and make new friends.

I smile and say something friendly.

I might ask, "What's happening?" or "What do you like to play?"

I invite others to join in.

I can include others and make new friends.

Izzy Iguana includes others.
Izzy Iguana makes new friends.

★ · ★
UNIT 9

❷ SMART Practice Cards

Using the Unit 10 Practice Cards, have partners practice SMART Including Others.

- Read Practice Card 1. Then have partners practice including others.

READ PRACTICE CARD 1

Partner 1. Pretend you are a new student. It's recess, and you don't know what to do.

Partner 2. Make your partner feel welcome. Show your partner what you will do and say.

Lesson 3
SMART FRIENDS

- **Discuss what Partner 2 did to make Partner 1 feel included. Say something like:**
  [Dejohn], how did your partner make you feel? (welcome, happy, included . . .) Excellent, what did your partner do to make you feel included? (smiled, asked if I liked my new school, asked me if I wanted to play)

- **Repeat with Practice Cards 2–5.**

READ PRACTICE CARD 2

Partner 1. It's choice time, and you notice that your partner hasn't found anything to do. Your partner has tried a couple of activities, but the centers are full.

Partner 1. Make your partner feel included. Show your partner what you will do and say.

READ PRACTICE CARD 3

Partner 2. It's time for recess. Your partner has been sick and has just gotten back to school.

Partner 2. Make your partner feel happy to be back at school. Show your partner what you will do and say.

READ PRACTICE CARD 4

Pretend Partner 2 is having a bad day. Things aren't going well. It's time for lunch.

Partner 1. Make your partner feel included and better about the day. Show your partner what you will do and say.

READ PRACTICE CARD 5

Partner 2. Pretend you are a Student Greeter. You've noticed that your partner eats lunch alone and has been spending recess wandering around the playground. Give your partner a morning greeting and say something that will help your partner feel included.

---

❸ Review Unit 10 Poster
Have students practice the Social Story with gestures.

★ · · · · · · · · · SMART · · · · · · · · · ★
Friends

I can be a good friend.
I ask to join in.
I play nicely with my friends.
I take turns and share.
I cheer my friends along.
I show my friends I care.
I can be a good friend.

Jada Jackrabbit joins in and plays nicely.
Jada Jackrabbit is a good friend.

UNIT 10

❹ Brainstorm What Friends Do
Using what they've learned from SMART Including Others and SMART Friends, have students generate a list of what friends do. Write responses on the board. (Save this list as it can be used in Lesson 4 with a Read Aloud.)

- **On the board or a chart, write "We know how to be good friends. We can . . ."**
- **Have students brainstorm what they can do to be good friends. Say something like:**
  You know a lot about making and keeping friends. Let's make a list of all the things we can do to be good friends. Let's see. You know how to give a warm greeting, so I'll write that on the board. What else can you do to be a good friend?

135

Lesson Outline

❶ Practice Unit 10 Poster

Have students practice the Social Story with gestures.

❷ SMART Friends Read Aloud

For this lesson, select a favorite Read Aloud from your library. Choose a book that describes what good friends do. After reading, compare students' list of what friends do with what they learned in the book.

❸ Reasons for SMART Friends

Discuss the reasons for using the steps in SMART Friends.

Special Preparation Note
Read Alouds

For this lesson, select a favorite Read Aloud from your library. Choose a book that describes what good friends do.

Suggestions:

Friends
by Helme Heine

Charlie Rooster, Johnny Mouse, and Percy Pig are best of friends. They spend from dawn to dusk riding through the countryside, discovering new things, sharing, and deciding things together. When Charlie complains that Percy Pig has gotten too many cherries, they work it out—because that's what best friends do. Best friends stick together.

Henry and Mudge
by Cynthia Ryland

Mudge is Henry's best friend. Like friends do, Henry and Mudge walk to school together. They wait for each other. They eat together. The friends keep each other from worrying, and they worry about each other. Like all good friends, Henry and Mudge take care of each other.

Pumpkin Soup
by Helen Cooper

Cat, Squirrel, and Duck live together. They make soup and play songs together. They are the best of friends until one day Duck decides he wants Squirrel's job. A terrible squabble ensues. When Duck takes off, Cat and Squirrel learn that friends let each other help. Friends share and take turns.

❶ Practice Unit 10 Poster

Have students practice the Social Story with gestures.

- Have students repeat each line after you.
- Then read the poster using a cloze procedure.

★ • • • • • • • • • SMART • • • • • • • • • ★

Friends

I can be a good friend.
I ask to join in.
I play nicely with my friends.
I take turns and share.
I cheer my friends along.
I show my friends I care.
I can be a good friend.

Jada Jackrabbit joins in and plays nicely.
Jada Jackrabbit is a good friend.

UNIT 10   © 2010 The Mulkey Company and Marilyn Sprick - Pacific Northwest Publishing

❷ SMART Friends Read Aloud

For this lesson, select a favorite Read Aloud from your library. Choose a book that describes what good friends do. After reading the book, compare students' list (from Lesson 3) of what friends do with what they learned in the book.

- Ask questions and discuss lessons learned about friendship as you read.

- Discuss why students wish the main characters were their friends or not.

- Using the list from Lesson 3 of what friends do, compare what the friends in the book did. Students may wish to add to the list.

❸ Reasons for Using SMART Friends

Discuss the reasons for using the steps in SMART Friends. Using the poster, go through each step and discuss why they are important.

- **For joining in, say something like:**
  We learned it's important to ask to join in. Let's think about why. Do you want to play with someone who is pouting and hanging out alone? (probably not)

  That person may want to join in, but doesn't know how. It's important to ask to join in.

- **For playing nicely, say something like:**
  We learned it's important to play nicely. Let's think about why. Is it fun to play with someone who gets angry, fights, and wants his or her own way? (probably not)

  It's important to play nicely. It's more fun.

- Repeat with taking turns and sharing and cheering others along.

- Brainstorm ways to show you care.

- Summarize why the steps in SMART Friends are important.
  When we follow the steps in SMART Friends, we have a lot of people who want to work and play with us. We get along with each other because we treat each other like we want to be treated. Being a SMART Friend means we're being respectful and kind. We are following our Guidelines for Success!

Lesson 5

SMART FRIENDS

★ ······· Lesson Outline ······· ★

❶ Sing "Make New Friends but Keep the Old"

Have students sit in a friendship circle. Sing "Make New Friends but Keep the Old."

❷ Brainstorm What Friends Do

Have partners review what friends do with each other. Then, have the group generate a new list.

❸ *My SMART Book* Unit 10 Coloring Page

Have students color their SMART Friends Coloring Pages for their *My SMART Books.*

❹ SMART Friends Checkouts and Recognition

While other students are coloring, bring groups of five or six students together to do an activity of your choice such as playing with clay, putting together a puzzle, etc.

Check out each student's SMART Friends Skills while students play. Award SMART Friends Recognition Cards as individuals demonstrate the skills.

CHAMPS
ATTITUDES, TRAITS, & BEHAVIORS

"Develop a plan to actively share with your students guidelines that describe basic attitudes, traits, and behaviors that will help students be successful in your classroom and through their lives."

—Sprick, 2009, p. 34

SMART Skills help your students develop attitudes and traits through specific behaviors that will help them be successful in your classroom and throughout their lives.

Small Celebrations

❶ Sing "Make New Friends but Keep the Old"

- Have students sit in a friendship circle. Sing "Make New Friends but Keep the Old."
- Congratulate students on all they've learned. Provide positive descriptive feedback. Say something like:
  You've done a remarkable job learning about SMART Friends. I'm so proud of you all. Everyone, look at [Isabella].
  [Isabella], what do you do if you want to join in? (I say, "That looks like fun. Could I join in?")
  Class, what should [Isabella] say if they say "Yes"? (That's great. Thanks!)
  Class, what should [Isabella] do if they say "No"? (Say "Okay." Find something else to do.)

★ ★
★ ★
★ ★

UNIT

Lesson 5

10

SMART FRIENDS

Repeat with: playing nicely, taking turns and sharing, cheering friends along, and showing we care.

❷ Brainstorm What Friends Do

- Have partners review what friends do with each other.
- Then, have the group generate a new list. Write the list on a chart or the board. (Write the names of partners by each item they share.)

❸ *My SMART Book* Unit 10 Coloring Page

Have students color their SMART Friends Coloring Pages.

❹ SMART Friends Checkouts and Recognition

- While other students are coloring, bring groups of five or six students together to do an activity of your choice such as playing with clay, putting together a puzzle, etc.

- Check out each student's SMART Friends Skills while students play. Award SMART Friends Recognition Cards as individuals demonstrate the skills.

Note: Friendship skills are complex—skills that people learn across years and years of positive interactions. This unit makes overt what socially adept students have already begun to do and encourages those less adept at making friends to begin the process.

End-of-Unit Tip

SMART FRIENDS

As you move forward, work on . . .

·············· Generalization ···············

Everyday Use: Students can use the skills in SMART Friends in any situation that involves playing or working in groups.

Continue to Encourage Efforts by:
- Quietly prompt the skills in SMART Friends.
  Say things like:
  [Berto], when you are partner reading, you can cheer [Caden] along by complimenting [his] reading. What are some things that you could say that you really mean?

- Catching and acknowledging the efforts of students at being a good friend.
  [Ethan], I noticed you shared your crayons during our art activity. You were a good friend.

- Re-teaching periodically.
- Using SMART Recognition Cards to acknowledge student efforts.
- Using literature to reinforce the importance of friends.
- Referring to your Guidelines for Success.

·············· Intervention ···············

- Friendship Groups: Periodically during choice times, at recess, or during indoor recess, create diverse Play Groups. Prompt the skills of SMART Friends. Then reinforce those actions with positive descriptive feedback.
- Video Lesson: Record the Play Group. Play the video back for students, pointing out students as they use the skills of SMART Friends.

ENCOURAGE STUDENTS TO USE SMART FRIENDS SKILLS IN MULTIPLE SETTINGS

It's important for all young children to learn how to be a good friend. The skills in SMART Friends can be used across a lifetime.

SMART Accepting "No"

Student Objectives

Targeted Objectives
I can accept "No" for an answer.

Review Objectives
I join in, play nicely, and cheer my friends along.

I can include others and make new friends.

I can take turns.

I give compliments to others.

I say "Please" when I want something and "Thank you" when I get it.

I follow directions right away.

I look and listen when someone is talking.

I greet others with a smile and a "Hello."

★ ★ ★ ★ ★ ★ ★ ★ ★

······· Teaching Objectives ·······

Students practice Steps 1 through 3 and demonstrate competency by using two of the three steps below:

1. Keeping a quiet body
2. Taking a deep breath
3. Saying "OK" in a calm voice

Teaching Materials

School Materials

- Puppet of your choice
- Colors

SMART Materials

- Units 10 and 11 Posters
- *My SMART Book* Unit 11 Coloring Page
- Recognition Cards for Accepting "No" and previous units
- Unit 11 Reproducibles:
  11-3 Practice Cards
  11-4 No PAWS Symbol

············· Teaching Tips ·············

Positive Interactions

By teaching students SMART Accepting "No," students learn a strategy for keeping their interactions primarily positive.

When you must tell a student "No," be sure to follow with friendly noncontingent interactions.

Positive Feedback and Reinforcement

Provide descriptive feedback. Say things like:

I know hearing "No" wasn't easy, but you listened and kept your body calm. Nice job!

Use SMART Recognition Cards to acknowledge student efforts.

Connections

Reference your Guidelines for Success and other skills such as SMART Friends whenever possible.

·········· Intervention ··········

If a student has difficulty accepting "No," prompt an acceptable response. Say something like:

I know hearing "No" isn't easy. Remember to keep your body calm and quiet. You can take a deep breath and then you need to say "OK."

SMART ACCEPTING "NO" SKILLS ARE . . . OH, SO IMPORTANT!
The ability to gracefully accept "No" is very important in getting along with family, friends, teachers, and eventually supervisors in the workplace.

Lesson Planner

Lesson	Activities	Materials and Materials Preparation
1 •••	**SMART/Not-So-SMART Role Play** **Introduce Unit 11 Poster** **When and Where to Use SMART Accepting "No"**	**Unit 11 Poster** Reproducible: Print the Unit 11 Poster (2 pages) and affix to 11" x 17" poster board. (Or order premade color posters.)
2 ▲▲▲	**Practice Unit 11 Poster** **SMART Accepting "No" Description and Modeling** **SMART/Not-So-SMART Puppet Play**	• **Unit 11 Poster** • **A puppet**
3 ◆◆◆	**Review Unit 10 Poster** **Review What SMART Friends Do** **SMART Practice Cards**	• **Unit 10 Poster** • **Unit 11 Practice Cards** Reproducible 11-3: Make one copy of each card.
4 ■■■	**Practice Unit 11 Poster** **Reasons for Using SMART Accepting "No"** **Introduce No PAWS**	• **Unit 11 Poster** • **No PAWS Symbol** Reproducible 11-4: See Special Preparation Note, p. 151.
5 ★★★	**Practice SMART Accepting "No"** *My SMART Book* **Unit 11 Coloring Page** **SMART Accepting "No" Checkouts and Recognition**	• *My SMART Book* **Unit 11 Coloring Page** • **Colors** • **SMART Accepting "No" Recognition Cards** Reproducible: On card stock, make several copies of the cards. Then cut and hole punch each card.

❶ SMART/Not-So-SMART Role Play

Model and explain SMART and Not–So–SMART Accepting "No." Discuss why accepting "No" is an important skill.

- **Tell students SMART kids know what to do or say when they don't get what they want. Say something like:**
  Whether you are seven or eighty-seven years old, there will be times when you can't do what you want, or can't have what you want.

- **Role play and have students give you a thumbs up or thumbs down.**
  Let's pretend I have to go to a meeting. I'm grumpy so I call the principal and ask to be excused. [She] says, "No, I'm sorry. It's a very important meeting. You must be there." What should I do? Thumbs up or thumbs down. Should I pout, argue, and whine? **[Demonstrate.]**
  Oh, do I have to go? That's stupid. I don't need to be there! Don't make me go!

  Thumbs up or thumbs down. **[Demonstrate with a pleasant face and voice.]**
  Should I say, "OK. No problem. I'll be there"?

- **Discuss why one response is SMART and the other Not-So-SMART.**
  Why is pouting, arguing, and whining Not-So-SMART? (It makes you sound like a baby. It doesn't sound good. It's not grown up.)
  Why is saying "OK" SMART?
  (It's better. You want to keep your job . . .)
  Yes. Think about our Guidelines for Success. What does "OK" show? (being cooperative, getting along with others, being responsible)

❷ Introduce Unit 11 Poster

Introduce Achmed Alligator, then read and rehearse the Social Story with gestures. Say:

Let's look at our SMART Accepting "No" Poster. It says, "Achmed Alligator graciously accepts 'No.'" What is Achmed Alligator doing? (graciously accepting "No")

"Graciously" means that he can accept "No" with a pleasant face and quiet body. "Gracious" means he has good manners.

- **Read the Social Story to students.**
  Remember SMART Looking and Listening. Sometimes, I can't do or have what I want . . .

- **Have students repeat each line after you.**

- **Then read poster with a cloze procedure.**

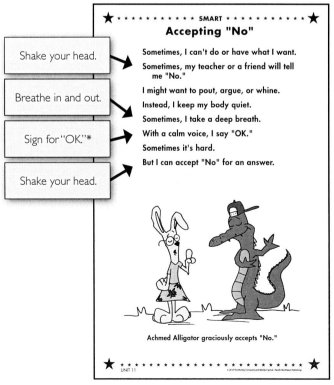

| Shake your head. |
| Breathe in and out. |
| Sign for "OK."* |
| Shake your head. |

★ • • • • • • • • ★ SMART ★ • • • • • • • • ★
Accepting "No"

Sometimes, I can't do or have what I want.
Sometimes, my teacher or a friend will tell me "No."
I might want to pout, argue, or whine.
Instead, I keep my body quiet.
Sometimes, I take a deep breath.
With a calm voice, I say "OK."
Sometimes it's hard.
But I can accept "No" for an answer.

Achmed Alligator graciously accepts "No."

★ ★ • • • • • • • • • • • • • • • • • • ★ ★
UNIT 11

* See "How to Teach the Program" for gestures and ASL.

❸ When and Where to Use SMART Accepting "No"

Explain and discuss when and where SMART Accepting "No" should be used.
Say something like:

You can accept "No" when it's important to cooperate.

If you ask for an extra recess and your teacher says, "No, we have work to do," what should you do? (say "OK")
Yes. You can say "OK" and get to work with a pleasant face and voice.

If you ask to stay up late and your parents say "No," what can you say? (OK)
What will you look and sound like? (pleasant and calm . . .)

If you ask to borrow your friend's bike and your friend says "No," what can you do? (say "OK")
What will you look and sound like? (pleasant and calm . . .)

What are other times you could use SMART Accepting "No"?
(when dad says I can't stay up later, when the bus driver says "No, you can't sit at the back of the bus" . . .)

145

▲········ Lesson Outline ········▲

❶ Practice Unit 11 Poster

Have students practice the Social Story with gestures.

❷ SMART Accepting "No" Description and Modeling

Have students help identify the steps in SMART Accepting "No." Then model accepting "No" using the poster steps.

❸ SMART/Not-So-SMART Puppet Play

Use a puppet to show SMART and Not-So-SMART Accepting "No."

❶ Practice Unit 11 Poster

Have students practice the Social Story with gestures.

- Have students repeat each line after you.
- Then read the poster using a cloze procedure.

★·········· SMART ··········★
Accepting "No"

Sometimes, I can't do or have what I want.
Sometimes, my teacher or a friend will tell me "No."
I might want to pout, argue, or whine.
Instead, I keep my body quiet.
Sometimes, I take a deep breath.
With a calm voice, I say "OK."
Sometimes it's hard.
But I can accept "No" for an answer.

Achmed Alligator graciously accepts "No."

★ ★···★ ★
UNIT 11

❷ SMART Accepting "No" Description and Modeling

Have students help identify the steps in SMART Accepting "No." Then model accepting "No" using the poster steps.

When you accept "No," you use a SMART face, body, and voice. That means you use a pleasant face, voice, and body.

You keep your body . . . quiet.
You might take a deep . . . breath.
Then you use a calm voice and say . . . OK.

146

It's OK to be disappointed.
Do you pout, argue, or whine? (no)
Do you cry and stomp your feet? (no)

❸ **SMART/Not-So-SMART Puppet Play**

Use a puppet to show SMART and Not-So-SMART Accepting "No."

• **Have students watch the puppet use the steps for SMART Accepting "No" after asking to pass out papers.**

The puppet asks: May I please pass out papers?
You say: No. I'm sorry. It's [Dimitre]'s turn.
Have the puppet look at you, take a deep breath, and stay calm.
The puppet says: OK.

Next, ask students:
What did the puppet do? (The puppet asked if he could pass out papers.)
What did the teacher say?
(No, it's [Dimitre]'s turn.)
What did the puppet do? (The puppet looked at you, stayed calm, and said "OK.")
Did the puppet use a pleasant face, body, and voice? (yes)
Did the puppet pout, argue, or whine? (no)
That's right! The puppet was doing a SMART job taking "No" for an answer.

• **Have students watch the puppet use Not-So-SMART Accepting "No" after asking if he can take the ball out to recess.**

The puppet asks: May I please take the ball out to recess?
You say: No. I'm sorry. It's [Madison]'s turn.

Have the puppet put [his] head down, cry, and beat the floor with [his] fists.
The puppet says:
You never let me help!

Next, ask students:
When the teacher said "No," what did the puppet do? (The puppet started to cry. [He] hit the floor. [He] said "You never let me help!")
Did the puppet use a SMART face, body, and voice? (no)

Do you think the teacher thought the puppet was doing a SMART and grown-up job of accepting "No"? (no)
Thumbs up if you think SMART Accepting "No" is a more grown up way to act than pouting, arguing, and whining.

147

Lesson 3

SMART ACCEPTING "NO"

◆ ········ Lesson Outline ········ ◆

❶ Review Unit 10 Poster

Have students practice the Social Story with gestures.

❷ Review What SMART Friends Do

Have partners share and practice what SMART Friends do.

❸ SMART Practice Cards

Using the Unit 11 Practice Cards, have students review and practice the poster steps for SMART Accepting "No."

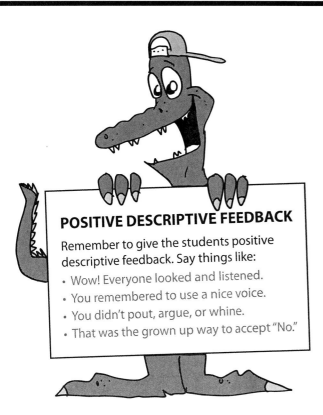

POSITIVE DESCRIPTIVE FEEDBACK

Remember to give the students positive descriptive feedback. Say things like:

• Wow! Everyone looked and listened.
• You remembered to use a nice voice.
• You didn't pout, argue, or whine.
• That was the grown up way to accept "No."

---

❶ Review Unit 10 Poster

Have students practice the Social Story with gestures.

• Have students repeat each line after you.
• Then read the poster using a cloze procedure.

★ ·········· SMART ·········· ★
Friends

I can be a good friend.
I ask to join in.
I play nicely with my friends.
I take turns and share.
I cheer my friends along.
I show my friends I care.
I can be a good friend.

Jada Jackrabbit joins in and plays nicely.
Jada Jackrabbit is a good friend.

★ ····················· ★
UNIT 10

❷ Review What SMART Friends Do

Have partners share and practice what SMART Friends do. Say something like:

Partner 1, tell Partner 2 one thing about SMART Friends.

Repeat with Partner 2.

Have partners share their answers with the group, then practice what SMART Friends do. Say something like:

[Emma], what did your partner say about

SMART Friends? (They ask if they can play.) Yes, that's what SMART Friends do! Everyone, turn to your partner and ask if you can play.

Encourage students to generate many ideas. Practice responses as appropriate. What else do SMART Friends do? (play nicely, take turns, share, cheer each other along— give compliments that they really mean, decide things together, stick together . . .)

❸ SMART Practice Cards

Using the Unit 11 Practice Cards, have students review and practice the poster steps for SMART Accepting "No."

- **Review the steps for SMART Accepting "No." Say something like:**
  Remember, when a teacher or a friend tells you "No," it's OK to be disappointed, but it's important to stay calm.
  You can keep your body . . . quiet.
  You can take a . . . deep breath.
  With a calm voice, you can say . . . OK.

- **Read Practice Card 1. Have a student practice accepting "No."**

> **READ PRACTICE CARD 1**
>
> Pretend you've just asked your Mom if you can have a new bike. Your mom says, "No, maybe for your birthday . . ."
>
> Show us what you will do and say.

- **Discuss whether the student showed SMART or Not-So-SMART Accepting "No." Say something like:**
  Did [Dakota] keep his body quiet, use a calm voice, and say "OK"?

- **Repeat with Practice Cards 2–5.**

> **READ PRACTICE CARD 2**
>
> Pretend that you haven't been Student Greeter for a long time. You've just asked me if you could be Student Greeter. I say, "No, sorry. It isn't your turn yet."
>
> Show us what you will do and say.

> **READ PRACTICE CARD 3**
>
> Pretend you don't want to work because it's your birthday. You ask the teacher if you can play instead. The teacher says, "No, it's important for you to do your work—even on your birthday."
>
> Show us what you will do and say.

> **READ PRACTICE CARD 4**
>
> Pretend you want to stay up late to see a very special TV show. Your parents say, "No. You will be too tired for school tomorrow."
>
> Show us what you will do and say.

> **READ PRACTICE CARD 5**
>
> Pretend you don't like your lunch and want to trade with a friend. Your friend says, "No. I like my lunch just fine."
>
> Show us what you will do and say.

■ ········ Lesson Outline ········ ■

❶ Practice Unit 11 Poster

Have students practice the Social Story with gestures.

❷ Reasons for Using SMART Accepting "No"

Discuss the reasons for using SMART Accepting "No."

❸ Introduce No PAWS

Show students the No PAWS Symbol. Explain that it's a symbol of a great day—a day without pouting, arguing, or whining. Post the symbol at the end of each day that goes by without pouting, arguing, or whining.

❶ Practice Unit 11 Poster

Have students practice the Social Story with gestures.

- Have students repeat each line after you.
- Then read the poster using a cloze procedure.

★ ············ SMART ············ ★
Accepting "No"

Sometimes, I can't do or have what I want.

Sometimes, my teacher or a friend will tell me "No."

I might want to pout, argue, or whine.

Instead, I keep my body quiet.

Sometimes, I take a deep breath.

With a calm voice, I say "OK."

Sometimes it's hard.

But I can accept "No" for an answer.

Achmed Alligator graciously accepts "No."

UNIT 11

❷ Reasons for Using SMART Accepting "No"

Discuss the reasons for using SMART Accepting "No." Have students discuss what happens when people pout, argue, and whine. Say something like:

Achmed Alligator knows how to accept "No" graciously.

Does he pout, argue, or whine? (no)

Let's think about why accepting "No" graciously is important.

- **Discuss what happens when people pout.**

  Everyone, show me what it looks like to pout.

  Thumbs up if you like to be around someone who is pouting.

  Thumbs down if you don't like to be around someone who is pouting.

  I agree with you. It isn't very fun.

  If you always got your way, I wonder what would happen? For example, if you always got to play and never had to work, what would happen? (You wouldn't get smart. You wouldn't learn how to read. You would have to stay in [kindergarten]. You would get spoiled . . .)

  Ah, it sounds like it's better to keep your body . . . quiet.
  Take a deep . . . breath.
  And with a calm voice say . . . OK.

- **Discuss what happens when people argue.**

  Everyone, show me what it looks like to argue.

  Put your hands on your hips and frown.
  Now say, "I don't want to work. It's stupid."

  Thumbs up if you like to be around someone who is arguing.
  Thumbs down if you don't like to be around someone who is arguing.

  If you argue when people say "No" or you don't get your way, what do you think will happen? (People may not want to play with you, or work with you . . .)
  That's right. And we waste a lot of time.

Arguing might keep us from doing what you want to do!

Ah, it sounds like it's better to keep your body . . . quiet.
Take a deep . . . breath.
And with a calm voice say . . . OK.

- **Repeat with whining if appropriate.**

Special Preparation Note · · · · · · · · · ·
No PAWS Symbol

Determine where you can post No PAWS symbols (one per day). You will post this symbol each day students successfully have a No PAWS Day.

- **You may wish to use your calendar to post a No PAWS symbol. If so, copy the small No PAWS symbols (page 1 of the reproducible).**
- **You may wish to post the No PAWS symbol across the bottom of a bulletin board, on a clothes line, or on your door. If so, copy the large No PAWS symbols on page 2.**
- **Show students the No PAWS Symbol.**
- **Explain that a No PAWS Day is a great day—a day without pouting, arguing, or whining.**
- **Post the symbol at the end of No PAWS Day. Periodically, make it a small celebration.**

---

❸ **Introduce No PAWS**

Show students the No PAWS Symbol. Explain that it's a symbol of a great day. Post the symbol at the end of each day that goes by without pouting, arguing, or whining.

Lesson 5

SMART ACCEPTING "NO"

★········ Lesson Outline ········★

❶ Practice SMART Accepting "No"

Have a few students practice SMART Accepting "No" in preparation for their checkouts.

❷ *My SMART Book* Unit 11 Coloring Page

Have students color their SMART Accepting "No" Coloring Pages for their *My SMART Books*.

❸ SMART Accepting "No" Checkouts and Recognition

Check out each student by having the student respond to "No, you can't have free time." Award SMART Accepting "No" Recognition Cards to individuals as they demonstrate the skill.

CHAMPS
TEACH!

"Provide lessons to teach [students] to behave responsibly."

—*Sprick, 2009, p. 22*

Accepting "No" can be difficult, but with SMART Lessons your kids have learned how. SMART Units are consistent with the CHAMPS behavior management principle—teach, teach, and re-teach.

Small Celebrations

❶ Practice SMART Accepting "No"

Have a few students practice SMART Accepting "No." Say something like:

You've all done a great job learning about SMART Accepting "No."
Everyone, look at [Xavier].
[Xavier] doesn't always get to do what [he] wants. Sometimes I tell [him] "No."
Watch what [Xavier] does when I say "No."
[Xavier], sorry. The answer is "No." (OK)
Class, did [Xavier] pout, argue, or whine? (no)
Did [he] keep his body quiet? (yes)
Did [he] use a calm voice and say "OK"? (yes)

❷ *My SMART Book* Unit 11 Coloring Page

Have students color their SMART Accepting "No" Coloring Pages. Say something like:

You all know how to accept "No" for an answer. You can [be responsible] and [treat others with respect].

You've earned another page for your *My SMART Book*.

★ ★
★ ★
★ ★

UNIT
11

Lesson 5

SMART ACCEPTING "NO"

❸ SMART Accepting "No" Checkouts and Recognition

Check out each student by having the student respond to "No, you can't have free time." Award SMART Accepting "No" Recognition Cards to individuals when they demonstrate the skill. Say something like:

While you are coloring your SMART Coloring Page, I'm going to have you show me what to do if I say, "No, I'm sorry. You can't have free time. You need to finish your work first."

If a student has difficulty, model and then have the student try again.

Celebrate each child's success with positive descriptive feedback.

Let me shake your hand. You can accept "No" in a very grown up way. I know you can use SMART Accepting "No" even when you are disappointed.

End-of-Unit Tip

SMART ACCEPTING "NO"

As you move forward, work on . . .

·············· Generalization ··············

Everyday Use: Have students practice SMART Accepting "No" when the situation arises. You may wish to prompt the skill. [Sophia], this would be a great time to use your SMART Accepting "No" Skills.

Encourage Efforts: Catch students using Smart Accepting "No" and encourage their efforts with Recognition Cards.

Guidelines for Success: Provide descriptive feedback, referencing your Guidelines for Success.

Added Practice: Set up little practice sessions to practice SMART Accepting "No" with students who like to negotiate or who tend to pout if they don't get their way. Prompt students by pointing to the SMART Accepting "No" Poster or by saying, "Remember to use the steps in SMART Accepting 'No.'"

PRE-CORRECTIONS

Try to anticipate when a student will have difficulty not getting his or her way. Coach the student through SMART Accepting "No." Then, cheer the student along.

SMART Cooling Down

 Student Objectives

Targeted Objectives
When I'm upset, I can cool down.

Review Objectives
I can accept "No" for an answer.

I join in, play nicely, and cheer my friends along.

I can include others and make new friends.

I can take turns.

I give compliments to others.

I say "Please" when I want something and "Thank you" when I get it.

I follow directions right away.

I look and listen when someone is talking.

I greet others with a smile and a "Hello."

SMART COOLING DOWN
Overview

······· Teaching Objectives ·······

Students practice Steps 1 through 3 to cool down when upset. Students demonstrate competence by using at least two of the three steps:

1. Counting to three
2. Taking a deep breath
3. Thinking a happy thought

Teaching Materials

School Materials

- Puppet of your choice
- Colors

SMART Materials

- Units 11 and 12 Posters
- *My SMART Book* Unit 12 Coloring Page
- Recognition Cards for Cooling Down and previous units
- Unit 12 Reproducibles:
  12-3 Respect and Kindness Scroll

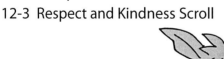

SMART COOLING DOWN IS . . . OH, SO IMPORTANT!

Learning how to cool down helps young children learn two important lessons.

- Everyone feels upset at one time or another, and that's OK.
- Even when you're upset, you can be in control. Learning how to cool down gives students the positive opposite of being out of control.

······· Teaching Tips ·············

Positive Interactions

Periodically gather students into a friendship circle. Have students make positive statements such as:

- **We are all friends and treat each other nicely.**
- **We use cool tools when we get upset.**
- **Cool talk helps me take care of myself.**
- **Mads come and mads go.**
- **I can let my anger go.**

Positive Feedback and Reinforcement

Provide descriptive feedback. Say things like:
That was a nice way to cool down.
You stopped and took deep breaths.
Then you said a happy thought.

Use SMART Recognition Cards to acknowledge student efforts at cooling or calming down.

Connections

Reference your Guidelines for Success.
You can make good choices.
You are responsible for your behavior!
I saw some SMART choices this morning. You know how to cool down when you are upset.

··········· Intervention ···········

Make an overt effort to practice SMART Cooling Down with students who are emotionally volatile.

- **Set up role plays and have student practice.**
- **Anticipate problems. Then, prompt and coach the student before the situation occurs.**

Lesson	Activities	Materials and Materials Preparation
1 •••	**Make Positive Statements in a Friendship Circle** **Introduce SMART Cooling Down, Description and Modeling** **Introduce Unit 12 Poster**	**Unit 12 Poster** Reproducible: Print the Unit 12 Poster (2 pages) and affix to 11"x 17" poster board. (Or order premade color posters.)
2 ▲▲▲	**Practice Unit 12 Poster** **SMART/Not-So-SMART Puppet Play**	• **Unit 12 Poster** • **A puppet**
3 ◆◆◆	**Review Unit 11 Poster in a Friendship Circle** **Practice SMART Cooling Down With Partners** **Recite "Respect and Kindness"**	• **Unit 11 Poster** • **Respect and Kindness Scroll** Reproducible 12-3: Make one copy.
4 ■■■	**Practice Unit 12 Poster** **Reasons for Using SMART Cooling Down** **Brainstorm Happy Thoughts**	**Unit 12 Poster**
5 ★★★	**Practice SMART Cooling Down in a Friendship Circle** *My SMART Book* **Unit 12 Coloring Page** **SMART Cooling Down Checkouts and Recognition**	• *My SMART Book* **Unit 12 Coloring Page** • **Colors** • **SMART Cooling Down Recognition Cards** Reproducible: On card stock, make several copies of the cards. Then cut and hole punch each card.

Lesson 1

SMART COOLING DOWN

> ● ······· Lesson Outline ······· ●
>
> **❶ Make Positive Statements in a Friendship Circle**
> Have students sit in a circle and identify their SMART Skills.
>
> **❷ Introduce SMART Cooling Down, Description and Modeling**
> Discuss reasons for cooling down. Model cooling down.
>
> **❸ Introduce Unit 12 Poster**
> Introduce Carl Coyote, then read and rehearse the Social Story with the poster pictures. Have students role play with the pictures.

❶ Make Positive Statements in a Friendship Circle

Have students gather in a friendship circle.

• Have students sit in a circle.

• Have students identify their SMART Skills.
Let's think about the SMART Skills you know. Think about your Recognition Cards. What makes you a SMART Kid and us a SMART Class?
(We greet one another. We look at each other and listen. We invite others in . . .)

❷ Introduce SMART Cooling Down, Description and Modeling

Describe why people get upset. Then describe and model SMART Cooling Down.

• Explain that it's OK to get upset. Say something like:
You are SMART Kids!
But, even SMART people get upset. Sometimes, I get upset if I'm late.

"CALM DOWN" VS. "COOL DOWN"
The words "calm down" and "cool down" are used interchangeably. Our goal is for students to understand both. We use "cool down" as the primary reference because students who have repeatedly heard "calm down" may be more receptive to this wording.

I can get upset when my plans change. Sometimes, I get mad when someone else is mad. It's OK to get upset—mad or even angry. Is it OK to get upset? (yes)

- **Model cooling down.**
  Show an angry expression.
  When I get upset . . . I can cool down.
  Show relaxed expression and speak in a pleasant voice.
  I use a calm face, body, and voice.
  Sometimes, I count to three. 1, 2, 3.
  I slowly breathe in and out.
  Breathe in and then out.
  Then I think or say a happy thought.
  I might think about your smiling faces or sitting on a beach.

  Remember, it's OK to get upset.
  But it's important to cool down. It's important to be cool and calm.

❸ **Introduce Unit 12 Poster**

Introduce Carl Coyote, then read and rehearse the Social Story using the pictures. Say something like:
I have a new poster that shows how to cool down. Look at the first picture. That's Carl Coyote. How do you think he feels? (mad, upset, unhappy)
Yes, Carl is upset about something, but he says, "When I'm upset, I can calm down."
Let's read the story and find out how he calms down.

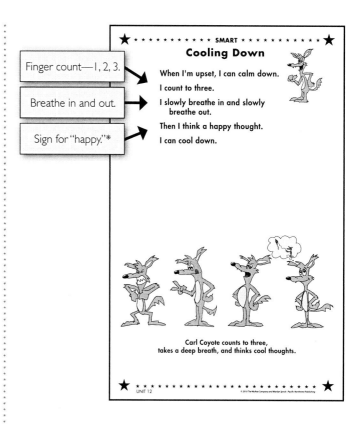

- **Read the Social Story to students pointing to each picture.**

- **Next, have students repeat each line after you, role playing (acting out) each step.**

- **Then, read the poster using a cloze procedure on the last word or words of each line.**
  When I'm upset, I can . . . calm down.

* See "How to Teach the Program" for gestures and ASL.

Lesson 2

SMART COOLING DOWN

▲ ······· Lesson Outline ······· ▲

❶ Practice Unit 12 Poster

Have students practice the Social Story with the poster pictures.

❷ SMART/Not-So-SMART Puppet Play

Use a puppet to show SMART/Not-So-SMART Cooling Down. Use the poster steps to help students determine whether the puppet was SMART or Not-So-SMART.

❶ Practice Unit 12 Poster

Have students practice the Social Story with the poster pictures.

- Have students repeat each line after you. Have students act out each step.
- Then read the poster using a cloze procedure.

★ ········· SMART ········· ★

Cooling Down

When I'm upset, I can calm down.

I count to three.

I slowly breathe in and slowly breathe out.

Then I think a happy thought.

I can cool down.

Carl Coyote counts to three,
takes a deep breath, and thinks cool thoughts.

★ ·········
UNIT 12

PACING AND SCRIPTING

The detailed scripting in each lesson provides a model for how to explicitly teach the lesson. Review the scripts before instruction. During instruction, use the lesson outline.

❷ SMART/Not-So-SMART Puppet Play

Use a puppet to show SMART and Not-So-SMART Cooling Down.

- **Have students watch the puppet use the steps for SMART Cooling Down when [he]'s told to put his toys away and clean up. Have students say:**
  It's time to clean up. Put your toys away.

  Have the puppet count to three.
  1, 2, 3.

  Have the puppet take a deep breath. Have the puppet think out loud about a happy thought.
  I don't want to clean up, but I can think a happy thought. I'm thinking about going to my Grandpa's. I'm cool. I can follow directions and put my toys away. I'm a SMART Kid.

  Next, use the poster to help students evaluate whether that was a SMART way to cool down. Ask students:
  Did the puppet count to three? (yes)
  Did the puppet slowly breathe in and out? (yes)
  What were some of the things the puppet said? (I'm a SMART Kid. I can cool down. I can think a happy thought. I can think about going to my Grandpa's. I can follow directions right away . . .)
  Did the puppet cool down when he was upset? (yes)
  Yes, the puppet was responsible!

- **Have students watch the puppet be Not-So-SMART when asked to put [his] toys away. Have students say:**
  It's time to clean up. Put your toys away.

  Have the puppet yell and pump its hands up and down.
  That's not fair. I'm not done playing!

  Next, use the poster steps to help students evaluate whether that was a SMART way to cool down. Ask students:
  Was the puppet upset? (yes)
  Did the puppet count to three? (no)
  Did the puppet slowly breathe in and out? (no)
  Did the puppet think a happy thought? (no)
  Did the puppet cool down when [he] was upset? (no)
  The puppet wasn't responsible for [his] behavior.

- **Have students practice SMART Cooling Down. (Guide practice—do it with them.) Say something like:**
  Let's pretend I kicked the ball and it accidentally hit you in the face!
  How would you feel? (upset, mad . . .)
  Show me an upset face.
  When you feel that way, what should you do? (count to three)
  Everyone, count to three. (1, 2, 3)
  What's next? (breathe slowly in and out)
  Everyone, take a deep breath.
  Now, think a happy thought. I'm thinking about eating my favorite dinner.
  [Cailey], what are you thinking about?
  Did we cool down? (yes)

Lesson 3

SMART COOLING DOWN

◆ · · · · · · · Lesson Outline · · · · · · · ◆

❶ Review Unit 11 Poster in a Friendship Circle

Have students sit in a circle and practice the Social Story. Make connections between SMART Accepting "No" and SMART Cooling Down.

❷ Practice SMART Cooling Down With Partners

Have partners practice SMART Cooling Down.

❸ Recite "Respect and Kindness"

Have students recite the Respect and Kindness Scroll.

---

❶ Review Unit 11 Poster in a Friendship Circle

Have students sit in a circle and practice the Social Story.

- Have students sit on the floor in a friendship circle.
- Have students repeat each line after you.
- Then read the poster using a cloze procedure.

★ · · · · · · · · · · SMART · · · · · · · · · · ★
Accepting "No"

Sometimes, I can't do or have what I want.

Sometimes, my teacher or a friend will tell me "No."

I might want to pout, argue, or whine.

Instead, I keep my body quiet.

Sometimes, I take a deep breath.

With a calm voice, I say "OK."

Sometimes it's hard.

But I can accept "No" for an answer.

Achmed Alligator graciously accepts "No."

UNIT 11

- **Make connections between SMART Accepting "No" and SMART Cooling Down. Say something like:**

Everyone, do you like to be told "No"? (no)

I think almost everyone feels that way.

I'd rather hear "Yes" than "No"!

Nod your head if you sometimes feel upset, mad, or even angry if someone tells you "No."

When someone says "No" and you feel upset, it's a great time to cool down.

❷ Practice SMART Cooling Down With Partners

Have partners practice SMART Cooling Down.

- **Have Partner 1 pretend Partner 2 took his or her crayon. Say something like:**
  Partner 1, you are going to pretend that you are upset because Partner 2 took your crayon.

- **Have students say what they will do. Guide students through the steps for cooling down.**
  After Partner 2 takes your crayon, what are you going to do? (count to three)
  What's next? (breathe in and breathe out)
  Then think a happy thought!

  Have students share the happy thoughts they used to cool down.
  (I thought about going to the beach. I thought about going on a sleepover. I thought about my birthday . . .)

- **Have partners switch roles. Have Partner 2 pretend he or she was bumped by Partner 1.**

❸ Recite "Respect and Kindness"

Have students recite positive statements using the Respect and Kindness Scroll.
- **Unroll the Respect and Kindness Scroll.**
- **Explain to students that this is a very important document because it tells how they are respectful and kind.**
- **Read one sentence. Then have students repeat.**

Respect and Kindness Scroll

We treat people with respect and kindness.
We use cool tools when we're upset.
Cool talk helps us take care of ourselves.

We can make mads go away!
We can say goodbye to anger.

We use helpful words and happy thoughts—
not hurtful words or fists.
We are proud to be responsible for our behavior!

Our classroom is happy and safe—
because we use our SMART Skills.
We don't lose our cool—we cool down.

Lesson 4

SMART COOLING DOWN

■ ⋯⋯⋯ Lesson Outline ⋯⋯⋯ ■

❶ Practice Unit 12 Poster

Have students practice the Social Story with the poster pictures.

❷ Reasons for Using SMART Cooling Down

Discuss the reasons for using SMART Cooling Down. Reference your Guidelines for Success.

❸ Brainstorm Happy Thoughts

Review and practice the steps in SMART Cooling Down. Use the poster steps to guide instruction. Then brainstorm happy thoughts with partners. Have students share, "I'm happy when . . ." Then have everyone repeat the statement.

---

❶ Practice Unit 12 Poster

Have students practice the Social Story with the poster pictures.

- Have students repeat each line after you.
- Then read the poster using a cloze procedure.

★ ⋯⋯⋯⋯ SMART ⋯⋯⋯⋯ ★
Cooling Down

When I'm upset, I can calm down.
I count to three.
I slowly breathe in and slowly
　breathe out.
Then I think a happy thought.
I can cool down.

Carl Coyote counts to three,
takes a deep breath, and thinks cool thoughts.

UNIT 12

❷ Reasons for Using SMART Cooling Down

Discuss the reasons for using SMART Cooling Down. Reference your Guidelines for Success. Say something like:

It's important to use SMART Cooling Down. When you use SMART Cooling Down, you can take care of yourself.

You are following our guidelines—[treating others with respect] and [being responsible].

It's important to cool down because . . .
People like to be around others who can cool down. Would you rather be around someone who is happy or mad?

❸ Brainstorm Happy Thoughts

Review and practice the steps in SMART Cooling Down. Use the poster steps to guide instruction. Then brainstorm happy thoughts with partners. Have students share, "I'm happy when . . ." Then, have everyone repeat the statement.

- **Review the steps in SMART Cooling Down. Say something like:**
  Is it okay to get upset? (yes)
  When we get upset, we usually have bad feelings that bubble up inside of us.

  We can stop the bad feelings and cool down—just like Carl Coyote.

  What can we do first? (count to three)
  Practice counting to three. (1, 2, 3)
  What can we do next?
  (slowly breathe in and out)
  Everyone, slowly breathe in and breathe out. Then we can think . . . happy thoughts.

- **Brainstorm happy thoughts.**
  Today, we're going to think of lots of happy thoughts. Happy thoughts can help us feel better.

  Model a happy thought.
  I'm happy when . . . someone tells me I'm doing a good job.
  I'm happy when . . . I'm eating with friends.
  Think of a time when you're happy, but

keep it a secret.
Think of something that makes you smile.
Make a sentence in your head that begins with "I'm happy when . . ."

Give students several seconds to think and then share with partners.
When you have a cool, happy thought, touch your head.
Turn to your partner. Say "I'm happy when . . ."

- **Call on several students to share their happy thought or their partner's happy thought. After each response, have everyone repeat the student's happy thought. Provide assistance and correction as needed.**

- **Celebrate each child's success.**

- **Review with individuals as needed. If a student struggles with cooling down, at a neutral time have the student practice "I'm happy when . . ." statements.**
  Good job [Jabaar]. I hope everybody heard [Jabaar]'s happy thought. Let's all repeat it.

PRACTICE SMART COOLING DOWN THROUGHOUT THE DAY

Provide quick prompts for cooling down throughout the day. Practice at neutral times so students can use the steps when they are angry. For example, say things like:
If you're upset, mad, or even angry . . .
- Check your thinking—is it mad or happy?
- Think of a cool tool you can use if you're upset.
- Ask yourself, "Am I taking care of myself?"
- Ask yourself, "Am I being friendly or hurtful?"
- Think of a happy, cool thought.

UNIT 12

Lesson 5

SMART COOLING DOWN

★ · · · · · · · Lesson Outline · · · · · · · ★

❶ Practice SMART Cooling Down in a Friendship Circle

Use the poster to quickly review the steps for cooling down. Practice positive statements related to cool, happy thoughts.

❷ *My SMART Book* Unit 12 Coloring Page

Have students color their SMART Cooling Down Coloring Pages for their *My SMART Books*.

❸ SMART Cooling Down Checkouts and Recognition

Check out each student's SMART Cooling Down Skills by having the student tell you something that is upsetting. Then have the student show you the steps in cooling down. Award SMART Cooling Down Recognition Cards to students as they demonstrate the skill.

CHAMPS
NEW BEHAVIORS

"If the student is capable of the behavior but does not know how to exhibit it, your intervention must involve teaching the student."

—Sprick, 2009, p. 390

Many young children are capable of calming down but don't know how. With SMART Cooling Down, students practice a strategy they can use when upset.

Small Celebrations

❶ Practice SMART Cooling Down in a Friendship Circle

Use the poster to quickly review the steps for cooling down. Practice positive statements related to cool, happy thoughts.

- Have students sit in a friendship circle.
- Have students review the steps for cooling down. Say something like:
  If you get angry and upset, what can you do to cool down?
  First . . . count to three. 1, 2, 3.
  Then, breathe . . . in and breathe out.
  Finally, think . . . a happy thought.

- **Have individuals share a happy thought.**
  Here is a happy thought for me today. I feel happy when I think of a sunny day.

  Close your eyes and think of something happy.
  [Xiang], tell us your happy thought for today.

❷ *My SMART Book* Unit 12 Coloring Page

Have students color their SMART Cooling Down Coloring Pages. Say something like:

You can cool down when you are upset.

It's so important to be in control when you are upset.

That means you have earned the next page for your *My SMART Book!*

❸ SMART Cooling Down Checkouts and Recognition

Check out each student's SMART Cooling Down Skills by having the student tell you something that is upsetting. Then have the student show you the steps in cooling down.

Award SMART Cooling Down Recognition Cards to students as they demonstrate the skill. Say something like:

While you are coloring your SMART Coloring Page, I'm going to have you show me SMART Cooling Down.

When you show me SMART Cooling Down, you will earn a Recognition Card to add to your ring.

- **While students are coloring, circulate and have each student show you SMART Cooling Down.**

- **Have each student tell you something that is upsetting. Have the student show you an unhappy face. Then have the student show you the steps in SMART Cooling Down.**

- **Model and guide as needed. Award SMART Recognition Cards when they demonstrate the skill.**

Note: If needed, finish this informal assessment during free time activities or independent work periods. Keep track of students who would benefit from more guided practice.

End-of-Unit Tip

SMART COOLING DOWN

As you move forward, work on . . .

················ Generalization ················

Everyday Use: Periodically gather in a friendship circle. Have students greet the person next to them and give them a compliment. Then have students practice positive statements that begin with "I'm happy when . . ."

Continue to Encourage Efforts by:
- Praising and providing descriptive feedback when students show efforts to cool down.
- Reminding students that everyone feels upset at one time or another and that's OK. It's what we do when we're upset that's important.
- Providing gentle corrections and guided practice as needed.
- Re-teaching periodically.
- Using SMART Recognition Cards to acknowledge student efforts.

················ Intervention ················

When a student or students have difficulty cooling down:

Add Practice With the Puppet
- Work one-to-one with the student. Pretend the puppet is upset and having trouble cooling down. Have the student teach the puppet how to cool down. Use the poster or prompt each step. For example, hold up three fingers, then take a deep breath, then point to your head and smile.

- Work in small groups to master the steps in cooling down. Have students look at themselves in a mirror using a calm face. Have students hold up three fingers to remind them of the next step. Prompt students to touch their head and smile to remind them to think a happy thought.

Add Reinforcement
Each time you catch the student using a small step toward cooling down, provide the student with one of the following: a cool note, an opportunity to be your special helper for a job, a positive note home.

SMART Review

Student Objectives

Review Objectives

When I'm upset, I can cool down.

I can accept "No" for an answer.

I join in, play nicely, and cheer my friends along.

I can include others and make new friends.

I can take turns.

I give compliments to others.

I say "Please" when I want something and "Thank you" when I get it.

I follow directions right away.

I look and listen when someone is talking.

I greet others with a smile and a "Hello."

★ ★ ★ ★ ★ ★ ★ ★ ★ ★

Let's Review!

SMART REVIEW
Overview

······· Teaching Objectives ·······

1. SMART Greetings
2. SMART Looking and Listening
3. SMART Following Directions
4. SMART Polite Requests
5. SMART Compliments
6. SMART Taking Turns
7. SMART Including Others
8. SMART Friends
9. SMART Accepting "No"
10. SMART Cooling Down

Teaching Materials

School Materials

- Read Aloud book of your choice (See Lesson 1 for suggested titles.)
- Colors, scissors, glue for each student
- Two craft sticks for each student
- Compliments Can (from Unit 6)

SMART Materials

- Units 6 and 9–12 Posters
- Recognition Cards for Units 1–3, 5–7, and 9–12
- Unit 12 Respect and Kindness Scroll
- Unit 13 Reproducibles:
  - 13-2 Compliment Cards
  - 13-3 Accepting "No" Stick Puppets
  - 13-4 Happy Thoughts
  - 13-5a SMART/Not-So-SMART Cards
  - 13-5b *Sharing Book 3*

Teaching Tips ·············

Positive Interactions

- Student Greeters welcome other students.
- Model the use of SMART Compliments when students use SMART Skills.
- Gather students in a friendship circle. Have students make positive statements about including others and using the steps in SMART Friends.

Positive Feedback and Reinforcement

Provide positive descriptive feedback to the class and individuals.

Use SMART Recognition Cards to intermittently (unpredictably) acknowledge all ten SMART Skills.

Connections

Reference your Guidelines for Success.

·········· Intervention ··········

Target skills and set up positive practice in small groups or individually.

Catch individuals using SMART Skills. Then, use the student as a model. Reinforce with positive descriptive feedback.

REVIEW IS OH, SO IMPORTANT!

Keep practicing! SMART Skills are great habits.

Students who interact positively are happy kids. Greetings, compliments, making polite requests, taking turns, including others, using SMART Friends, and cooling down are all skills that help kids be happy kids.

Lesson	Activities	Materials and Materials Preparation
1 •••	**Sing "Make New Friends" in a Friendship Circle** **Review Units 9 and 10 Posters** **Read Aloud Book of Your Choice**	• **Units 9 and 10 Posters** • **Read Aloud book of your choice** See Lesson 1 for suggested titles.
2 ▲▲▲	**Sing "Make New Friends" in a Friendship Circle** **Review Unit 6 Poster** **SMART Can of Compliments**	• **Unit 6 Poster** • **Compliments Can (from Unit 6)** • **Unit 13 Compliments Cards** Reproducible 13-2: See Special Preparation Note, p. 174.
3 ◆◆◆	**SMART Greetings Daily Routine** **SMART Accepting "No" Stick Puppets** **Review Unit 11 Poster**	• **SMART Greetings Recognition Cards** • Reproducible: Make additional cards as needed. • **SMART Accepting "No" Stick Puppets** Reproducible 13-3: Copy one SMART Accepting "No" Stick Puppet page per student on 8.5 x 11 inch card stock. Make a sample of each puppet. • **Colors, scissors, and glue for each student** • **Two craft sticks for each student** • **Unit 11 Poster**
4 ■■■	**Review Unit 12 Poster** **Recite "Respect and Kindness"** **Happy Thoughts Picture**	• **Unit 12 Poster** • **Unit 12 Respect and Kindness Scroll** • **Unit 13 Happy Thoughts Picture** Reproducible 13-4: Copy one per student.
5 ★★★	**SMART/Not-So-SMART Cards** ***I'm a SMART Kid Sharing Book 3*** **SMART Review Checkout**	• **Unit 13 SMART/Not-So-SMART Cards** Reproducible 13-5a: Make one copy of each card. • ***Sharing Book 3*** Reproducible 13-5b: Copy one book per student on 8.5 x 11 inch paper. • **SMART Recognition Cards** Reproducible: Make additional cards from previous units as needed.

Lesson 1

SMART REVIEW

•······· Lesson Outline ·······•

❶ Sing "Make New Friends" in a Friendship Circle

Have students sit in a friendship circle. Sing "Make New Friends but Keep the Old."

❷ Review Units 9 and 10 Posters

With each poster, have students practice the Social Story.

❸ Read Aloud Book of Your Choice

Read aloud a book about friends. While reading, have students discuss how the story relates to SMART Including Others and SMART Friends.

Special Preparation Note ··········
Read Alouds

For this lesson, select a favorite Read Aloud from your library. Choose a book about friendship.

Suggestions:

The Recess Queen
by Alexis O'Neil, illustrated by Laura Huliska-Beith

Meet Mean Jean—the Recess Queen. If kids ever crossed her, she would push 'em, and smooth 'em, and lollapaloosh 'em! No one ever crossed the Recess Queen—until little Katie Sue arrived. And, then . . . things changed. Now Jean is having fun "rompity-romping with her FRIENDS." Read why things changed. (It's about a very important SMART Skill.)

How to Lose All Your Friends
by Nancy Carlson

This is a Not-So-SMART book. Have your students tell these Not-So-SMART kids how to make and keep good friends. They have the SMART Skills to evaluate.

Suggestions from Unit 10:

Friends
by Helme Heine

Henry and Mudge
by Cynthia Rylant

Pumpkin Soup
by Helen Cooper

❶ Sing "Make New Friends" in a Friendship Circle

Have students sit in a friendship circle. Sing "Make New Friends but Keep the Old."

❷ Review Units 9 and 10 Posters

With each poster, have students practice the Social Story.

- Have students repeat each line after you.
- Then read the poster using a cloze procedure on the last word or words of each line.

❸ Read Aloud Book of Your Choice

Read aloud a picture book about friends. While reading, have students discuss how the story relates to SMART Including Others and SMART Friends.

- Ask questions and discuss lessons learned about friendship as you read.
- Discuss why students wish the main characters were friends or not.
- Help your students make connections with SMART Including Others and SMART Friends.

★ • • • • • • • • • SMART • • • • • • • • • ★
Including Others

I can include others and make new friends.
I smile and say something friendly.
I might ask, "What's happening?" or "What do you like to play?"
I invite others to join in.
I can include others and make new friends.

Izzy Iguana includes others.
Izzy Iguana makes new friends.

★ • • • • • • • • SMART • • • • • • • • • ★
Friends

I can be a good friend.
I ask to join in.
I play nicely with my friends.
I take turns and share.
I cheer my friends along.
I show my friends I care.
I can be a good friend.

...bit joins in and plays nicely.
...rabbit is a good friend.

Lesson 2

SMART REVIEW

▲ ········ Lesson Outline ········ ▲

❶ **Sing "Make New Friends" in a Friendship Circle**

Have students sit in a friendship circle and sing "Make New Friends but Keep the Old."

❷ **Review Unit 6 Poster**

Have students practice the Social Story for SMART Compliments.

❸ **SMART Can of Compliments**

Have students review how to give a SMART Compliment. Then, draw (take out) a premade Compliment Card about each student from a can.

Special Preparation Note ··········
Can of Compliments

Reuse the Compliments Can from Unit 6.

• Print the Unit 13 Compliment Cards reproducible so you have one Compliment Card per student.

• Write a compliment for each student and put the cards in the Compliments Can.

Examples of compliments:

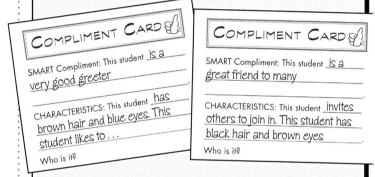

COMPLIMENT CARD

SMART Compliment: This student _is a very good greeter_

CHARACTERISTICS: This student _has brown hair and blue eyes. This student likes to ..._

Who is it?

COMPLIMENT CARD

SMART Compliment: This student _is a great friend to many_

CHARACTERISTICS: This student _invites others to join in. This student has black hair and brown eyes_ .

Who is it?

❶ Sing "Make New Friends" in a Friendship Circle

Have students sit in a friendship circle and sing "Make New Friends but Keep the Old."

❷ Review Unit 6 Poster

Have students practice the Social Story for SMART Compliments.

- Have students repeat each line after you.
- Read the poster using a cloze procedure.

★ • • • • • • • • • • SMART • • • • • • • • • • ★
Compliments

I can give a compliment when I notice something nice.

My face is pleasant.

I look at the person.

I say something nice—something that I really mean with a happy voice.

I can help someone feel happy and important.

I can give a compliment.

Carlos Cougar gives cool compliments.

★ • ★
UNIT 6

❸ SMART Can of Compliments

Have students review how to give a SMART Compliment. Then draw (take out) a premade Compliment Card about each student from a can. Have students guess who the compliment is about.

Note: This activity should be completed across a few days. Read a few cards in the morning, a few after lunch, and a few before students go home.

- **First, have students review the steps for SMART Compliments.**

  Show me what you will look like when you give a compliment.

  Excellent, I see smiles and pleasant faces.

  Where will you look? (at the person)

  Then you'll say something . . . nice.

  You'll say something that you really . . . mean.

  You will use a happy . . . voice.

  You will make your friends happy by cheering them along with compliments.

- **Draw the premade Compliment Cards about each student from a can.**

  Read the compliment clue. Then have students guess who the compliment is about.

◆ ‥‥‥‥ Lesson Outline ‥‥‥‥ ◆

❶ SMART Greetings Daily Routine

Have SMART Student Greeters at the door each morning giving morning greetings. Award SMART Greetings Recognition Cards to Student Greeters.

❷ SMART Accepting "No" Stick Puppets

Have students make stick puppets of Achmed Alligator and Jada Jackrabbit.

❸ Review Unit 11 Poster

Have students use their stick puppets to act out the SMART Accepting "No" Social Story. Then have students practice SMART Accepting "No" with their puppets.

❶ SMART Greetings Daily Routine

Have SMART Student Greeters at the door each morning giving morning greetings. Award SMART Greetings Recognition Cards to Student Greeters.

❷ SMART Accepting "No" Stick Puppets

Have students make stick puppets of Achmed Alligator and Jada Jackrabbit.

- Show students samples of completed SMART Accepting "No" Stick Puppets.

- Give each student a copy of the SMART Accepting "No" reproducible and two craft sticks.

- Have students color the puppets, cut them out, and glue each puppet to a craft stick.

MANAGEMENT TIP

If time is limited, have puppets already cut out. Students will only need to color and glue them on their sticks.

❸ Review Unit 11 Poster

Have students use their stick puppets to act out the SMART Accepting "No" Social Story. Use the poster steps to guide instruction.

- **Tell students what their puppets are going to do. Say something like:**
  We're going to practice the SMART Accepting "No" Social Story with your puppets.
  Everyone, hold up Jada Jackrabbit.
  Now hold up Achmed Alligator.

- **Read the Social Story to students using a cloze procedure. Have students act out the social story with their puppets.**
  Get your puppets ready to help tell our Social Story.

Sometimes, I can't do or have . . . what I want.
Sometimes, my teacher or friend will
tell me . . . no.
I might want to pout . . . argue, or whine.

Instead, I keep my body . . . quiet.
I take a deep . . . breath.
With a calm voice, I say . . . "OK."

- **Have students act out a SMART Polite Request with the puppets.**
  Everyone, have Jada look at Achmed.
  Let's have Jada ask Achmed if she can ride his bike. Start with "May I please."
  (May I please ride your bike?)

  Now hold up Achmed.
  Everyone, have Achmed say, "No, I'm sorry."
  (No, I'm sorry.)

  Now hold up Jada.
  What will Jada say? (OK)

- **Repeat with Achmed asking Jada if he can use her crayons. Have Jada say, "No, sorry. I'm going to use them, but you can use them when I'm done." Have Achmed say "OK."**

- **Repeat with Jada asking Achmed if he would like to come over after school. Have Achmed say, "That sounds like fun, but I can't. Please, ask again another day." Have Jada say "OK."**

Lesson 4

SMART REVIEW

■ .... Lesson Outline .... ■

❶ Review Unit 12 Poster

Have students practice the Social Story for Cooling Down with the poster pictures.

❷ Recite "Respect and Kindness"

Have students recite positive statements using the Respect and Kindness Scroll from Unit 12.

❸ Happy Thoughts Picture

Have students brainstorm and draw pictures of happy thoughts.

❶ Review Unit 12 Poster

Have students practice the Social Story with the poster pictures.

- Have students repeat each line after you.
- Then read the poster using a cloze procedure.

★ ••••••••• SMART ••••••••• ★
Cooling Down

When I'm upset, I can calm down.
I count to three.
I slowly breathe in and slowly breathe out.
Then I think a happy thought.
I can cool down.

Carl Coyote counts to three,
takes a deep breath, and thinks cool thoughts.

❷ Recite "Respect and Kindness"

Have students recite positive statements using the Respect and Kindness Scroll from Unit 12.

- Unroll the Respect and Kindness Scroll.
- Remind students that this is a very important document because it tells how they are SMART Kids—respectful and kind people.
- Read one sentence. Then have students repeat.

Respect and Kindness Scroll

We treat people with respect and kindness.
We use cool tools when we're upset.
Cool talk helps us take care of ourselves.

We can make mads go away!
We can say goodbye to anger.

We use helpful words and happy thoughts—
    not hurtful words or fists.
We are proud to be responsible for our behavior!

Our classroom is happy and safe—
    because we use our SMART Skills.
We don't lose our cool—we cool down.

Special Preparation Note · · · · · · · · · ·
Happy Thoughts

Using a copy of the Unit 13 Reproducible, draw your face, then an example of a happy thought.

❸ **Happy Thoughts Picture**

Have students brainstorm and draw pictures of happy thoughts.

- **Make connections between the Social Story and the Respect and Kindness Scroll. Say something like:**
  The Respect and Kindness Scroll tells us we are respectful and kind to others when we make our mads go away. It says we use helpful words and happy thoughts—not hurtful words and fights. What do we use to cool down? (helpful words and happy thoughts)

  Yes, if we need to, we know we can count to three, breathe slowly in and out. Then, we think . . . happy thoughts.

- **Model and then have partners brainstorm happy thoughts.**

- **Show students your Happy Thoughts picture.**

- **Explain how you added hair, eyes, nose, and a mouth—to make the face look like you. Then, explain your Happy Thought picture.**

- **Have students draw a Happy Thought picture that they can use to help them when they get upset.**

★ ★
★ ★
★ ★

Lesson 5

SMART REVIEW

★········ Lesson Outline ········★

❶ SMART/Not-So-SMART Cards

Using the Unit 13 SMART/Not-So-SMART Cards, have students identify whether a character is being SMART or Not-So-SMART.

❷ *I'm a SMART Kid Sharing Book 3*

Have students complete an *I'm a SMART Kid Sharing Book 3*.

❸ SMART Review Checkout

Recheck each student's SMART Skills. Focus on students who are less socially adept. Award Recognition Cards as appropriate.

 CHAMPS
THREE STEPS

CHAMPS identifies a three-step teaching cycle: 1) Teach your expectations. 2) Observe student behavior. 3) Provide positive and corrective feedback.

—*Sprick, 2009, pp. 209–215*

Keep re-teaching SMART Skills with these three steps.

---

❶ SMART/Not-So-SMART Cards

Using the Unit 13 SMART/Not-So-SMART Cards, have students identify whether a character is being SMART or Not-So-SMART. Say something like:

Remind students that Ms. Smart knows it's OK to make mistakes. When Ms. Smart sees a mistake, she just helps her kids practice being SMART instead of Not-So-SMART.

Read each SMART Card. (Card text and sample student responses are shown here.)

SMART CARD 1

READ SMART CARD 1   Accepting "No" and Cooling Down

When Ms. SMART tells Jada it's time to work, Jada pouts, "Can't I play a little longer?"

Ms. Smart says, "No, it's time to work now."

Jada jumps up, clenches her fists, and yells, "That's not fair! You said we could play!"

Thumbs up or thumbs down? Did Jada remember how to accept "No"?

Tell Jada what she should do to be a SMART Kid. (Say "OK." Keep her body quiet. Take a deep breath.)

That's right, but Jada has the mads. She is upset! Tell Jada what she should do to cool down. (Count to 3. Breathe in and breathe out slowly. Think a happy thought.)

★ ★
★ ★
★ ★

UNIT
13

Lesson 5
SMART REVIEW

READ SMART CARD 2
Including Others

Carl Coyote stays in during recess to work on his project. When he goes out to recess, everyone is already playing. Carl doesn't know what to do, so he just stands near the door.
Achmed Alligator sees Carl. He smiles and says, "Hey, Carl. Come on out and play with us."

Thumbs up or thumbs down? Did Achmed remember to include others?

Thumbs up or thumbs down? Would you like to be Achmed's friend? Why or why not?

READ SMART CARD 3
Friends

One Saturday, Gregory Gopher and Li Lizard decide to play together at Gregory's house.

Both boys play nicely. What are some things they might do?

Gregory and Li might . . .

READ SMART CARD 4
Greetings, Including Others, Friends

Theodore Thunderbird is moving to a new house. He is moving to another state. Before he leaves, Ms. Smart says, "You are a SMART Kid, so I know you will have fun making new friends."

Let's help Theodore remember all the things he can do to make new friends.

When Theodore meets a new kid, he can give a SMART Greeting. What could he say?

When Theodore sees others playing, he can ask to join in. What might he say?

When Theodore plays with others, what can he do to keep new friends?

Small Celebrations

❷ *I'm a SMART Kid Sharing Book 3*

Have students complete an *I'm a SMART Kid Sharing Book 3.*

- Guide students through the book.
- Demonstrate how to trace the "I" statements.
- Have students complete their books by coloring each picture. Have students use at least three colors.
- Have students take their books home to share with their families.

❸ **Recheck Students' SMART Skills**

Recheck each student's SMART Skills. Focus on students who are less socially adept. Award Recognition Cards as appropriate.

End-of-Unit Tip

SMART REVIEW

As you move forward, work on . . .

·············· **Generalization** ···············

Everyday Use: Have students practice across settings and situations the SMART Skills they've learned—Greetings, Looking and Listening, Following Directions, Polite Requests, Compliments, Taking Turns, Including Others, Friends, Accepting "No," and Cooling Down.

These skills are important to success in school, at home, and in the workplace.

Continue to Encourage Efforts by:
* Providing positive descriptive feedback.
* Providing gentle corrections and guided practice as needed.
* Re-teaching periodically.
* Using SMART Recognition Cards to acknowledge student efforts.
* Referring to your Guidelines for Success.

················ **Intervention** ···············

When a student or students have difficulty with any of the ten skills learned to date:

Target one or two skills—Greetings, Looking and Listening, Following Directions, Taking Turns, Friends, or Cooling Down.

Scaffold Practice
For the targeted social skill, identify the easiest step for the student. Practice and reinforce this step. Then add another step. Practice and reinforce both steps. Then add another step and practice in multiple contexts.

KEEP WALKING THE TALK

Be explicit. Model the skills you've taught. Guide practice, and acknowledge student efforts.

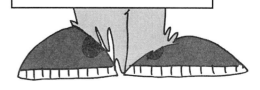

SMART Apologies

 Student Objectives

Targeted Objectives
I can apologize when I'm wrong, and I can accept an apology.

Review Objectives
When I'm upset, I can cool down.

I can accept "No" for an answer.

I join in, play nicely, and cheer my friends along.

I can include others and make new friends.

I can take turns.

I give compliments to others.

I say "Please" when I want something and "Thank you" when I get it.

I follow directions right away.

I look and listen when someone is talking.

I greet others with a smile and a "Hello."

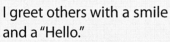

SMART APOLOGIES
Overview

······· Teaching Objectives ·······

Students practice and demonstrate competency on all the steps below when making or accepting an apology.

1. Looking at the person
2. Saying, "I'm sorry that . . ." or "That's OK"
3. Using an honest voice and meaning what is said

Teaching Materials

School Materials

- Puppet of your choice
- Building blocks
- Colors
- Masking tape

SMART Materials

- Units 12 and 14 Posters
- *My SMART Book* Unit 14 Coloring Page
- Recognition Cards for Apologies and previous units
- Unit 14 Reproducibles:
  14-3 SMART/Not-So-SMART Cards

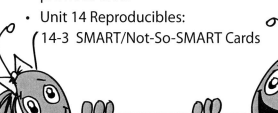

SMART APOLOGY SKILLS ARE . . . OH, SO IMPORTANT!
Everyone makes a mistake now and then. Knowing how to make an apology and accept an apology helps students learn to deal positively with things that happen.

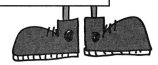

······· Teaching Tips ·············

Positive Interactions

Model how to apologize and accept apologies. This important skill helps students learn how to turn a negative interaction into a positive interaction.

Positive Feedback and Reinforcement

Notice students when they apologize and accept apologies with grace. Encourage their efforts with feedback and tangible reinforcers (e.g., Recognition Cards, Kid Badges, Home Notes located on the CD in Teacher Resources).

Connections

Reference your Guidelines for Success. (For example, treat others with respect.)

·········· Intervention ··········

When you notice the need for an apology, prompt the student by pointing to the SMART Apologies Poster or guide practice and then have the student apologize.

"Remember to say something like: 'I'm sorry I hurt your feelings. I shouldn't have left you out.' Can you say that and mean it? What else can you say?"

Lesson	Activities	Materials and Materials Preparation
1 • • •	**Introduce SMART Apologies** **Introduce Unit 14 Poster**	**Unit 14 Poster** Reproducible: Print the Unit 14 Poster (2 pages) and affix to 11"x 17" poster board. (Or order premade color posters.)
2 ▲▲▲	**Practice Unit 14 Poster** **SMART/Not-So-SMART Puppet Play**	• **Unit 14 Poster** • **A puppet** • **Building blocks**
3 ◆◆◆	**Review Unit 11 Poster** **Practice SMART Accepting "No" With Partners** **SMART/Not-So-SMART Cards**	• **Unit 11 Poster** • **SMART/Not-So-SMART Cards** Reproducible 14-3: Make one copy of each card.
4 ■■■	**Practice Unit 14 Poster** **When and Where to Use SMART Apologies** **"Five Little Monkeys" Variation**	• **Unit 14 Poster** • **Masking tape**
5 ★★★	**Practice and Discuss Reasons for SMART Apologies** *My SMART Book* **Unit 14 Coloring Page** **SMART Apologies Checkouts and Recognition**	• *My SMART Book* **Unit 14 Coloring Page** • **Colors** • **SMART Apologies Recognition Cards** Reproducible: On card stock, make several copies of the cards. Then cut and hole punch each card.

Lesson 1
SMART APOLOGIES

Lesson Outline

❶ Introduce SMART Apologies
Discuss and model SMART Apologies—making and accepting apologies.

❷ Introduce Unit 14 Poster
Introduce Annie Ant and Alejandro Ant, then read and rehearse the Social Story with gestures.

❶ Introduce SMART Apologies

Discuss and model SMART Apologies.

- **Discuss mistakes and making an apology.**
  Everyone makes a mistake now and then.

  Sometimes our mistakes can bother someone or hurt their feelings. If that happens, it's important to say "I'm sorry" and mean it.
  An apology is saying "I'm sorry" and meaning what you say.
  What's an apology? (saying "I'm sorry" and meaning what you say)

  A SMART Apology can help you keep friends when you make a mistake.

- **Discuss accepting an apology.**
  If someone else makes a mistake and says "I'm sorry," it's also important to accept the apology. You can do that by saying "That's OK" and meaning what you say.

  Accepting an apology can help you keep a friend and start over again.

- **Set up a role play. Model making an apology.**
  Let's pretend I was walking behind [Isabella] and stepped on [her] heel by accident.
  Everyone, do you think that would have hurt or bothered [her]? (yes)
  What should I do? (make an apology)

  Yes. Watch me make a SMART Apology. [Isabella], I'm sorry that . . . I stepped on your heel. I hope you are OK.

Have the student say:

That's OK. It was an accident.

Describe why SMART Apologies are important and what you will try to do next. Say something like:

I just made a SMART Apology, and [Isabella] just accepted my apology.

Am I mad at [Isabella]? (no)

Is [Isabella] mad at me? (no)

That's right. We're happy with each other.

And I'll try not to step on [her] heel again!

❷ Introduce Unit 14 Poster

Introduce Annie Ant and Alejandro Ant, then read and rehearse the Social Story with gestures. Say something like:

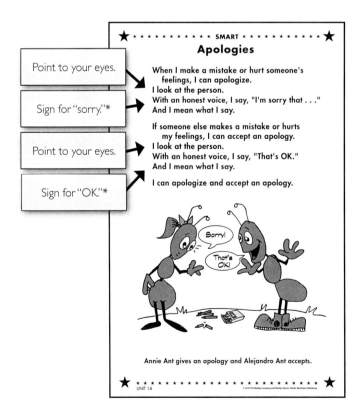

Annie Ant gives an apology and Alejandro Ant accepts.

Let's look at our SMART Apologies Poster. Annie Ant bumped into Alejandro. He threw his crayons up into the air and they spilled on the ground. Annie Ant is very sorry.

She says, "Alejandro, I'm sorry. I didn't mean to make you spill your crayons."

What do you think Alejandro Ant is doing?

(He's saying "That's OK," "Don't worry," "It's no big deal . . .")

Does it look like Annie is really sorry? (yes)

Does it look like Alejandro is really OK. (yes)

- **Read the Social Story to students.**

  Listen to me read about SMART Apologies. "When I make a mistake or hurt someone's feelings, I can apologize . . ."

- **Next, have students repeat each line after you.**

- **Then, read the poster using a cloze procedure.**

  When I make a mistake or hurt someone's feelings . . . I can apologize.

* See "How to Teach the Program" for gestures and ASL.

▲ ······ Lesson Outline ······· ▲

❶ Practice Unit 14 Poster

Have students practice the Social Story with gestures.

❷ SMART/Not-So-SMART Puppet Play

Have students evaluate whether you and a puppet are demonstrating SMART or Not-So-SMART Apologies—making and accepting apologies. Use the poster steps to guide students.

❶ Practice Unit 14 Poster

Have students practice the Social Story with gestures.

- Have students repeat each line after you.
- Then read the poster using a cloze procedure.

★ ········· SMART ········· ★
Apologies

When I make a mistake or hurt someone's feelings, I can apologize.
I look at the person.
With an honest voice, I say, "I'm sorry that . . ."
And I mean what I say.

If someone else makes a mistake or hurts my feelings, I can accept an apology.
I look at the person.
With an honest voice, I say, "That's OK."
And I mean what I say.

I can apologize and accept an apology.

Annie Ant gives an apology and Alejandro Ant accepts.

❷ SMART/Not-So-SMART Puppet Play

Have students evaluate whether you and a puppet are demonstrating SMART or Not-So-SMART Apologies—making and accepting apologies. Use the poster steps to guide students.

- Have students watch you apologize to the puppet. Explain to students that you said the puppet was silly. You need to apologize because the puppet's feelings were hurt. Say something like:

I made a mistake and told the puppet it was silly. Now, the puppet feels bad. I need to apologize because I want the puppet to be my friend. Use SMART Looking and Listening while I make an apology.

Look at the puppet and say:
[Mr. Puppet], I'm sorry that . . . I hurt your feelings. I didn't mean to make you feel bad.

Using the poster steps, have students identify whether you made a SMART or Not-So-SMART Apology.
Did I look at the puppet? (yes)
Did I say, "I'm sorry that . . ."? (yes)
Did I use an honest voice and mean what I said? (yes)
Thumbs up or thumbs down. Did I make a SMART Apology?

- Repeat and have students watch you make a Not-So-SMART Apology to the puppet. Use an insincere voice to tell the puppet you are sorry you stepped on it's paper.

- Repeat, using blocks for a prop. Pretend you are making a block tower and the puppet accidentally knocks it over. Have students watch you deliver a Not-So-SMART response to the puppet's apology. Have the puppet say:
Oh, no! I'm sorry that I knocked the tower down. Let's make another tower. It will be fun.
Say to the puppet.
No! I don't want to play with you anymore.

Using the poster steps, have students identify whether you accepted the apology.
Did I look at the puppet? (yes)
What did I say? (No! I don't want to play with you anymore.)
Did I use an honest voice and mean what I said? (yes)
Thumbs up or thumbs down. Did I accept the puppet's SMART Apology? (no)
Do you think the puppet will want to play with me anymore? (no, maybe not)

The puppet said, "I'm sorry that I knocked the tower down. Let's make another tower. It will be fun." Who can tell me how to accept the puppet's apology?
(That's OK. It will be fun to make another tower.)

- Repeat and have students watch you accept an apology. Have the puppet get upset, call you stupid, and then apologize for getting angry and calling you a name. Accept the apology.

Lesson 3
SMART APOLOGIES

◆ ······· Lesson Outline ······· ◆

❶ **Review Unit 11 Poster**

Have students practice the Social Story Accepting "No."

❷ **Practice SMART Accepting "No" With Partners**

Guides students through SMART Accepting "No," then have students practice with partners.

❸ **SMART/Not-So-SMART Cards**

Read the Unit 14 SMART/Not-So-SMART Cards. Have students identify whether Ms. Smart's students are using SMART Apologies or being Not-So-SMART.

❶ **Review Unit 11 Poster**

Have students practice the Social Story.
- Have students repeat each line after you.
- Then read the poster using a cloze procedure.

★ ·········· SMART ·········· ★
Accepting "No"

Sometimes, I can't do or have what I want.

Sometimes, my teacher or a friend will tell me "No."

I might want to pout, argue, or whine.

Instead, I keep my body quiet.

Sometimes, I take a deep breath.

With a calm voice, I say "OK."

Sometimes it's hard.

But I can accept "No" for an answer.

Achmed Alligator graciously accepts "No."

★ ★
UNIT 11

❷ **Practice SMART Accepting "No" With Partners**

Have students practice SMART Accepting "No" with partners.
- Have students practice SMART Accepting "No." Say something like:

Pretend to ask me if you can [take the ball barrel out for recess].

Everybody ask, "May I [take the ball barrel out for recess], please?" (May I [take the ball barrel out to recess], please?)

No. Not today.

What will you do with your body—stomp your feet and clench your fists or keep your body quiet? (keep my body quiet)

Then, you might take a . . . deep breath. That means you breathe in and breathe out.
Everyone, take a deep breath.
Finally, you say "OK."
What kind of voice will you use—pleasant or not-so-pleasant? (pleasant)

Great—you know how to accept "No" for an answer!

- **Have students practice SMART Accepting "No" with a partner. Say something like:**
Partner 1, ask Partner 2 if you can borrow a pencil. (May I borrow a pencil, please?)
Partner 1, say, "No, I'm sorry. I need it."
(No, I'm sorry. I need it.)
Partner 2, turn to Partner 1.
What will you say? (OK)

- **Reverse roles. Have Partner 2 ask if they can sit with Partner 1 at lunch. Have Partner 1 say, "No, I'm sorry. I'm already sitting with [Riley] and [Berto]. But you can sit at our table."**

❸ **Unit 14 SMART/ Not-So-SMART Cards**

Read the Unit 14 SMART/ Not-So-SMART Cards and have students identify whether a character is being SMART or Not-So-SMART. (Card text and sample student responses are shown here.)

READ SMART CARD 1   Making an Apology

Achmed Alligator is so excited about the big game that he pushes Felicia Frog out of his way. When Achmed and Felicia get to the field, Achmed sees Felicia. She is not happy.

Achmed says, "Felicia, you are being dumb. So, OK! I'm sorry."

Thumbs up or thumbs down? Was Achmed making a SMART or Not-So-SMART Apology?

Who can tell Achmed what he should do and say? (Achmed, you need to tell Felicia that you are sorry, but you need to mean it. You need to use a pleasant voice.)

READ SMART CARD 2   Cooling Down and Accepting an Apology

Felicia is very upset. Even after Achmed makes a SMART Apology, Felicia is still angry.

Who can tell Felicia how to cool down? (Count to three. Take a deep breath. Think a happy thought.)

Once Felicia has cooled down, what can she say to Achmed after he's apologized—if she really means it? (Achmed, it's OK.)

Yes, and she can also say, "Please watch where you are going."

READ SMART CARD 3   Taking Turns, Apologizing, Accepting an Apology

Carl Coyote has just started talking when Jada starts talking at the same time.

Thumbs up or thumbs down? Did Jada treat Carl with respect?

Thumbs up or thumbs down? Did Jada use SMART Taking Turns?

Who can tell Jada what she should say and do? (She should say, "I'm sorry. I didn't mean to take your turn. I will try to listen and wait.")

Carl is a good friend. What do you think he might say? (That's OK. Thanks for the apology.)

Lesson 4

SMART APOLOGIES

---

❶ Practice Unit 14 Poster

Have students practice the Social Story with gestures.

- Have students repeat each line after you.
- Then read the poster using a cloze procedure on the last word or words of each line.

★ · · · · · · · · · · SMART · · · · · · · · · · ★
Apologies

When I make a mistake or hurt someone's
feelings, I can apologize.
I look at the person.
With an honest voice, I say, "I'm sorry that . . ."
And I mean what I say.

If someone else makes a mistake or hurts
my feelings, I can accept an apology.
I look at the person.
With an honest voice, I say, "That's OK."
And I mean what I say.

I can apologize and accept an apology.

Annie Ant gives an apology and Alejandro Ant accepts.

❷ When and Where to Use SMART Apologies

Discuss when and where to use SMART Apologies.

- **Model why you sometimes need to apologize. Say something like:**

  Apologies are important because we all make mistakes. Apologies are important because sometimes things just happen and someone gets hurt or bothered.

Let's think about when and where apologies might be important.

Sometimes, I need to apologize to you because I've forgotten something. Yesterday, I forgot to [bring my stop watch, so we couldn't run our relay races]. So, what did I do? (You said you were sorry that we couldn't [run our races]. You said you would [bring the stopwatch] today.) Yes, I made a SMART Apology, and you were all great. You said, "That's OK. We can have a free recess and [run our races tomorrow]."

- Have partners share with each other and then the group when they've needed to apologize.

❸ "Five Little Monkeys" Variation

Review and practice SMART Apologies with a variation of "Five Little Monkeys." Teach students the chant and have them act it out.

- With masking tape, mark off an area on the floor about 6 x 6 feet square. Have students sit in a circle around the square. Explain that the square represents a bed.

- Tell students they are going to act out a new chant. Teach students the chant.

Have students listen to the chant.
Five little monkeys jumping on a bed.
One got bumped and said, "Good-bye!"
So, four little monkeys said, "We're so sorry that you got bumped.
Please come back and play some more!"

Have students repeat each line after you. Have students say the chant with you.

- Have five students stand on the "bed."

Tell students they get to jump on the bed, then show them how.

Tell these students when the chant says, "One got bumped," they will *gently* bump into [Dejohn]. Show them how to gently bump into [Dejohn].

Tell [Dejohn] that [he] will step off the butcher paper and pretend to fall down. Then, with the chant [he] should wave "good-bye."

Next, tell students on the bed they will motion for [him] to come back when the chant says, "Please come back and play some more."

When the chant is done, tell [Dejohn] [he] should accept their apology by saying something like, "OK. It's fun." Then, [he] should return to the bed and jump some more.

- Have all students say the chant while the five little monkeys act out the chant.

- As time permits, repeat with other groups of five students.

193

UNIT 14

Lesson 5

SMART APOLOGIES

★········ Lesson Outline ········★

❶ Practice and Discuss Reasons for SMART Apologies

Sing "Make New Friends but Keep the Old" in a friendship circle. Practice SMART Apologies with partners. Discuss why SMART Apologies are important.

❷ *My SMART Book* Unit 14 Coloring Page

Have students color their SMART Apologies Coloring Pages for their *My SMART Books.*

❸ SMART Apologies Checkouts and Recognition

Check out each student with a partner. See p. 195. Award SMART Apologies Recognition Cards to individuals as they demonstrate the skill.

 CHAMPS LEARNING TRAITS

"Certainly, some tendencies and personality traits seem to be present from birth, but most human behavior is learned . . ."

—Sprick, 2009, p. 17

The ability to forgive and traits of humility and honesty can be developed by teaching students to make and accept apologies.

Small Celebrations

❶ Practice and Discuss Reasons for SMART Apologies

Sing "Make New Friends but Keep the Old" in a friendship circle. Practice SMART Apologies with partners. Discuss why SMART Apologies are important.

- Have students sit in a friendship circle.
- Sing "Make New Friends but Keep the Old."
- Review and practice SMART Apologies with partners.

  You've all done a great job of learning about SMART Apologies. Let's review. [Logan], what do you do when you make a mistake or hurt someone's feelings? (I look at the person and say, "I'm sorry for what I did.") [Xavier], what do you do when someone else makes a mistake or hurts your feelings? (I accept [his] apology. Then I look at [him], use a nice voice, and say, "That's OK.") Excellent—you know how to do SMART Apologies!

  Partner 1, pretend you bumped into Partner 2. Turn to Partner 2 and make a SMART Apology.

  Partner 2. Turn to Partner 1 and graciously accept your partner's apology.

- **Discuss why SMART Apologies are important. Say something like:**

  Our song says, "Make new friends but keep the old. One is silver and the other gold." Tell me about friends. Why are they important? (They play with you, invite you in, cheer you up . . .)

That's right, but even friends make mistakes.

Nod your head if you've ever made a mistake. Touch your nose if you've ever hurt someone's feelings by accident. Touch your ear if you've ever made someone mad.

Yes, we all make mistakes now and then, and things happen that make us upset.

Who would you rather have as a friend—someone who says, "I'm sorry" or just says things like, "You're stupid" or "It's your fault"?

Who would you rather have as a friend when you make a mistake—someone who says, "That's OK" or "It's not OK! I'll never play with you again!"?

Why are SMART Apologies so important? (They help us keep our friends. They help people cool down . . .)

❷ *My SMART Book* **Unit 14 Coloring Page**

Have students color their SMART Apologies Coloring Pages.

You can all do SMART Apologies.

You can [treat others with respect and kindness]. You've earned another page for your *My SMART Book.*

Annie Ant gives an apology and Alejandro Ant accepts.

UNIT 14 ⑪

❸ **SMART Apologies Checkouts and Recognition**

Check out each student with a partner. Award SMART Apologies Recognition Cards to individuals as they demonstrate the skill.

Say something like:

While you are coloring your SMART Coloring Page, I'm going to have partners show me SMART Apologies.

When each partner shows me SMART Apologies, you will each earn a Recognition Card to add to your ring.

- **While students are coloring, circulate and have them show you SMART Apologies.**

- **Have partners role play. Possible situations:**
  Partner 1 left Partner 2 out of a game.
  Partner 2 lost Partner 1's toy.
  Partner 1 stepped on Partner 2's jacket and made it dirty.
  Partner 2 got mad and yelled at Partner 1.

- **Model and guide as needed. Award SMART Recognition Cards when they demonstrate the skill.**

Note: If needed, finish this informal assessment during free time activities, or independent work periods. Keep track of students who would benefit from more guided practice.

End-of-Unit Tip

SMART APOLOGIES

As you move forward, work on . . .

··············· Generalization ···············

Everyday Use: Periodically gather in a friendship circle. Have students greet others and give them a compliment. Have students practice positive statements that begin with, "I'm happy when . . ." or practice apologizing and accepting an apology. (Practice during neutral times can help students use SMART Apologies when something happens.)

Continue to Encourage Efforts by:

- Praising and providing descriptive feedback when students use SMART Apologies in natural contexts.
- Reminding students that everyone makes mistakes at one time or another and that's OK. It's what we do after we make mistakes that makes a difference.
- Prompting SMART Apologies in natural contexts and providing gentle corrections and guided practice as needed.
- Re-teaching periodically.
- Using SMART Recognition Cards to acknowledge student efforts.

················ Intervention ················

When a student or students have difficulty making and accepting apologies:

Add Practice

- Work one-to-one with the student. Pretend the puppet has done something wrong. Have the student teach the puppet how to make an apology. Use the poster or prompt each step with words or gestures.

- Work with partners to master the steps in SMART Apologies. Use examples of situations that have occurred in your classroom, on the playground, in the cafeteria, and at home.

Add Reinforcement

Each time you catch the student apologizing or accepting an apology, provide the student with: a cool note, an opportunity to be your special helper for a job, or a positive note home.

SMART Interruptions

Student Objectives

Targeted Objectives
I can interrupt when something is important.

Review Objectives
I can apologize when I'm wrong, and I can accept an apology.

When I'm upset, I can cool down.

I can accept "No" for an answer.

I join in, play nicely, and cheer my friends along.

I can include others and make new friends.

I can take turns.

I give compliments to others.

I say "Please" when I want something and "Thank you" when I get it.

I follow directions right away.

I look and listen when someone is talking.

I greet others with a smile and a "Hello."

UNIT 15 — SMART INTERRUPTIONS
Overview

······· Teaching Objectives ·······

Students practice Steps 1 through 3 and demonstrate competency by showing the ability to use Steps 1 and 2.

1. Knowing when to interrupt and when to wait
2. Using a signal to get an adult's attention right away
3. Calmly explaining the problem

Teaching Materials

School Materials

- Puppet of your choice
- Colors

SMART Materials

- Units 14 and 15 Posters
- *My SMART Book*
- *My SMART Book* Unit 15 Coloring Page
- Recognition Cards for Interruptions and previous units
- Unit 15 Reproducibles:
  15-4 Practice Cards

SMART INTERRUPTION SKILLS ARE . . . OH, SO IMPORTANT!

There are times when it is important for a young child to interrupt. Knowing when and how helps children avoid a sense of hopelessness and provides a strategy for getting an adult's attention and help when needed.

 Teaching Tips ·············

Positive Interactions

Keep positive interactions with all students high. Greet them, show an interest in them, and acknowledge their presence. Noncontingent positive interactions reduce the likelihood that students unconsciously interrupt to get attention.

Positive Feedback and Reinforcement

Provide positive descriptive feedback to help students who interrupt only when appropriate.

[Isabella], you showed great maturity. You waited until we had a private moment to tell me about your Grandpa's visit.

Connections

Pair positive feedback with your Guidelines.

··········· Intervention ··········

If a student interrupts inappropriately and frequently:

- Provide noncontingent positive interactions throughout the day. For example, make an effort to greet the student in the morning and to chat with the student during free time. Let the student be line leader so you can informally talk with the student.
- Work with the student on examples of when it was appropriate to interrupt and when it was not.
- Make sure the student has a strategy for getting help but waiting. (For example, see the Help Card, introduced in Unit 5.)
- Award Recognition Cards when you catch this student using SMART Skills.

Lesson	Activities	Materials and Materials Preparation
1 •••	**Introduce Unit 15 Poster** **When and Where to Use SMART Interruptions**	**Unit 15 Poster** Reproducible: Print the Unit 15 Poster (2 pages) and affix to 11"x 17" poster board. (Or order premade color posters.)
2 ▲▲▲	**Practice Unit 15 Poster** **SMART Interruptions Description and Modeling** **SMART/Not-So-SMART Puppet Play**	• **Unit 15 Poster** • **A puppet**
3 ♦♦♦	**Review Unit 14 Poster** **Review SMART Skills in a Friendship Circle** **Practice SMART Interruptions**	• **Unit 14 Poster** • **My SMART Book** Each student will need all their Coloring Pages from previous units (assembled in a book).
4 ■■■	**Practice Unit 15 Poster in a Friendship Circle** **SMART Practice Cards** **Reasons to Use SMART Interruptions**	• **Unit 15 Poster** • **Unit 15 Practice Cards** Reproducible 15-4: Make one copy of each card.
5 ★★★	**Practice SMART Interruptions** **My SMART Book Unit 15 Coloring Page** **SMART Interruptions Checkouts and Recognition**	• **My SMART Book Unit 15 Coloring Page** • **Colors** • **SMART Interruptions Recognition Cards** Reproducible: On card stock, make several copies of the cards. Then cut and hole punch each card. **Prep for your Graduation Party. Send invitations. See Unit 18.**

Lesson 1

SMART INTERRUPTIONS

```
•········ Lesson Outline ········•
```

❶ Introduce Unit 15 Poster

Introduce Isaac Inchworm and the words *interrupt* and *intelligently*. Then read and rehearse the Social Story with gestures.

❷ When and Where to Use SMART Interruptions

Explain and discuss when and where to use SMART Interruptions and when not to use them.

---

❶ Introduce Unit 15 Poster

Introduce Isaac Inchworm and the words *interrupt* and *intelligently*. Then read and rehearse the Social Story with gestures. Say something like:

Let's look at our SMART Interruptions Poster. Isaac Inchworm is waving his hands at Ms. Smart.

It says, "Isaac Inchworm interrupts intelligently."

What is Isaac Inchworm doing? (interrupting intelligently)

Wow! Those are two big words.

- **Teach students what *interrupt* means.**

  When you interrupt others, you stop them from doing what they are doing.

  You might interrupt others when they are talking. That means you might stop them from . . . talking.

  You might interrupt others when they are eating. That means you might stop them from . . . eating.

  You should only interrupt others when you really need their help.

  Look at the picture. Ms. Smart is teaching, and Isaac is interrupting her. So, Isaac is stopping Ms. Smart from . . . teaching.

- **Teach students what *intelligently* means.**

  The poster says Isaac is interrupting intelligently. *Intelligently* means smartly. What does *intelligently* mean? (smartly)

  Isaac must have something very important to tell Ms. Smart. Would he be smart if he interrupted her with something that wasn't very, very important? (no)

- **Read the Social Story to students.**
  Listen to me read about SMART Interruptions.
  "When something is very important . . ."

- **Next, have students repeat each line after you.**

- **Then, read the poster using a cloze procedure.**
  When something is very . . . important, possibly awful, dangerous, or even . . . scary . . . I can interrupt and get help . . . right away.
  I signal an . . . adult.
  I calmly say, "I need your help because . . ."
  I can interrupt and get help right away.

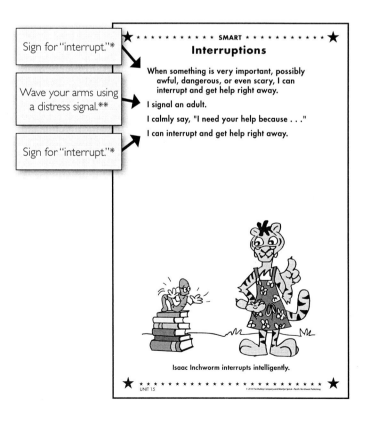

Sign for "interrupt."*

Wave your arms using a distress signal.**

Sign for "interrupt."*

★ ✶ ✶ ✶ ✶ ✶ ✶ ✶ ✶ SMART ✶ ✶ ✶ ✶ ✶ ✶ ✶ ✶ ✶ ★
Interruptions

When something is very important, possibly awful, dangerous, or even scary, I can interrupt and get help right away.

I signal an adult.

I calmly say, "I need your help because . . ."

I can interrupt and get help right away.

Isaac Inchworm interrupts intelligently.

★ ✶ ✶ ✶ ✶ ✶ ✶ ✶ ✶ ✶ ✶ ✶ ✶ ✶ ✶ ✶ ✶ ✶ ★
UNIT 15

❷ **When and Where to Use SMART Interruptions**

Explain and discuss when and where SMART Interruptions should be used.

You can use SMART Interruptions when other people are busy and you have something very important to say that cannot wait.

Remember, things that cannot wait are very . . . important, possibly awful, dangerous, or even . . . scary!

Let's think about something that is very important and possibly awful, dangerous or scary—if you don't get adult help right away.

If you really need to use the restroom—right away . . . If you really can't wait, that would be a time to use SMART Interruptions!

If another student got very angry, forgot about SMART Cooling Down, and ran off the playground, would that be a time to use SMART Interruptions? (yes)
Yes, that would be a very smart thing to do. Why? (The student could get hurt or lost.)

If you need help with a math problem and I'm busy working with others, would that be a time to use SMART Interruptions or to wait? (wait)
Yes, you could wait. How would you get help? (Put up a Help Card. Sit in the question chair. Ask someone at my table . . .)

Repeat with (1) A student wanting to tell you about his or her birthday party and (2) Someone getting hurt on the playground.

---

* See "How to Teach the Program" for gestures and ASL.
** Put your arms to your side, then move them up and down in a jumping jack motion.

Lesson 2
SMART INTERRUPTIONS

▲ ······· Lesson Outline ······· ▲

❶ Practice Unit 15 Poster
Have students practice the Social Story with gestures.

❷ SMART Interruptions Description and Modeling
Describe and have students practice SMART Interruptions using the poster steps.

❸ SMART/Not-So-SMART Puppet Play
Use a puppet to show SMART and Not-So-SMART Interruptions. Use the poster steps to guide instruction.

❶ Practice Unit 15 Poster
Have students practice the Social Story with gestures.
- Have students repeat each line after you.
- Then read the poster using a cloze procedure.

★ · · · · · · · · · · SMART · · · · · · · · · · ★
Interruptions

When something is very important, possibly awful, dangerous, or even scary, I can interrupt and get help right away.

I signal an adult.

I calmly say, "I need your help because . . ."

I can interrupt and get help right away.

Isaac Inchworm interrupts intelligently.

❷ SMART Interruptions Description and Modeling
Describe and have students practice SMART Interruptions using the poster steps.
Say something like:
First, you decide whether you can wait or if you need to use a SMART Interruption.

Then, if you need to make a SMART Interruption, you use a quiet signal to show you need an adult's attention. Like Isaac Inchworm, we are going to wave our hands quickly—to show we need help right away.

Everyone, watch me wave my hands back and forth very quickly. If you saw me doing this, what would you think? (You need our attention. Something is important . . .)
Wave your hands quickly—back and forth.

When the other person sees you, use a calm voice and say, "I'm sorry. This can't wait."
Then say what you need. You might say, "I need to use the restroom right away."
Everyone, try saying the whole thing with me.
I'm sorry. This . . . can't wait.
I need to . . . use the restroom right away.

Let's try another one. Let's pretend [Emma] got hurt on the playground, and needs an adult's help. You see me, so you run to me and wave your hands very quickly.

I look at you. You use a calm voice and say, "It's an emergency." Then say what you need. "[Emma] got hurt and needs help right away."

Let's try that. It's an . . . emergency.
[Emma] got hurt and needs . . . help right away.

❸ **SMART/Not-So-SMART Puppet Play**
Use a puppet to show SMART and Not-So-SMART Interruptions. Use the poster steps to guide your instruction.
- **Have students watch the puppet use the steps for SMART Interruptions.
  Have a student start reading to you. Then, have the puppet wave his hands quickly back and forth. Say:**
  Excuse me, [Abrianna].
  Look at the puppet. Have the puppet say:
  I'm sorry. This can't wait. I need your help because the paint spilled on the rug.

Next, say: Let's decide whether the puppet needed my help right away.

Remember, things that can't wait are very . . . important, possibly awful, dangerous, or even . . . scary!
Did the puppet need my help right away? (yes)
Yes, it was very important to get my help right away because paint can soak into the rug.
Did the puppet use our signal and get my attention? (yes)
Did the puppet [calmly] tell me what [he] needed? (yes)

Was that a SMART or Not-So-SMART Interruption? (SMART)

- **Have students watch the puppet use a Not-So-SMART Interruption.
  Repeat the same situation as before.
  Have the puppet tug on your clothes and yell:**
  Teacher, teacher, [Joey] spilled the paint!

Ask: Was it important for the puppet to interrupt me? (yes)
Did the puppet use our signal to get me attention? (no)
What did the puppet do?
(tugged on your clothes)
Did the puppet use a calm voice?
(No, he shouted, yelled . . . screeched!)
Was that a SMART or Not-So-SMART Interruption? (Not-So-SMART)

- **Repeat as time allows with:
  "My reading partner and I can't figure out a word."
  "Someone fell down and is crying."**

Lesson 3

SMART INTERRUPTIONS

Lesson Outline

❶ Review Unit 14 Poster

Have students practice the SMART Apologies Social Story with gestures.

❷ Review SMART Skills in a Friendship Circle

Have students sing "Make New Friends but Keep the Old." Then have students review their SMART Skills using their *My SMART Books*. Summarize or use cloze procedures. Make connections between SMART Skills and what friends do.

❸ Practice SMART Interruptions

Have students review and then practice the poster steps for SMART Interruptions.

RIGHT AWAY OR WAIT?
Learning to differentiate between situations when an interruption is necessary or is not necessary can be difficult for young children. When a student interrupts, help the student identify whether to wait or whether help is needed right away.

❶ Review Unit 14 Poster

Have students practice the Social Story with gestures.

- Have students repeat each line after you.
- Then read the poster using a cloze procedure.

★ SMART ★
Apologies

When I make a mistake or hurt someone's feelings, I can apologize.
I look at the person.
With an honest voice, I say, "I'm sorry that . . ."
And I mean what I say.

If someone else makes a mistake or hurts my feelings, I can accept an apology.
I look at the person.
With an honest voice, I say, "That's OK."
And I mean what I say.

I can apologize and accept an apology.

Sorry!

That's OK!

Annie Ant gives an apology and Alejandro Ant accepts.

UNIT 14

❷ Review SMART Skills in a Friendship Circle

Have students sing "Make New Friends but Keep the Old." Then have students review their SMART Skills using their *My SMART Books*. Summarize or use cloze procedures. Make connections between SMART Skills and what friends do.

- Have students sit in a circle.

- Have students sing "Make New Friends but Keep the Old."

- Have students turn to Unit 1, SMART Greetings, in their *My SMART Books*. Review the steps in a SMART Greeting. Then discuss how SMART and Not-So-SMART Greetings make one feel.
  The first SMART Skill we learned was Greetings. Thumbs up if friends give each other a warm greeting.

  Partner 1, look at Partner 2 and give a SMART Greeting. Remember to look, smile, wave, say "Hi," and say something friendly.

  How does a SMART Greeting make you feel? (happy, welcome, like a friend . . .)

- Have students turn to Unit 2, SMART Looking and Listening. Review, using a cloze procedure. Discuss what friends do.
  Look at Li Lizard and Penelope Parrot. They are showing us how to do a SMART Skill. What was our second SMART Skill? (Looking and Listening)
  Remember, when you use SMART Looking and Listening, you sit . . . up.
  Your face is . . . pleasant.
  You look with . . . your eyes.
  You listen with . . .

  If someone didn't use SMART Looking and Listening while you were talking, would you think he or she was your friend? Why or Why not? (Friends cheer each other along. Friends encourage each other. Friends look at and listen to each other.)

As time permits, repeat with any of the SMART Skills you've taught. Friends use: Polite Requests (Unit 5), Compliments (Unit 6), Taking Turns (Unit 7), Including Others (Unit 9), Friends (Unit 10), Accepting "No" (Unit 11), Cooling Down (Unit 12), and Apologies (Unit 14).

❸ Practice SMART Interruptions

Have students review and then practice the poster steps for SMART Interruptions.

- **Review the steps for SMART Interruptions.**
  Remember, when something is very . . . important, possibly awful . . . dangerous, or even scary, you need to tell an adult and get help. You . . . signal.
  You say, "I'm sorry but . . . this can't wait."
  Or say, "This is an . . . emergency."
  Then you say what you need and why.

- **Have students practice the steps for SMART Interruptions.**
  Let's pretend that [Dimitre] has skinned [his] knee. Show me your signal.
  Now say, "I'm sorry but this can't wait. [Dimitre] skinned his knee and needs help." (I'm sorry but this can't wait . . .)

  Give students positive feedback.
  That was perfect. [Dimitre] was hurt. You showed me our signal and then told me exactly what you needed and why.

  Provide corrective feedback when needed. (See Intervention Tips at the end of this unit.) Say something like:
  Is something awful, dangerous, or scary going to happen? (no)
  I'm glad you could tell. This would be a great time to put up your Help Card. What else could you do? (wait in the question chair)
  Excellent!

205

Lesson 4

SMART INTERRUPTIONS

■ · · · · · · · Lesson Outline · · · · · · · ■

❶ Practice Unit 15 Poster in a Friendship Circle

Have students practice the Social Story in a friendship circle.

❷ SMART Practice Cards

Read the Unit 15 Practice Cards to students and have them determine whether to interrupt or wait. When appropriate, have students practice making a SMART Interruption. Conclude the activity by summarizing why making SMART Interruptions is important.

❸ Reasons to Use SMART Interruptions

Discuss why it's important to interrupt only when it's important and possibly awful, dangerous, or scary.

❶ Practice Unit 15 Poster in a Friendship Circle

Have students practice the Social Story.

- Have students sit in a friendship circle.
- Have students repeat each line after you.
- Read the poster using a cloze procedure.

★ · · · · · · · · · · SMART · · · · · · · · · · ★
Interruptions

When something is very important, possibly awful, dangerous, or even scary, I can interrupt and get help right away.

I signal an adult.

I calmly say, "I need your help because . . ."

I can interrupt and get help right away.

Isaac Inchworm interrupts intelligently.

★ · ★
UNIT 15

❷ Unit 15 Practice Cards

Read the cards and have students determine whether to interrupt or wait. When appropriate, have students practice making SMART Interruptions. (Card text and sample student responses are shown here.)

READ PRACTICE CARD 1

Here's what happened. The ball rolled off the playground.

I'm going to count to three. Please stand up if you should make a SMART Interruption.

(continued)

READ PRACTICE CARD 1 (cont.)

Count quietly to 3.

Why was it important to make a SMART Interruption? (The ball might get lost. We can't leave the playground to get it . . .)

Show me our signal.
What might you say? (I'm sorry, but this can't wait. Our ball escaped and is rolling down the street.)

READ PRACTICE CARD 2

Here's what happened. We're doing math and you remember that you're going on a trip.

I'm going to count to three. Please put one hand on your head if you should make a SMART Interruption.

Count quietly to 3.

What should you do instead? (wait and tell you about my trip at recess, after school . . .)

READ PRACTICE CARD 3

Here's what happened. I'm at the door talking to a parent. You notice the pet gerbil from next door running into the closet.

I'm going to count to three. Please touch your toes if you should make a SMART Interruption.

Count quietly to 3.

Why is it important to make a SMART Interruption? (The gerbil might run somewhere else. The kids in Mr. Bell's room will be sad if they don't get it back.)

Show me our signal.

What might you say? (I'm sorry, but this can't wait. Mr. Bell's gerbil just ran into the closet.)

READ PRACTICE CARD 4

Here's what happened. We are on our way to the auditorium, but you notice that [Dakota] isn't back from the office.

I'm going to count to three. Please wave your hand if you should make a SMART Interruption.

(continued)

READ PRACTICE CARD 4 (cont.)

Count quietly to 3.

Why is it important to make a SMART Interruption? ([Dakota] might get back from the office and get scared. [Dakota] might not know where to go.)

Show me our signal.

What might you say? (I'm sorry, but this can't wait. [Dakota] isn't back from the office.)

❸ Reasons to Use SMART Interruptions

Discuss why it's important to interrupt only when it's important and possibly awful, dangerous, or scary. Say something like:
It's important to be able to interrupt because you may need help quickly, but it's also important not to interrupt if something can wait.

Let's think about what might happen if someone interrupts all the time—when it isn't important, possibly awful, dangerous, or scary.

Here's the first problem. I might quit listening. Would that be good or bad? (bad)

Here's the second problem. Kids in the class might not be able to learn as well. Would that be good or bad? (bad)

Here's the third problem. Interrupting might become a habit. Someone might start interrupting friends. Do friends interrupt each other or take turns? (take turns)
If interrupting became a habit, would it help you keep friends? (no)
Would that be good or bad? (bad)

Remember, a SMART Interruption should be used only when something is . . . very important, possibly awful, dangerous, or scary.

Lesson 5

SMART INTERRUPTIONS

★ ⋯⋯⋯ Lesson Outline ⋯⋯⋯ ★

❶ Practice SMART Interruptions

Review SMART Interruptions using the poster steps. Then have students practice with partners.

❷ *My SMART Book* Unit 15 Coloring Page

Have students color their SMART Interruptions Coloring Pages for their *My SMART Books.*

❸ SMART Interruptions Checkouts and Recognition

Check out each student by having the student tell you whether to interrupt or not and show you how. See p. 209. Award Recognition Cards to individuals as they demonstrate the skill.

CHAMPS
SMART AND NOT-SO-SMART

"The best way to help students understand your rules is to demonstrate specific examples of following and not following the rules."

—*Sprick, 2009, p. 118*

Part of learning social skills is knowing when and when not to do something. With SMART Interruptions, your students are on the way to learning judgments about appropriate and inappropriate use of interruptions.

Small Celebrations

❶ Practice SMART Interruptions

Review SMART Interruptions using the poster steps. Then have students practice with partners.

- **Review how to make a SMART Interruption.**

  You've done a great job learning about SMART Interruptions. I'm very proud of all of you.

  Everyone, look at [Malia].

  [Malia] knows how to interrupt the SMART way.

  [Malia], when is it okay to interrupt someone else who is busy? (when something is very important, possibly awful, dangerous, or scary)

  How do you interrupt, [Malia]? (I signal. Then I say "I'm sorry, but I need your help now. [Sophia] is stuck in the restroom.")

- **Have partners practice SMART Interruptions.**

  Class, show me our signal.

  Partner 1, pretend Partner 2 is a teacher and someone has gotten stuck in the bathroom. Turn to Partner 2, signal, then tell the teacher what you need.

  Partner 2, tell Partner 1 what you would do if I was busy and you finished your work.

★ ★
★ ★
★ ★

UNIT

Lesson 5

15

SMART INTERRUPTIONS

❷ *My SMART Book* Unit 15 Coloring Page

Have students color their SMART Interruptions Coloring Pages for their *My SMART Books*. **Say something like:**

You can all do SMART Interruptions. You can [be responsible] and [treat others with respect]. You've earned another page for your *My SMART Book*!

❸ SMART Interruptions Checkouts and Recognition

Check out each student by having the student tell you whether to interrupt or not and show you how. Award SMART Interruptions Recognition Cards to individuals as they demonstrate the skill.

Say something like:

While you are coloring your SMART page, I'm going to give each of you a SMART Interruptions Recognition Card.

- While students are coloring, work with individual students. Describe a situation that requires an interruption and another that does not. Have the student identify whether to use an interruption or not. Have the student act out a SMART interruption.

  Let's pretend I'm talking to the principal and you want to tell me about your trip to the beach. Would that be a good reason to use a SMART Interruption?

  Let's pretend [Caden] has gotten sick and needs help. Would that be a good reason to use a SMART Interruption?

  Show me what you would do and say.

- **Model and guide as needed. Award SMART Recognition Cards when they demonstrate the skill.**

End-of-Unit Tip

SMART INTERRUPTIONS

As you move forward, work on . . .

·············· Generalization ···············

Everyday Use: Make sure students have procedures for getting help when you're busy. You can teach them to use a Help Card. (See Unit 5.) Or, you can teach them to wait quietly in a Question Chair. The Question Chair is a place where one student can wait until you are free to help.

Continue to Encourage Efforts by:
- Praising and providing descriptive feedback when students show they know when to wait and when to interrupt.
- Providing gentle corrections and guided practice as needed.
- Re-teaching periodically.
- Using SMART Recognition Cards to acknowledge student efforts.

·············· Intervention ···············

When a student or students have difficulty knowing when to interrupt:

Add Practice With the Puppet
Work one-to-one with the student. Using examples similar to the types of interruptions the student makes and those that would be appropriate. Have the student teach the puppet when it's OK to interrupt.

Set Up a Reinforcement System
Have the student earn tickets for time with you. Determine the frequency with which the student seems to need attention. Award tickets intermittently, but frequently enough to meet the students needs. Tickets can be worth one to five minutes of time with you— to talk or play a game.

Increase Noncontingent Positive Interactions
Interact frequently with the student. Use the student's name. Greet the student. Give the student meaningful jobs and comment on the student's work and efforts.

SMART Disagreeing

 ## Student Objectives

Targeted Objectives
I can disagree respectfully.

Review Objectives
I can interrupt when something is important.

I can apologize when I'm wrong, and I can accept an apology.

When I'm upset, I can cool down.

I can accept "No" for an answer.

I join in, play nicely, and cheer my friends along.

I can include others and make new friends.

I can take turns.

I give compliments to others.

I say "Please" when I want something and "Thank you" when I get it.

I follow directions right away.

I look and listen when someone is talking.

I greet others with a smile and a "Hello."

UNIT 16

SMART DISAGREEING
Overview

······· Teaching Objectives ·······

Students practice all of the steps below and demonstrate competency by using at least Steps 2 and 3.

1. SMART Looking and Listening (pleasant face, looking at the person, listening without interrupting, hands and feet still)
2. Saying something to acknowledge the other person's thoughts
3. Expressing a different idea with a calm voice

Teaching Materials

School Materials

- Read Aloud book of your choice (See Lesson 2 for suggestsed titles.)
- Puppet of your choice
- Colors, scissors, glue for each student

SMART Materials

- Units 10, 15, and 16 Posters
- *My SMART Book* Unit 16 Coloring Page
- Recognition Cards for Disagreeing and previous units
- Unit 16 Reproducibles:
  16-3 SMART/Not-So-SMART Cards
  16-4a Finger Puppets
  16-4b Practice Cards

SMART DISAGREEING SKILLS ARE . . . OH, SO IMPORTANT!
When young children learn to disagree respectfully, they are learning a skill that will help them be valued classmates, coworkers, family members, and friends.

Teaching Tips ··············

Positive Interactions
Greet children, show an interest in them, and acknowledge their presence.

Positive Feedback and Reinforcement
Provide positive descriptive feedback when you notice students disagreeing with respect.

[Ethan], I'm glad you and [Xavier] can disagree respectfully. I saw pleasant faces. Even though you disagree, you can still be friends.

Use SMART Recognition Cards to acknowledge student efforts.

Connections
Pair positive feedback with your Guidelines for Success.

·········· Intervention ··········

If a student disagrees regularly and uses pouting, arguing, or whining:

- Provide noncontingent positive interactions throughout the day.
- Provide positive practice. At a neutral time, have the student practice SMART Looking and Listening (pleasant face), restating another person's ideas, and then stating his or her idea with a calm voice.
- Provide quick corrective feedback and then ignore pouting, arguing, or whining.
- Award Recognition Cards when you catch this student using any of the SMART Skills you've taught.

212

Lesson Planner

Lesson	Activities	Materials and Materials Preparation
1 ● ● ●	**Introduce Unit 16 Poster** **Model SMART Disagreeing With Puppet Play and Practice With Partners**	• **Unit 16 Poster** Reproducible: Print the Unit 16 Poster (2 pages) and affix to 11"x 17" poster board. (Or order premade color posters.) • **A puppet**
2 ▲ ▲ ▲	**Practice Unit 16 Poster** **When to Use SMART Disagreeing** **Practice SMART Disagreeing With a Read Aloud**	• **Unit 16 Poster** • **Read Aloud book of your choice** See Lesson 2 for suggested titles.
3 ◆ ◆ ◆	**Review Unit 15 Poster** **Review and Practice When and How to Use SMART Interruptions** **SMART/Not-So-SMART Cards**	• **Unit 15 Poster** • **SMART/Not-So-SMART Cards** Reproducible 16-3: Make one copy of each card.
4 ■ ■ ■	**Practice Unit 16 Poster in a Friendship Circle** **Review Unit 10 Poster in a Friendship Circle** **SMART Disagreeing Practice With Finger Puppets and Practice Cards**	• **Units 10 and 16 Posters** • **Finger Puppets** Reproducible 16-4a: Copy four finger puppets per student. • **Colors, scissors, glue for each student** • **Practice Cards** Reproducible 16-4b: Make one copy of each card.
5 ★ ★ ★	**Review SMART Skills in a Friendship Circle** *My SMART Book* **Unit 16 Coloring Page** **SMART Disagreeing Checkouts and Recognition**	• *My SMART Book* **Unit 16 Coloring Page** • **Colors** • **SMART Disagreeing Recognition Cards** Reproducible: On card stock, make several copies of the cards. Then cut and hole punch each card. **Prep for your Graduation Party. Send invitations. See Unit 18.**

Lesson 1

SMART DISAGREEING

<table>
<tr><td>

●······· Lesson Outline ·······●

❶ Introduce Unit 16 Poster

Introduce Deja Duck, Priscilla Penguin, and the word *disagree*. Then read and rehearse the Social Story with gestures.

❷ Model SMART Disagreeing With Puppet Play and Practice With Partners

Use a puppet to model the poster steps in SMART Disagreeing. Demonstrate with the puppet how to disagree about what story to read. Then have students practice with partners.

</td></tr>
</table>

❶ Introduce Unit 16 Poster

Introduce Deja Duck, Priscilla Penguin, and the word *disagree*. Then read and rehearse the Social Story with gestures.

- **Introduce and greet Deja Duck and Priscilla Penguin.**
  Let's look at our SMART Disagreeing Poster.
  It shows two of Ms. Smart's kids—Deja Duck and Priscilla Penguin. Wave and say "Hi" to Deja and Priscilla. (Hi, Deja and Priscilla)

  Deja and Priscilla are the best of friends. This picture says, "Deja Duck disagrees respectfully."
  Let's think about the word *disagree*.

  When two people have different ideas, they disagree. Deja and Priscilla disagree. What do you think that means?
  (They have different ideas . . .)
  That's right. Priscilla wants them to go to her house after school, but Deja wants to go to her house. What are the friends disagreeing about? (whose house to go to)

- **Explain that friends can disagree.**
  Deja and Priscilla have two different ideas, but that's OK. They can disagree nicely and respect one another.
  Do you think they get mad at each other? (no)

Lesson 1

SMART DISAGREEING

- Read the Social Story to students.

- Next, have students repeat each line after you.

- Then, read the poster using a cloze procedure on the last word(s) of each line.
  When I disagree, I can be . . . respectful.

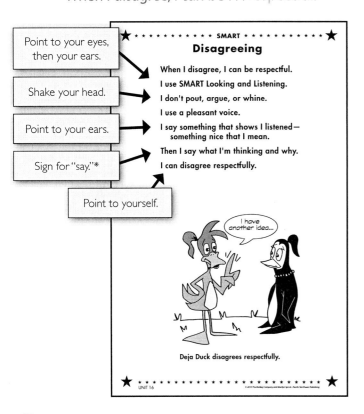

Point to your eyes, then your ears.

Shake your head.

Point to your ears.

Sign for "say."*

Point to yourself.

★ ★ ★ ★ ★ ★ ★ SMART ★ ★ ★ ★ ★ ★ ★ ★ ★
Disagreeing

When I disagree, I can be respectful.
I use SMART Looking and Listening.
I don't pout, argue, or whine.
I use a pleasant voice.
I say something that shows I listened—
    something nice that I mean.
Then I say what I'm thinking and why.
I can disagree respectfully.

I have another idea...

Deja Duck disagrees respectfully.

UNIT 16

❷ Model SMART Disagreeing With Puppet Play and Practice With Partners

Use a puppet to model the poster steps in SMART Disagreeing. Then have students practice with partners.

- Use the puppet to demonstrate how to disagree. Say:
  Let's you and I read *Toot and Puddle* together. I like that book.

Have the puppet say:
That's a good idea. *Toot and Puddle* is a good book, but I was hoping we could read *Enemy Pie*. It's really funny.

- Using the poster steps, have students identify the steps in SMART Disagreeing. Say something like:
  Let's think about how the puppet and I did. Nod your head if we disagreed about something.
  What did we disagree about?
  (which book to read)

  Touch your eyes and ears if the puppet used SMART Looking and Listening when I talked.

  Did the puppet say what I wanted? (yes)
  That's right. He said, "That's a good idea. *Toot and Puddle* is a good book."
  Did he use a pleasant voice? (yes)
  Did he say which book he wanted to read? (yes)
  Did he say why?
  Thumbs up or thumbs down. Did the puppet use SMART Disagreeing?

- Have partners practice SMART Disagreeing about whether to play soccer or T-ball.
  Partner 1, tell your partner you'd like to play soccer.
  Partner 2, look and listen, then disagree. Remember to say something nice about your partner's idea. Then say what you'd like to do and why.

Reverse roles and repeat.

* See "How to Teach the Program" for gestures and ASL.

215

Lesson 2

SMART DISAGREEING

▲ ······· Lesson Outline ······· ▲

❶ Practice Unit 16 Poster

Have students practice the Social Story with gestures.

❷ When to Use SMART Disagreeing

Discuss whether to use SMART Disagreeing or not.

❸ Practice SMART Disagreeing With a Read Aloud

Use a Read Aloud of your choice to practice SMART Disagreeing.

Special Preparation Note ··········
Read Alouds

For this lesson, select a favorite Read Aloud from your library. Choose a book that lends to making predictions and/or includes disagreements between the characters.

Suggestions:

Dear Mr. Blueberry
by Simon James

Emily is convinced that a whale is in her pond. In a series of letters, her teacher, Mr. Blueberry, politely disagrees. Students can give a thumbs up or a thumbs down for these very civil exchanges between a trusted teacher and student.

The Little Mouse, The Red Ripe Strawberry, and THE BIG HUNGRY BEAR
by Don and Audrey Wood
illustrated by Don Wood

Little Mouse must protect his red, ripe strawberry from a big, hungry bear. Ask whether little Mouse's attempts will keep the luscious treat safe. What else should he try? This wonderful text lends to rich literary discussions and different ideas.

Olivia
written and illustrated by Ian Falconer

Olivia has strong opinions and inspires strong opinions. Is she naughty or nice? Do you agree or disagree?

❶ Practice Unit 16 Poster

Have students practice the Social Story
with gestures.

- Have students repeat each line after you.
- Then read the poster using a cloze
  procedure on the last word(s) of each line.

★ · · · · · · · · · SMART · · · · · · · · · ★
Disagreeing

When I disagree, I can be respectful.
I use SMART Looking and Listening.
I don't pout, argue, or whine.
I use a pleasant voice.
I say something that shows I listened—
   something nice that I mean.
Then I say what I'm thinking and why.
I can disagree respectfully.

I have
another idea...

Deja Duck disagrees respectfully.

★ ★★★★★★★★★★★★★★★★★ ★
UNIT 16

❷ When to Use SMART Disagreeing

Discuss whether to use SMART Disagreeing.

- **Is it smart to disagree when it's time to clean up?**
  Pretend I've said, "It's time to clean up for lunch." But you want to keep [playing]. Would that be a good time to disagree? Why not? (We wouldn't get to eat. We wouldn't be following directions right away.)

  That's right. SMART Disagreeing includes knowing when to disagree and when it's important to follow directions right away.

- **Is it smart to disagree when deciding what to do for fun?**
  Let's pretend you and your family are deciding what to do on a Saturday.
  Your mom says, "What shall we do today?"
  Your sister says, "Let's go to the park."
  You disagree. What does that mean?
  (I have a different idea.)
  That's right. Should you yell, "That's stupid"?

  What else could you say? (That's a good idea. The park is fun, but it's raining. How about a movie?)

- **Is it smart to disagree about predictions?**
  Pretend we are reading a Read Aloud, and I have a prediction about what the story will be about. Is it OK for you to disagree? (yes)

  Yes! It's important for you to have ideas.

❸ Practice SMART Disagreeing With a Read Aloud

Use a Read Aloud of your choice to practice SMART Disagreeing—like Dear M. Blueberry.

- **Read the title and look at the picture, then predict what the book will be about. Use the poster steps to prompt SMART Disagreeing.**
  I think this book is going to be about a tiger. Nod your head if you agree.
  Shake your head "No" if you disagree.
  [Jabaar], make a SMART Disagreement. Say something nice, then what you think and why. (I think that's interesting, but I don't see a tiger. I think it's about writing a letter.)

- **Ask comprehension questions throughout. Share your ideas and encourage students to use SMART Disagreeing as appropriate.**

◆ ······· Lesson Outline ······· ◆

❶ **Review Unit 15 Poster**

Have students practice the Social Story about SMART Interruptions with gestures.

❷ **Review and Practice When and How to Use SMART Interruptions**

Have students identify when to use a SMART Interruption. Next, have students practice.

❸ **SMART/Not-So-SMART Cards**

Discuss the importance of different ideas. Then, have students identify whether the characters are using SMART or Not-So-SMART Disagreeing.

❶ **Review Unit 15 Poster**

Have students practice the Social Story with gestures.

- Have students repeat each line after you.
- Then read the poster using a cloze procedure on the last word or words of each line.

★ ★ ★ ★ ★ ★ ★ ★ ★ ★ SMART ★ ★ ★ ★ ★ ★ ★ ★ ★ ★
Interruptions

When something is very important, possibly awful, dangerous, or even scary, I can interrupt and get help right away.

I signal an adult.

I calmly say, "I need your help because . . ."

I can interrupt and get help right away.

Isaac Inchworm interrupts intelligently.

UNIT 15

❷ **Review and Practice When and How to Use SMART Interruptions**

Have students identify when to use a SMART Interruption. Next, have students practice.

- Have students discuss when it's important to interrupt. Say something like:

  Sometimes it's important to interrupt. Should you interrupt when you want to tell an adult about a TV Show you like? (no) What should you do? (wait until free time . . .)

Should you interrupt if someone is hurt? (yes)
Why? (They need help right away.)
That's right. If something is very important, possibly awful, dangerous, or scary, it is important to get help right away.
When should you interrupt an adult? (If there's a fire, a stranger around, someone says scary things . . .)

- **Have students practice making a SMART Interruption. Say something like:**
Let's pretend an older kid is scaring you, and you are afraid. What should you do?
(Use our signal, then say, "I'm sorry to interrupt. I'm afraid [Joe] will hurt me, and I need your help.")

- **Have partners practice making a SMART Interruption.**

❸ **SMART/Not-So-SMART Cards**
Discuss the importance of different ideas. Then, have students identify SMART or Not-So-SMART Disagreeing.

- **Discuss the importance of different ideas.**
People sometimes disagree when there 's more than one way to do things, or more than one way to think about something.

I think different ideas are good because we learn new things from each other. Why do you think lots of ideas are good?
(It's more interesting. You might try something new . . .)

- **Review the steps in a disagreement.**
Thinking different thoughts is a good thing. Remember how to disagree respectfully. First, you use SMART Looking and . . . Listening. Do you pout, argue, or whine? (no)

You use a pleasant voice and say something that shows you listened like, "That's a good idea," or "Good thinking . . ." Then you say what you are thinking and why.

Read each SMART Card and discuss. (Card text and sample students responses are shown here.)

READ SMART CARD 1

Carlos Cougar says he doesn't like the new TV Show. Before Carlos can finish, Tony Turtle interrupts and says, "Oh, I love that show. You're stupid not to like it."

Thumbs up or down? Is this a good time to have a different idea?

Did Tony use SMART Disagreeing?

Tell Tony what he might have done and said instead.
(looked and listened while Carlos talked, asked Carlos why he didn't like the show, then said why he liked it . . .)

READ SMART CARD 2

The class is discussing where to go on a field trip. Penelope suggests the zoo. Gregory suggests going underground. Felicia Frog gets upset, puts her hands on her hips, and says, "We have to go to the pond. It's dark underground and the zoo is full of dumb animals."

Thumbs up or down? Was it a good time to have a different idea?

Did Felicia use SMART Disagreeing?

Tell Felicia what she might have done and said instead.

READ SMART CARD 3

Ms. Smart and the kids are lining up for music. Li Lizard says, "Ms. Smart, I think it is nice that you are going to take us to music, but I think we should go to P.E. We get a lot of exercise in P.E."

Thumbs up or down? Was this a good time to disagree?

Tell Li why it wasn't a good time to disagree.
(Li just needs to follow directions. He is trying to do Ms. Smart's job. It's time for music . . .)

■······· Lesson Outline ······· ■

❶ Practice Unit 16 Poster in a Friendship Circle

Have students practice the Social Story with gestures.

❷ Review Unit 10 Poster in a Friendship Circle

Have students practice the Social Story SMART Friends in their friendship circle. Help students make connections between SMART Friends and SMART Disagreeing.

❸ SMART Disagreeing Practice With Finger Puppets and Practice Cards

Pass out two finger puppets to each student or have students make two finger puppets of their choice by coloring, cutting out, and gluing them. Model SMART Disagreeing. Then read the Practice Cards and have students practice.

❶ Practice Unit 16 Poster in a Friendship Circle

Have students practice the Social Story SMART Disagreeing with gestures.

• Have students sit in a friendship circle.
• Have students repeat each line on the poster after you.
• Read the poster using a cloze procedure.

★···········★ SMART ★···········★
Disagreeing

When I disagree, I can be respectful.
I use SMART Looking and Listening.
I don't pout, argue, or whine.
I use a pleasant voice.
I say something that shows I listened—
   something nice that I mean.
Then I say what I'm thinking and why.
I can disagree respectfully.

I have another idea...

Deja Duck disagrees respectfully.

★ ·· ★
UNIT 16

❷ Review Unit 10 Poster in a Friendship Circle

Have students practice the Social Story SMART Friends in their friendship circle.

• Have students repeat each line after you.
• Read the poster using a cloze procedure.
• Help students make connections between SMART Friends and SMART Disagreeing. Say something like:

Remember the last line of SMART Friends says, "I can show my friends . . . I care." Nod your head if you've ever made a mistake.

I nodded my head because I've made lots of mistakes. If a friend is about to make a mistake it's important to disagree. You can show you care by disagreeing.

★ • • • • • • • • SMART • • • • • • • • • ★
Friends

I can be a good friend.
I ask to join in.
I play nicely with my friends.
I take turns and share.
I cheer my friends along.
I show my friends I care.
I can be a good friend.

Jada Jackrabbit joins in and plays nicely.
Jada Jackrabbit is a good friend.

★ • ★
UNIT 10   © 2010 The Mailey Company and Marian Synch - Pacific Northwest Publishing

❸ **SMART Disagreeing Practice With Finger Puppets and Practice Cards**

Pass out two finger puppets to each student or have students make two finger puppets of their choice by coloring, cutting out, and gluing them. Model SMART Disagreeing. Then read the Practice Cards and have students practice.

• Model how to use the finger puppets.

Watch me. I'm going to put one finger puppet on each of my index fingers. I have [Deja Duck] and [Jada Jackrabbit] on my fingers. Look and listen to [Deja] and [Jada].
Have [Deja] say: I know we aren't supposed to, but no one is watching. I'm just going to run across the street and get our ball.
Have [Jada] say: We do need to get our ball back. Let's go ask mom to help us.

• **Read each Practice Card. Have everyone act it out. Then have a few students act out the scenario for the class.**

READ PRACTICE CARD 1

Have one puppet say: Look at Mrs. Cole's flowers. Let's go pick some to take to our moms.

Have your other puppet disagree by saying something nice and then offering a different idea.

READ PRACTICE CARD 2

Have one puppet say:
Here comes [Carl Coyote]. I don't want to sit with him. Let's move away.

Have your other puppet disagree by saying something nice and then offering a different idea.

READ PRACTICE CARD 3

Have one puppet say:
I think the very best part of the day is going to bed.

Have your other puppet disagree by saying something nice and then offering a different idea.

READ PRACTICE CARD 4

Have one puppet say: Let's play video games.

Have your other puppet disagree by saying something nice and then offering a different idea.

Lesson 5
SMART DISAGREEING

★ .... Lesson Outline .... ★

❶ Review SMART Skills in a Friendship Circle

Have students make positive statements about their SMART Skills and give compliments. Then practice SMART Disagreeing.

❷ My SMART Book Unit 16 Coloring Page

Have students color their SMART Disagreeing Coloring Pages for their My SMART Books.

❸ SMART Disagreeing Checkouts and Recognition

Check out each student by having the student pretend to disagree. See p. 223. Award SMART Disagreeing Recognition Cards to individuals as they demonstrate the skill.

CHAMPS
CULTURAL COMPETENCE

Cultural competence includes . . . "teaching students how to handle disagreements between teacher and students and between students . . ."

—Baldwin and Nieves, 2009, p. 9

SMART Disagreeing gives young children a start at learning how to disagree respectfully.

Small Celebrations

❶ Review SMART Skills in a Friendship Circle

Have students make positive statements about their SMART Skills and give compliments. Then practice SMART Disagreeing.

- Have students sit in a friendship circle.

- Have students repeat positive statements about their social skills.

  When you compliment one another, what do you do? (We say something nice that we really mean.)

  When you include others, what do you do? (We invite others to join us.)

  Select from and repeat with: greetings, looking and listening, making polite requests, taking turns, being friends, making and accepting apologies, interrupting, and disagreeing.

- Have students practice SMART Disagreeing.

  Let's pretend we are going to plan a celebration. I want to have a rest time and you want to have a party.

  I say, "To celebrate, let's have free time." Think about it. What might you say? (Remember, you want to mean what you say.) (A celebration is a great idea. What if we had a party? That would be fun!)

  That's excellent. You said something nice about my idea and you really meant it— "a celebration is a great idea." Then you came up with another idea, and you said it respectfully.

★ ★
★ ★
★ ★

UNIT

Lesson 5   16

SMART DISAGREEING

❷ *My SMART Book* Unit 16 Coloring Page

Have students color their SMART Disagreeing Coloring Pages.

Say something like:

You can all disagree respectfully—the SMART way. You've earned another page for your *My SMART Book*!

❸ SMART Disagreeing Checkouts and Recognition

Check out each student by having the student pretend to disagree. Award SMART Disagreeing Recognition Cards to individuals as they demonstrate the skill.

Say something like:

While you are coloring your SMART Coloring Page, I'm going to have you show me SMART Disagreeing. When you show me SMART Disagreeing, you will earn a Recognition Card to add to your ring.

- **While students are coloring, circulate and have them show you SMART Disagreeing.**

Say:

Let's pretend I've said, "I don't like treats. I think they waste our time."

What might you say? (I'm surprised you don't like treats. I love treats. They make me feel happy . . . Really? I love treats. I like to eat!)

- **Model and guide as needed. Award SMART Recognition Cards as students demonstrate the skill.**

Note: If needed, finish this informal assessment during free time activities, or independent work periods. Keep track of students who would benefit from more guided practice.

End-of-Unit Tip

SMART DISAGREEING

As you move forward, work on . . .

> ·············· Generalization ···············
>
> **Everyday Use:** Periodically gather in a friendship circle. Have students greet the person next to them and give them a compliment. Using disagreements that are similar to those you've heard, have students practice disagreeing politely. SMART Disagreeing is an art that requires lots and lots of practice.
>
> **Continue to Encourage Efforts by:**
> - Praising and providing descriptive feedback when students demonstrate SMART Disagreeing.
> - Reminding students that everyone disagrees with others from time to time and that's good. It's what we say and do that matters.
> - Providing gentle corrections and guided practice as needed.
> - Re-teaching periodically.
> - Using SMART Recognition Cards to acknowledge student efforts.
> - Using literature to reinforce the importance of disagreeing respectfully.
>
> ··············· Intervention ···············
>
> When a student or students have difficulty disagreeing:
>
> **Add Practice**
> - Work with partners or in a small group.
> - Set up scenarios that are similar to the disagreements you've heard. Have students practice what they might say or do to disagree respectfully.
> - Use SMART/Not-So-SMART examples with Ms. Smart's characters so students can correct the characters.
> - Once students become more adept at disagreeing respectfully, continue practice periodically to maintain skills.
>
> **Provide Positive Descriptive Feedback**
> - Catch the student or students disagreeing respectfully. Provide descriptive feedback. Say exactly what the student did that was respectful. Say things like:
>   Wow! You were honest. You told me what you liked and your idea. Your tone of voice was very pleasant. You sounded like a friend.

SMART Problem Solving

Student Objectives

Targeted Objectives
I can solve problems.

Review Objectives
I can disagree respectfully.

I can interrupt when something is important.

I can apologize when I'm wrong, and I can accept an apology.

When I'm upset, I can cool down.

I can accept "No" for an answer.

I join in, play nicely, and cheer my friends along.

I can include others and make new friends.

I can take turns.

I give compliments to others.

I say "Please" when I want something and "Thank you" when I get it.

I follow directions right away.

I look and listen when someone is talking.

I greet others with a smile and a "Hello."

SMART PROBLEM SOLVING
Overview

······· Teaching Objectives ·······

Students practice all of the steps below and demonstrate competency by using all three steps for problem solving with others.

1. Describing the problem
2. Thinking of ways to solve the problem
3. Picking an idea and trying it out

Teaching Materials

School Materials

- Puppet of your choice
- Colors

SMART Materials

- Units 10, 12, 16, and 17 Posters
- *My SMART Book* Unit 17 Coloring Page
- Recognition Cards for Problem Solving and previous units

SMART PROBLEM SOLVING SKILLS ARE . . . OH, SO IMPORTANT!

Problem solving is a complex and critical life skill. Getting a start on problem solving while children are young helps them learn to deal with problems as they arise. Knowing how to solve little problems gives children the confidence to tackle bigger problems.

 Teaching Tips ············

Positive Interactions

Greet children, show an interest in them, and acknowledge their presence.

Positive Feedback and Reinforcement

Provide positive descriptive feedback when students work together to solve problems.

[Isabella], I'm glad you and [Xiang] can work to solve problems. Even though you had a problem, you can still be friends.

Use SMART Recognition Cards to acknowledge student efforts.

Connections

Pair positive feedback with your Guidelines for Success.

·········· Intervention ··········

If a student has difficulty solving problems, target skills and provide positive practice.

- Have the student practice brainstorming solutions to problems—first with the puppet, then with an adult, and finally with peers.
- Practice problem-solving strategies such as Rock Paper Scissors at a neutral time. Then practice using this strategy to problem solve with a puppet, an adult, and then with peers.

Ask which skills are a priority for positive practice. For example:

- Would the student benefit from increased positive interactions? If yes, work on greetings, compliments, including others, and friends.
- Would the student benefit from learning how to cool down so he or she can problem solve? If yes, work on cooling down.

Lesson Planner

Lesson	Activities	Materials and Materials Preparation
1 • • •	**Explain and Model SMART Problem Solving** **Introduce Unit 17 Poster**	**IF YOU HAVEN'T PREPARED FOR YOUR GRADUATION PARTY, DO IT NOW! (See Unit 18.)** **Unit 17 Poster** Reproducible: Print the Unit 17 Poster (2 pages) and affix to 11" x 17" poster board. (Or order premade color posters.)
2 ▲ ▲ ▲	**Practice Unit 17 Poster** **Introduce Rock Paper Scissors** **SMART Problem Solving Results and Guided Practice**	**Unit 17 Poster**
3 ◆ ◆ ◆	**Review Unit 16 Poster** **Review Unit 12 Poster** **SMART/Not-So-SMART Puppet Play**	• **Unit 16 Poster** • **Unit 12 Poster** • **A puppet**
4 ■ ■ ■	**Unit 10 Poster in a Friendship Circle** **Practice Unit 17 Poster** **Brainstorm When to Use SMART Problem Solving and Discuss Why** **Practice SMART Problem Solving With Rock Paper Scissors**	• **Unit 10 Poster** • **Unit 17 Poster**
5 ★ ★ ★	**Practice SMART Problem Solving in a Friendship Circle** *My SMART Book* **Unit 17 Coloring Page** **SMART Problem Solving Checkouts and Recognition**	• *My SMART Book* **Unit 17 Coloring Page** • **Colors** • **SMART Problem Solving Recognition Cards** Reproducible: On card stock, make several copies of the cards. Then cut and hole punch each card.

Lesson 1

SMART PROBLEM SOLVING

❶ **Explain and Model SMART Problem Solving**

Explain and model SMART Problem Solving.

- **Discuss what a problem is.**
  Say something like:
  Problems are things that we need to solve. They can be big or small.

  If a problem is small, we can solve it quickly. If a problem is big, it may take longer. Remember this: No problem is too big or small for a SMART kid to solve. Everyone, say that. (No problem is too big or small for a SMART kid to solve.)

- **Model describing a problem.**
  Here is a problem I have. Maybe you can help me solve it. This is my problem. I'm always losing my keys.
  The first step is to describe the problem. What is my problem? (You keep losing your keys.)

  That's right! It's a problem because I can't drive anywhere, and I can't get into my house without my keys. It is definitely a problem to lose my keys.

- **Model and guide brainstorming ways to solve the problem. Write ideas on the board.**
  Next, we need to figure out different ways to solve my problem.

  Let's use SMART Looking and Listening while we think of things to help me quit losing my keys. I'll write our ideas on the board. Any idea is a great idea. Here's an idea: I could tell someone where I'm putting my keys.

What are some other things I could to do?
(Always put them in the same place. Keep them in your purse. Put up a hook for them. Get a beeper . . .)

- **Guide picking an idea to try by having students vote.**
  Wow! You've given me a lot of great ideas. The next thing we need to do is pick an idea. You can help me by voting for something you want me to try.

  I'm going to read the list two times. When you hear an idea you want me to try, keep it in your head. The second time I read the list, you will get to vote.

- **Tell students you will try the idea with the highest votes. Compliment students and thank them for their help.**

- **Implement the solution and report the results back to students.**

❷ Introduce Unit 17 Poster

Introduce Priscilla Penguin and Izzy Iguana, then read and rehearse the Social Story with gestures. Say something like:

Look at our SMART Problem Solving Poster. Priscilla Penguin and Izzy Iguana have a little problem. Izzy wants to go swimming, but Priscilla wants to play on the swings.

Priscilla Penguin and Izzy Iguana are playing a game called Rock Paper Scissors. If Priscilla wins, they will play on the swings. If Izzy wins, what will they do? (go swimming)

Our poster says "Priscilla Penguin and Izzy Iguana solve problems." What are the friends doing? (solving a problem)

- **Read the Social Story to students.**

- **Next, have students repeat each line after you.**

- **Then, read the poster using a cloze procedure.**
  Problems happen. But . . . that's OK.

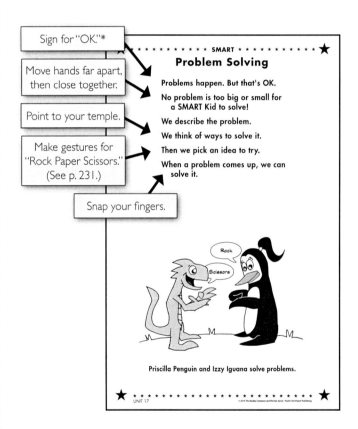

* See "How to Teach the Program" for gestures and ASL.

Lesson 2

SMART PROBLEM SOLVING

▲ ······· Lesson Outline ······· ▲

❶ Practice Unit 17 Poster

Have students practice the Social Story with gestures.

❷ Introduce Rock Paper Scissors

Teach students how to play Rock Paper Scissors. Practice using the game to solve problems.

❸ SMART Problem Solving Results and Guided Practice

Update students on the results of their problem solving with you. Review the poster steps and practice solving another problem.

❶ Practice Unit 17 Poster

Have students practice the Social Story with gestures.

- Have students repeat each line after you.
- Then read the poster using a cloze procedure.

★ · · · · · · · · · · SMART · · · · · · · · · · ★
Problem Solving

Problems happen. But that's OK.

No problem is too big or small for a SMART Kid to solve!

We describe the problem.

We think of ways to solve it.

Then we pick an idea to try.

When a problem comes up, we can solve it.

Priscilla Penguin and Izzy Iguana solve problems.

★ · ★
UNIT 17

❷ Introduce Rock Paper Scissors

Teach students how to play Rock Paper Scissors. Practice using the game to solve problems.

- Explain that Izzy Iguana and Priscilla Penguin used this game to solve their disagreement.
- Model and have students practice making a rock, paper, and scissors.
- Model playing the game with a student. Have students determine who is the winner.

Special Preparation Note · · · · · · · · · ·
Rock Paper Scissors

Players make a fist with their right hand. Their left hand is held flat. Players count to three, pounding their right fist on their left hand.

On the count of three, players use their right hand to make:

- A rock with a fist
- Paper with a flat hand
- Scissors cutting with the index and middle finger

The winner is determined as follows:

- Rock breaks scissors.
- Paper wraps around rock.
- Scissor cuts paper.

- **Have partners practice solving problems with Rock Paper Scissors.**

    Pretend you each want the ball. Play Rock Paper Scissors to decide who gets it.

    Pretend you are playing t-ball and you both want to pitch. Play Rock Paper Scissors to decide who gets to pitch.

❸ SMART Problem Solving Results and Guided Practice

Update students on the results of their problem solving. Review the poster steps and practice solving another problem.

- **Update students on your problem and review the poster steps.**

    Yesterday, I described a problem for you. What was it? (You keep losing your keys.)
    What did we do next? (came up with ideas)
    Then what did we do? (voted)

Yes, we decided I should have a special place for my keys, so last night I put my keys in a special dish by my door. Guess what? My keys were still there this morning. What should I do tonight? (Put your keys in the dish.)

- **Have students help you with a second problem—such as [your kids argue over whose turn it is to help with the dishes, your husband and you like to watch different TV shows . . .] Describe the problem.**

    You were such a big help with my keys. I think you can help me solve another problem. What do I need to do first? (describe the problem)
    OK, here's the problem. [My husband and I like to watch different TV shows. Both shows are on at the same time.]

Have students brainstorm ideas. Write their ideas on the board.

How can you help me problem solve? (think of ideas)
Yes, then I'll write them on the board. What should we do next? (vote)
Yes, and then I can try your idea. What should [my husband and I do when we each want to watch a different show]? (Take turns. Play Rock Paper Scissors . . .)

Have students vote. Try students' idea and then report the results.

What should [my husband and I do when we each want to watch a different show]? (Play Rock Paper Scissors . . .)

Have students vote. Try students' idea and then report the results.

UNIT 17

Lesson 3

SMART PROBLEM SOLVING

◆ ········ Lesson Outline ········ ◆

❶ Review Unit 16 Poster

Have students practice the Social Story about SMART Disagreeing with gestures.

❷ Review Unit 12 Poster

Have students practice the Social Story about SMART Cooling Down.

❸ SMART/Not-So-SMART Puppet Play

Review the poster steps and make connections with other SMART Skills. Use a puppet to have students identify SMART and Not-So-SMART Problem Solving and then assist the puppet with cooling down and problem solving.

---

❶ Review Unit 16 Poster

Have students practice the Social Story with gestures.

- Have students repeat each line after you.
- Then read the poster using a cloze procedure.

★ · · · · · · · · · · · SMART · · · · · · · · · · ★
Problem Solving

Problems happen. But that's OK.

No problem is too big or small for a SMART Kid to solve!

We describe the problem.

We think of ways to solve it.

Then we pick an idea to try.

When a problem comes up, we can solve it.

Priscilla Penguin and Izzy Iguana solve problems.

❷ Review UNIT 12 Poster

Have students practice the Social Story about SMART Cooling Down.

- Have students repeat each line after you.
- Then read the poster using a cloze procedure.

❸ **SMART/Not-So-SMART Puppet Play**

Review the poster steps and make connections with other SMART Skills. Use a puppet to have students identify SMART and Not-So-SMART Problem Solving. Then help the puppet cool down and problem solve.

- **Review the steps for Problem Solving and make connections with other SMART Skills. Say something like:**
  When you use SMART Problem Solving, what's the first thing you do?
  (describe the problem)
  What's the second thing you do?
  (think of ideas—ways to solve the problem)
  What's the third thing you do? (pick an idea)
  And finally you . . . try it.

  What kind of voice should you use?
  (pleasant, calm)
  That's right. You can use a lot of your SMART Skills when you are solving problems.

  If you are feeling angry, what should you do first? (cool down)
  If you are brainstorming ideas, what should you do while other people are talking?
  (look and listen, take turns . . .)

- **Have students identify whether the puppet is using the steps for SMART Problem Solving when [he] loses [his] jacket. Say something like:**
  Pretend the puppet has lost [his] jacket.

Have the puppet act frantic and say:
Oh, no . . . Oh, no!!! What am I going to do?

Have the puppet flop down, beat [his] hands on the ground, and then whine:
I'm going to get in trouble.

Then have the puppet yell at you:
It's all your fault! You told me to line up.

Have students identify whether the puppet is using SMART Problem Solving.
Is the puppet using SMART Problem Solving? (no)
What did [he] do? (pouted, argued, shouted)
Yes, [he] forgot No PAWS.
What should he do? (Cool down, describe the problem, think of ideas, and try it.)

Let's help him. Let's help the puppet cool down. Say, "[Mr. Puppet], count to three."
([Mr. Puppet], count to three.)
Have the puppet count.
1, 2, 3.
What's next? (take a deep breath)
Have the puppet take a deep breath.
What's next? (think a happy thought)
Close your eyes and imagine yourself wearing a nice red jacket.
Now we can help [Mr. Puppet] problem solve.

Have students help the puppet describe the problem, think of ideas, and pick one to try.

■ ········ Lesson Outline ········ ■

❶ Practice Unit 10 Poster in a Friendship Circle

Have students practice the Social Story about SMART Friends.

❷ Practice Unit 17 Poster

Have students practice the Social Story about SMART Problem Solving with gestures.

❸ Brainstorm When to Use SMART Problem Solving and Discuss Why

Brainstorm problems (when) and then have students discuss why (reasons) they could use SMART Problem Solving.

❹ Practice SMART Problem Solving With Rock Paper Scissors

Review Rock Paper Scissors. Select problems from the students' list that can be resolved with the game. Practice with partners.

❶ Practice Unit 10 Poster in a Friendship Circle

Have students practice the Social Story about SMART Friends.

- Have students sit in a circle.
- Have students repeat each line after you.
- Then read the poster using a cloze procedure.

★ · · · · · · · · · SMART · · · · · · · · · ★
Friends

I can be a good friend.
I ask to join in.
I play nicely with my friends.
I take turns and share.
I cheer my friends along.
I show my friends I care.
I can be a good friend.

Jada Jackrabbit joins in and plays nicely.
Jada Jackrabbit is a good friend.

★ · ★
UNIT 10

❷ Practice Unit 17 Poster

Have students practice the Social Story about Problem Solving with gestures.

- Have students repeat each line after you.
- Then read the poster using a cloze procedure.
- Make connections between SMART Friends and SMART Problem Solving. Say something like:

Sometimes friends disagree or have problems, but we know it's OK. We not only know that we can disagree but we can also problem solve when we can only use or do one thing. How do we disagree, then problem solve? (Listen and say what we think respectfully. Then problem solve. Play Rock Paper Scissors . . .)

❸ **Brainstorm When to Use SMART Problem Solving and Discuss Why**

Brainstorm problems (when) and then have students discuss why (reasons) they could use SMART Problem Solving.

Now that you know how to use SMART Problem Solving, we can solve a lot of problems. Remember, there's no problem too big or small for a SMART kid to solve!

You helped me fix my problem—losing my keys! It's great. I don't have to panic. My keys are in a special place by the door. You also helped [my husband and I figure out what TV show to watch]. We take turns!

- **Identify a class problem and have students help you identify why it's a problem.**
  Let's think about times we might want to use SMART Problem Solving at school. Here's a problem I've noticed. Some people only want to sit next to their best friends. Why is that a problem? (Some kids feel left out. It causes kids to argue. People get upset . . .)
  Nod your head if you think we could use SMART Problem Solving to help us.

- **Have partners identify and share classroom problems. Discuss why these are problems, and write them on the board.**
  Partner 1, tell Partner 2 about a problem you've noticed in our classroom—it can be big or small.

  Repeat with Partner 2. Then have partners share their ideas.

❹ **Practice SMART Problem Solving With Rock Paper Scissors**

Review Rock Paper Scissors. Select problems from the students' list that can be resolved with the game. Practice with partners.

- **Review Rock Paper Scissors.**

- **Select problems from the students' list that can be resolved with the game. Practice with partners.**
  Let's look at our list of problems. [Logan] said kids argue over who gets to use the red marker. Since there's only one red marker, it's a problem. Can we solve that problem with Rock Paper Scissors? (yes) Let's try it.

  Partners get your hands ready to play Rock Paper Scissors. Everyone, count. (1, 2, 3) Put your hand up if you get to be the one to use the red marker.

  Repeat with other examples (e.g., two people want to sit in the question chair at one time, partners argue over who reads first . . .)

Lesson 5

SMART PROBLEM SOLVING

★ ········ Lesson Outline ········ ★

❶ Practice SMART Problem Solving in a Friendship Circle

Have students sing "Make New Friends but Keep the Old." Then, have students practice solving a problem of your choice or a friendship problem (e.g., best friends want to sit next to each other and exclude others).

❷ *My SMART Book* Unit 17 Coloring Page

Have students color their SMART Problem Solving Coloring Pages for their *My SMART Books.*

❸ SMART Problem Solving Checkouts and Recognition

Check out each student by having the student pretend to solve a problem. See p. 237. Award SMART Problem Solving Recognition Cards to individuals as they demonstrate the skill.

CHAMPS VISION

"Give students a vision of what they will eventually be able to do."

—*Sprick, 2009, p. 47*

Problem solving is a complex task. However, with this start, your young children will have a vision that "no problem is too big or small" for a SMART Kid to solve.

Small Celebrations

❶ Practice SMART Problem Solving in a Friendship Circle

Have students sing "Make New Friends but Keep the Old." Then, have students practice solving a problem of your choice or a friendship problem (e.g., best friends only want to sit next to each other).

- Have students sing "Make New Friends but Keep the Old." (You may wish to teach students to practice the song in a round.)
- Compliment students on their SMART Skills.

  You've done a great job learning many SMART Skills. I've noticed [Ethan] cheering others along by giving SMART Compliments. [Connor], give [Ethan] a high five for us.

- Review the poster steps in problem solving and guide practice.
  Describe and discuss the problem.
  Today, we are going to work on solving a classroom problem. Sometimes best friends only want to sit next to each other in our friendship circle. Why is that a problem? (Other kids get left out . . .)
  It's very natural to want to sit next to a best friend, but it does leave out others.

  Have students identify the next step in problem solving and then brainstorm ideas. Write ideas on the board.
  I've described the problem.
  What do we do next? (Think of solutions. Come up with ideas . . .)

Lesson 5

SMART PROBLEM SOLVING

Yes, we can brainstorm. Here's an idea. I could assign seats.
Partners, think together, then we'll share.

[Riley], what did you and your partner come up with? (sitting in alphabetical order, sitting next to other people . . .)

Have students identify the next step in problem solving. Vote to select an idea.
Excellent ideas! What do we do next? (pick an idea)
Yes, we listen to each other. We describe the problem. We think of ways to solve the problem. Then, we pick an idea.
We could play Rock Paper Scissors, but there are too many of us. Let's vote.

Have students try the idea the next time you form a friendship circle.

❷ *My SMART Book* Unit 17 Coloring Page

Have students color their SMART Problem Solving Coloring Pages. Say something like:
You can all use SMART Problem Solving.
Today, you get to complete your *My SMART Book.*
Congratulations!

❸ SMART Problem Solving Checkouts and Recognition

Check out each student's SMART Problem Solving Skills by having the student pretend to solve a problem. Award SMART Problem Solving Recognition Cards to individuals as they demonstrate the skill.

- **While students are coloring, have individual students help you problem solve. Say something like:**
  [Cailey], let's pretend you are having trouble remembering to bring your homework back. What's the problem? (remembering my homework)
  Now, what should you do? (come up with ideas)
  Great, let's see if you can think of two ideas. (Put it in my backpack. Have my mom help me remember . . .)
  Nice, what do you do next? (pick an idea)
  If you had a homework problem, what idea would you pick to try?

- **Model and guide as needed. Award a SMART Recognition Card when a student demonstrates the skill.**

End-of-Unit Tip

SMART PROBLEM SOLVING

As you move forward, work on . . .

················· Generalization ···············

Everyday Use: When a problem occurs, have your students use the problem solving process to resolve it. Practice makes perfect!

Continue to Encourage Efforts by:
- Praising and providing descriptive feedback when students initiate or problem solve with prompting.
- Providing gentle corrections, prompting, and guided practice as needed.
- Re-teaching periodically.
- Using SMART Recognition Cards to acknowledge student efforts.

················· Intervention ···············

When a student or students have difficulty knowing how to problem solve:

Add Practice
Practice at a neutral time with examples that are similar to those the students encounter.
- Work one-to-one with the student. Have the student teach the puppet how to problem solve.
- Work with partners.
- Work with small groups.

Set Up a Reinforcement System
Use Recognition Cards whenever the students engage in problem solving.

Increase Noncontingent Positive Interactions
Interact frequently with the student or students. Use the student's name. Greet the student. Give the student meaningful jobs and comment on the student's work and efforts.

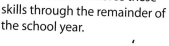

CONGRATULATE YOURSELF!
Your students have learned many skills that will hold them in good stead as they progress through school and into the world of work. Congratulate yourself on what you have done to contribute to their success. In the next unit, you will have a big celebration with your students. If you are finishing SMART midyear, be sure to continue to review and reinforce these skills through the remainder of the school year.

SMART Graduation

 ## Student Objectives

Review Objectives

I can solve problems.

I can disagree respectfully.

I can interrupt when something is important.

I can apologize when I'm wrong, and I can accept an apology.

When I'm upset, I can cool down.

I can accept "No" for an answer.

I join in, play nicely, and cheer my friends along.

I can include others and make new friends.

I can take turns.

I give compliments to others.

I say "Please" when I want something and "Thank you" when I get it.

I follow directions right away.

I look and listen when someone is talking.

I greet others with a smile and a "Hello."

It's Time to Graduate!

······· SMART Graduation ·······
Planning and Overview

Off to a SMART start with:

1. SMART Greetings

2. SMART Looking and Listening

3. SMART Following Instructions

4. SMART Polite Requests

5. SMART Compliments

6. SMART Taking Turns

7. SMART Including Others

8. SMART Friends

9. SMART Accepting "No"

10. SMART Cooling Down

11. SMART Apologies

12. SMART Interruptions

13. SMART Disagreeing

14. SMART Problem Solving

A CELEBRATION IS . . . OH, SO IMPORTANT!

Your students are off to a SMART start learning the skills of social grace, good manners, and respectful talk. May your SMART kids go through life with a positive outlook and joyful interactions with others.

For this unit, you and your students will prepare for their graduation ceremony—using their SMART Skills in the process. Excitement will fill the air!

Advance Preparation · · · · · · · · · · · ·
Graduation

1. Two to three weeks in advance of the ceremony, send invitations to family members and VIP staff members—principal, custodian, cook, secretary, counselor . . . (Invitations and RSVP Cards are available in the Unit 18 Reproducibles.)

2. Using your classroom procedures, arrange for refreshments.

3. Ask the principal or another administrator to read names, hand graduates their diplomas, and move tassels from the right to the left of the mortar board.

4. Determine who will provide the ceremony opening and closing. (You may wish to do both.) Prepare an opening and closing.

5. Customize the celebration. Determine your own room set-up and celebration details. Consider how and whether you will:
   - Decorate
   - Set up a temporary/mini stage
   - Use music (e.g., "Pomp and Circumstance")
   - Have a procession of graduates
   - Seat the audience
   - Set up for refreshments
   - Serve guests

Have fun! Be creative!

6. Graduation caps will need to be made by adults. See the next page for instructions. Determine who will measure each student's head and who will make the caps.

Unit Summary: Heads Up

In the Unit Lessons, you and your students will:
- Select and rehearse three posters to present with gestures
- Prepare Graduation Programs (adding names and details before copying and coloring)
- Run a dress rehearsal
- Have a big celebration

(Graduation Ceremony to include: Opening, Performance of Three Posters, Graduate Procession, Presentation of Diplomas, Closing, refreshments and passing out of *My SMART Books* to take home)

Teaching Materials

School Materials

- 11" x 11" cardboard (or black poster board), one per student
- Black butcher paper, gold yarn, packing tape or long-arm stapler, glue, regular tape or stapler, markers, sack
- Music selection (e.g., "Pomp and Circumstance") and player
- Stage or table
- Entrance table
- Seating for visitors
- Refreshments

SMART Materials

- Units 1–3, 5–7, 9–12, 14–17 Posters
- *My SMART Book* (completed)
- Unit 18 Reproducibles:
  18-1a Graduation Invitation
  18-1b Graduation RSVP Card
  18-2 Graduation Student Name Tags
  18-3a Graduation Program Option 1
  18-3b Graduation Program Option 2
  18-5a Diploma Option 1
  18-5b Diploma Option 2
  18-5c Graduation Visitor Name Tags

Special Preparation Note ··········
Graduation Caps

Top of the Hat:
For each student, one 11" x 11" piece of cardboard wrapped in black butcher paper, or one piece of black poster board

Tassel
- Cut gold yarn into 12" lengths. For each tassel, fold several strands in half.
- Wrap toward the top with another piece of yarn to create the tassel.
- Using another piece of yarn, attach the tassel to the top of the cap with packing tape or use a long-arm stapler to staple it.

Band: Black butcher paper band
- Measure the circumference of each student's head.
- Cut a strip of butcher paper 11 inches wide and the length of the child's head size plus two inches.
- Fold the paper in half (lengthwise) for increased strength.
- Fold the top of the band down 1 inch. Cut this fold (1 inch down) several times so it can be glued to the board.
- Tape or staple the band ends together.
- Glue the band to the board.

Lesson Planner

Lesson	Activities	Materials and Materials Preparation
1 ●●●	**Positive Statements in a Friendship Circle** **Select Posters to Perform** **Practice Selected Posters** — **Graduation Invitations and RSVP Cards** Reproducibles 18-1a and 18-1b: These should have been sent out in advance. If not, consider modifying the ceremony to a class-only performance.	**Units 1–3, 5–7, 9–12, and 14–17 Posters**
2 ▲▲▲	**Practice Selected Posters in a Friendship Circle** **Pass Out Graduation Student Name Tags and Assign Poster Groups**	• **Posters for Groups 1, 2, and 3** • **Graduation Student Name Tags** Reproducible 18-2: Copy one per student.
3 ◆◆◆	**Practice Selected Posters in a Friendship Circle** **Play *Pass the Sack*** — **Graduation Program Option 1 or 2** Reproducible 18-3a or 18-3b: Customize (add names and activities) then prepare one for each student and visitor.	• **Posters for Groups 1, 2, and 3** • **Graduation Student Name Tags** • **Sack** See Special Preparation Note on p. 248.
4 ■■■	**Discuss the Ceremony in a Friendship Circle** **Dress Rehearsal**	• **Posters for Groups 1, 2, and 3** • **Graduation Student Name Tags** • **Graduation Caps** See Special Preparation Note, p. 250. • **Music selection and player** Suggested selection: "Pomp and Circumstance" • **Stage or table** • **Diploma Option 1 or 2** Reproducible 18-5a or 18-5b: Copy one per student and sign.
5 ★★★	**Before Guests Arrive** **When Guests Arrive** **Begin the Program** **Refreshments**	• **Graduation Visitor Name Tags, table and markers** • **Seating for visitors** • **Graduation Programs** • **Posters for Groups 1, 2, and 3** • **Graduation Student Name Tags** • **Graduation Caps** • **Music selection and player** • **Stage or table** • **Diplomas** • ***My SMART Book* (completed)** • **Refreshments**

☰ ········ Lesson Outline ········ ☰

❶ Positive Statements in a Friendship Circle

Have students sit in a friendship circle with all 14 posters on display. Discuss the Graduation Ceremony. Have students make positive statements about their SMART Skills. Sing "Make New Friends but Keep the Old."

❷ Select Posters to Perform

Have students select three favorite posters to recite with gestures at the ceremony.

❸ Practice Selected Posters

Begin practice with gestures.

---

❶ Positive Statements in a Friendship Circle

Have students sit in a friendship circle with all 14 posters on display. Discuss the Graduation Ceremony. Have students make positive statements about their SMART Skills. Sing "Make New Friends but Keep the Old."

- **Tell students when the Graduation Ceremony will be. Say something like:**
Our big celebration is [this week]. We are going to honor you for being SMART Kids! Our principal [Mr. Sweet] will present you with diplomas, and some of your family members will be here too. We want to honor you for being SMART Kids.

- **Model and have students make positive statements about their SMART Skills. Say something like:**
I'm very proud of you and all the skills you've learned. I'm proud of the way you greet people. Nod if you can give a warm greeting.

    [Oksana], what skill are you proud of? Start with "I'm proud that . . ."
    (I'm proud that I include others.)
    I'm very proud of you too. You help make our classroom a nice place. Everyone, touch your nose if you include others.

    Repeat with individuals as time and attention span allow.

- **Sing "Make New Friends but Keep the Old."**

❷ Select Posters to Perform

Have students select three favorite posters to recite with gestures at the ceremony.

- Group the posters.
  Group 1: Greetings, Looking and Listening, Following Directions, Polite Requests, Compliments

  Group 2: Taking Turns, Including Others, Friends, Accepting "No"

  Group 3: Cooling Down, Apologies, Interruptions, Disagreeing, Problem Solving

- Tell students they will pick their three favorite posters to perform at the ceremony.

- Show students the posters from the first group. Think aloud (model) your reason for liking one or two of the posters. Have partners discuss which poster they would like to perform. Say something like:

  It's going to be hard for me to choose which of these posters to perform. I love Gregory, but I love the SMART Looking and Listening Poster. When you look and listen, you are showing respect for others.

  Think about which poster you will vote for and why. Partners share your ideas with each other.

- Have students share their ideas. Remind students that different ideas are great. They can use their SMART Disagreeing Skills.

- Have students vote for one poster out of the group.

  Repeat with each group of posters.

❸ Practice Selected Posters

Begin practice with gestures.

- Have students practice the first selected poster using a cloze procedure and gestures.

- Have students recite the first poster with gestures.

- Have students *stand* and recite the poster with gestures.

  Repeat with the second and third selected posters.

▲ ········ Lesson Outline ········ ▲

❶ **Practice Selected Posters in a Friendship Circle**

Have students practice each of the three posters with gestures.

❷ **Pass Out Graduation Student Name Tags and Assign Poster Groups**

Pass out Graduation Student Name Tags. Explain to students they will each perform in one of the three poster groups. Pass out name tags with poster groups written in the top right corner. Have students practice introducing their group.

❶ **Practice Selected Posters in a Friendship Circle**

Have students practice each of the three posters with gestures. Cheer each other along with applause following the third practice on each poster.

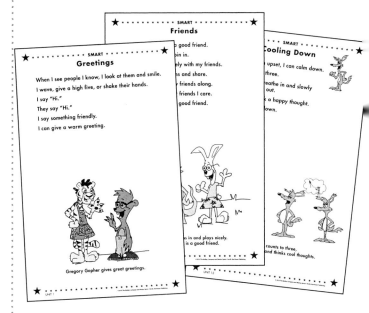

- Have students practice the first selected poster using a cloze procedure and gestures.

- Have students recite the first poster with gestures. Compliment students and practice any difficult lines.

- Have students *stand* and recite the poster with gestures. Cheer each other along with applause following the third practice on each poster. Say something like:
Everyone, clap for yourselves. Clapping is like a compliment. It says you've done a nice job. It's something friends do to cheer each other along.

Repeat with the second and third selected posters.

❷ Pass Out Graduation Student Name Tags and Assign Poster Groups

Pass out Graduation Student Name Tags. Explain to students they will each perform in one of the three poster groups. Pass out name tags with poster groups written in the top right corner.

- Tell your class which students will be in Group 1. Have students in Group 1 stand up and practice introducing themselves. Have students repeat after you:

  We are SMART Kids. We will perform SMART [Greetings] for you.

  Repeat with Group 2 and Group 3.

- Collect name tags by having students take them off and pass them to the right. Have students count while name tags are being collected to keep everyone busy. Congratulate students on SMART Taking Turns, Looking and Listening, and Following Directions.

Lesson 3

SMART GRADUATION

◆ ········ Lesson Outline ········ ◆

❶ Practice Selected Posters in a Friendship Circle

Pass out Graduation Student Name Tags. Have all students practice each of the three posters with gestures. Have each group practice performing their poster for the group. Cheer each other along.

❷ Play *Pass the Sack*

Play *Pass the Sack* to determine who gets to be Student Greeters and ushers.

Special Preparation Note ··········
Pass the Sack and Greeter Jobs

For this lesson, you will need a sack.

- Determine how many Student Greeters you would like at the door and how many ushers to pass out programs.

- Write each job on a slip of paper. (For example, you might have four Student Greeters and three ushers—totaling seven jobs and seven slips of paper.)

- Put the slips of paper in the sack.

❶ Practice Selected Posters in a Friendship Circle

Pass out Graduation Student Name Tags. Have students practice each of the three posters with gestures. Cheer each other along with applause following the third practice on each poster.

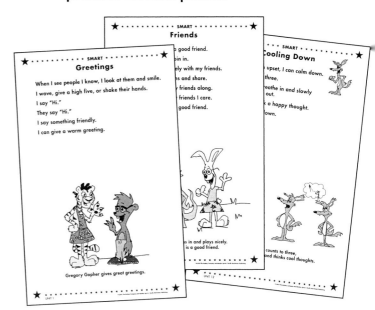

248

- Have all students practice the first selected poster using a cloze procedure and gestures.

- Have all students recite the first poster with gestures. Compliment students and practice any difficult lines.

- Have Group 1 *stand* and recite the poster with gestures. Cheer the group along with applause. Say something like:
  Everyone, clap for Group 1. When we clap, what are we doing? (cheering each other along, being good friends)

  Repeat with Group 2 and 3.

❷ Play *Pass the Sack*

Play *Pass the Sack* to determine who gets to be Student Greeters and ushers. Have students pass the sack while music plays. When the music stops, the student with the sack picks a job slip from the sack.

- Describe the jobs and how many students will be greeters and how many students will be ushers.

- Use the poster steps to remind students to use SMART Taking Turns. Say something like:
  We're going to play *Pass the Sack*. If the music stops and you have the sack, you get to reach in and pick a job.

  While we're playing, we can use SMART Taking Turns. Remember, sometimes it's your turn first, sometimes last, and sometimes . . . not at all.

What kind of face will you use if someone else gets a job—pleasant or not-so-pleasant? (pleasant)

Will you pout, argue, or whine? (no) That's right. You'll watch and listen and keep your hands and feet still. You are SMART Kids!
You watch and listen, and you keep your hands and feet still.

- **Play the game. Compliment students for using SMART Taking Turns.**

■ ·········· Lesson Outline ········· ■

❶ **Discuss the Ceremony in a Friendship Circle**

Pass out Graduation Student Name Tags and caps.

❷ **Dress Rehearsal**

Discuss and practice the program.

Special Preparation Note ···········
Set Up the Room for a Dress Rehearsal

In advance of this lesson:

- Have caps ready with names clearly marked on the inside bands.

- Determine what students who are not greeters or ushers will be doing as guests arrive.

- Determine the order in which students will receive their diplomas (for example, in alphabetical order, or by poster group and then by alphabetical order). You may wish to add numbers to student name tags.

- Download a music selection (e.g., "Pomp and Circumstance") to play during graduates' processional.

- Have your room set up for the celebration. You may wish to have:

  a) Guest seating—a designated area (partially set up)

  b) Aisle for processional

  c) Stage or table where students can receive their diplomas

Note: You may wish to have one or two adults assist with the rehearsal.

❶ **Discuss the Ceremony in a Friendship Circle**

Pass out Graduation Student Name Tags and caps. Explain the dress rehearsal.

❷ **Dress Rehearsal**

Have students practice each step of the celebration including:

Guest arrival, greetings, and passing out of programs

- Have the class pretend to be guests.
- Have the class practice giving SMART Compliments to the greeters and ushers.

Welcome and Introduction by an adult

- Have students practice SMART Looking and Listening. For the Introduction, you may wish to say something like:

On behalf of my class, we are happy to have you here and want to welcome you. Many of our working families were unable to attend, but they are thinking of us and cheering us along.

This year we have been working on fourteen SMART Skills that will help your children be great friends, be successful in school, and get good jobs. We have learned and will keep learning to:

- Give warm greetings
- Look and listen
- Follow directions right away
- Make polite requests
- Give compliments
- Take turns
- Include others
- Join in, play nicely, encourage others, and be good friends
- Accept "No"
- Cool down when we're upset
- Make and accept apologies
- Interrupt intelligently
- Disagree respectfully, and
- Solve problems

We are very proud of our accomplishments! And now, please applaud for the graduates!

Processional of graduates and seating with music ("Pomp and Circumstance")

- Have students practice SMART Following Directions.

Presentation of Social Story Posters

- Have students practice SMART Friends— cheering each other along.

Presentation of Diplomas

- Have students practice SMART Taking Turns and thank yous. Have presenters (or stand-in presenters) shake hands, pass students their diplomas, and practice moving student tassels from right to left. Have students give each student a quick round of applause.

Closing by an adult with a request for all adults to read the Graduation Poem on the back of the Program.

- For the closing, you may wish to say something like:

We know our kids will do well in life as they continue to work and grow with their SMART Skills. Please turn to the back of your program and help me read the Graduation Poem in honor of our SMART Kids.

Reading of Graduation Poem

- Explain to students that following the ceremony, they will have refreshments and time to visit with their guests.

Lesson 5
SMART GRADUATION

★········ Lesson Outline ········★

❶ Before Guests Arrive

Pass out Graduation Student Name Tags and caps.

❷ When Guests Arrive

Remind students what they will be doing as guests arrive. Have visitors fill out Graduation Visitor Name Tags. Have Student Greeters at the door. Have ushers direct guests to their seats and pass out programs.

❸ Begin the Program

If at all possible, begin the celebration on time. Follow the program and have fun!

❹ Refreshments

Serve refreshments to visitors and students. Remind students to demonstrate their SMART Polite Requests (and thank yous). Mingle with guests and students. Congratulate students on their accomplishments and award *My SMART Books* to take home.

CHAMPS
CELEBRATE SUCCESS!

"When students are successful, their sense of accomplishment can be so satisfying that they are more motivated to behave responsibly."

—*Sprick, 2009, p. 44*

With success and this celebration, your SMART Kids will be motivated to continue being SMART Kids in the future.

Special Preparation Note ··········
Getting Ready for the Celebration

The following should be all ready to go:

- **Room set up**

- **Music ready to play**

- **Graduation Student Name Tags, caps, and SMART Diplomas ready to quickly pass out**

- **Programs ready for each student and visitor**

- *My SMART Book* **ready to give out to students to take home**

- **Visitors' table with Graduation Visitor Name Tags and markers set up just outside the classroom**

- **Refreshments ready to serve**

A Big Celebration

❶ Before Guests Arrive

Pass out Graduation Student Name Tags and caps.

❷ When Guests Arrive

Remind students what they will be doing as guests arrive. Have visitors fill out Graduation Visitor Name Tags before they enter the room. Have Student Greeters greet guests. Have ushers direct guests to their seats and give them programs.

❸ Begin the Program

If at all possible, begin the celebration on time. Follow the program and have fun!

❹ Refreshments

As refreshments are being served, remind students to demonstrate their SMART Polite Requests (and thank yous). While students are eating, mingle with guests and students. Congratulate each student and award his or her *My SMART Book* to

take home. Make an effort to congratulate each student on a specific SMART Accomplishment. Say things like:

[Berto], I am very proud of you. Here is your *SMART Book* to take home and share with your family. You are really great at all the SMART Skills, but I've noticed you making an effort to include others. That shows how kind you are.

253

Tips for Moving Forward

SMART GRADUATION

····· Generalization ·····

Positive Interactions: Continue to interact positively with students when they demonstrate social grace, manners, and respectful talk. These are the best times to interact!

Positive Feedback, Reinforcement, and Connections: Provide ongoing positive descriptive feedback. Your feedback helps students understand how their actions translate into responsible, kind, and respectful acts. Continue to use SMART Recognition Cards, awards, notes to the kids, and notes home to acknowledge efforts.

····· Intervention ·····

Continue to prompt targeted skills with students who have difficulty. NEVER GIVE UP!

Catch individuals using SMART Skills. Reinforce with positive descriptive feedback. Then, use the student as a model.

Set up positive practice.

Give the student meaningful jobs that encourage responsibility and respectful interactions.

CONGRATS AND BEST WISHES!

With continued encouragement, your students SMART Skills will grow and deepen. They are off to a SMART start, thanks to you!

Our best wishes for your students are reflected in the SMART Graduation Poem.

We are here to celebrate
Our SMART well-mannered kids.
They studied hard and now it's time
To graduate! So we say:

May you grow with social grace.
May your manners serve you well.
May you speak with respect
To everyone you know.

RESOURCES *for* TEACHERS
from PACIFIC NORTHWEST PUBLISHING

CHAMPS: *A Proactive and Positive Approach to Classroom Management (2nd ed.)*

RANDY SPRICK, PH.D.

CHAMPS helps classroom teachers design or fine-tune a proactive and positive classroom management plan that will overtly teach students how to behave responsibly. The new edition includes tips and resources to make this definitive guide to classroom management even more user friendly. *CHAMPS* strategies are easy to implement and will:

- Reduce classroom disruptions and office referrals
- Improve classroom climate
- Increase student on-task behavior
- Establish respectful and civil interactions

030-6 978-1-59909-030-6 / 2009 / 520 pages and 1 CD (502 fillable reproducible forms and classroom icons)

Teach All, Reach All: Instructional Design & Delivery With TGIF!

SUSAN L. MULKEY, M.ED., KAREN A. KEMP, M.A.

If you are serious about filling your bag of tricks with proven ideas, this is the instructional strategy book for you. *Teach All, Reach All* provides more than 175 practical classroom strategies with a companion CD of reproducible forms, plus a reproducible form to guide effective lesson design. This book is about high-quality instruction and interventions that are available for all students and grade levels. *Teach All, Reach All* complements the fundamental premise of RTI.

029-0 978-1-59909-029-0 / 2009 / 240 pages and 1 CD (115 digital reproducible pages)

Shop online: PacificNWPublish.com
Phone: 866-542-1490

THE TOUGH KID SERIES

Books and programs in *The Tough Kid* series help you manage and motivate Tough Kids with evidence-based, effective tools. You will learn practical, easy-to-implement strategies for dealing with tough problems like aggression, noncompliance, lack of motivation, and poor academic performance.

The Tough Kid Book: Practical Classroom Management Strategies (2nd ed.)

The original *Tough Kid* book by Ginger Rhode, Bill Jenson, and H. Kenton Reavis is newly revised and updated with more creative techniques that you can use immediately to deal with tough classroom behaviors.

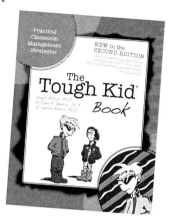

042-9　978-1-59909-042-9 / April 2010 / 256 pages (spiral bound) and 1 CD (90 pages reproducible forms)

The Tough Kid Tool Box

The Tough Kid Tool Box supplies straightforward, classroom-tested, ready-to-use materials for motivating and managing tough-to-teach students. The book and companion CD contain blackline masters and detailed directions for implementing self-monitoring programs, behavioral contracting, Mystery Motivators, and other effective, positive procedures to address problem behavior in the classroom.

034-4　978-1-59909-034-4 / 2009 / 131 pages (spiral bound) and 1 CD (250 pages reproducible forms in English and Spanish)

The Tough Kid Bully Blockers Book: 15-Minute Lessons for Preventing and Reducing Bullying

This positive and proactive program guides you through implementing a bully-blocking program in your school or classroom. A field-tested set of 15-minute lessons is designed to equip students—whether bullies, victims, or bystanders—with six skills to reverse bullying behavior.

019-1　978-1-59909-019-1 / 2008 / 286 pages (spiral bound) and 1 CD (69 pages reproducible forms)

The Tough Kid Social Skills Book

This book by Susan M. Sheridan contains a variety of tools, lessons, and strategies to help you identify Tough Kids in need of direct social skills training and lead productive social skills groups in small group, classroom, or schoolwide settings.

041-2　978-1-59909-041-2 / 2010 / 208 pages (spiral bound) and 1 CD (50 pages fillable reproducible forms)

SMART KID SOCIAL SKILLS POSTERS

Teach your students to be SMART with the skills of **S**ocial grace, **M**anners, **A**nd **R**espectful **T**alk. Save valuable preparation time by purchasing these colorful, ready-to-use *SMART Kid* Social Skills Posters. There are fourteen 11.5″ x 15″ posters in all.

044-3   978-1-59909-044-3 / 14 posters